JESUS

AND THE ECONOMIC QUESTIONS

OF HIS DAY

Douglas E. Oakman

Studies in the Bible and Early Christianity
Volume 8

The Edwin Mellen Press
Lewiston/Queenston

Library of Congress Cataloging-in-Publication Data

Oakman, Douglas E.
  Jesus and the economic questions of his day.

  (Studies in the Bible and early Christianity ; v. 8)
  Bibliography: p.
  Includes index.
  1. Jesus Christ--Teachings--Economic aspects.
2. Jesus Christ--Historicity. 3. Palestine--Economic
conditions. 4. Economics in the Bible. I. Title.
II. Series.
BS2417.E3034 1986   226'.067   86-23518
ISBN 0-88946-608-4 (alk. paper)

This is volume 8 in the continuing series
Studies in the Bible and Early Christianity
Volume 8 ISBN 0-88946-608-4
SBEC Series ISBN 0-88946-913-X

The Edwin Mellen Press   The Edwin Mellen Press
Box 450   Box 67
Lewiston, New York   Queenston, Ontario
USA 14092   L0S 1L0 CANADA

Printed in the United States of America

TO DEBORAH LYNN

*". . . keep seeking God's
reign and these things
will belong to you too."*

Luke 12:31

TABLE OF CONTENTS

PART ONE

THE ECONOMIC CONTEXT
OF THE HISTORICAL JESUS

PART TWO

AN EXPLORATION OF THE JESUS TRADITION FROM AN ECONOMIC PERSPECTIVE

LIST OF ILLUSTRATIONS

PREFACE

This monograph represents the substance of my
doctoral dissertation submitted in 1986 to the Graduate
Theological Union, Berkeley, California. Publication
has permitted the correction of several minor errors in
the original manuscript and the inclusion of additional
comments and references pertinent to the argument. The
main conclusions of the book, however, remain
unchanged.

There is no need to repeat here what is already
said in the Introduction about the genesis of this
study. However, a few comments are in order beyond
what is expressed in the Introduction or Conclusion
regarding some general issues raised by this monograph.

This is an interdisciplinary work crossing the
boundaries of biblical studies, ancient history, economic anthropology, peasant studies, scientific agronomy, and several other provinces of learning. I have
painted on a broad canvas. Undoubtedly, specialists in
each of these areas will find points to quibble about
in the following pages. Nonetheless, I hope they will
also find the effort to synthesize the larger picture
worthwhile and the result perhaps even convincing.

Methodologically, it seemed more helpful for me
to use conceptual models heuristically and inductively
rather than to work from general theories categorically
and deductively. Thus I employed, but did not con-
strictively define, the notions of "economy" and

"social class."   Enough is already made of the household character of the ancient economy in the book.   I
wanted to do some macroeconomic and quantitative
analysis of taxation and production, which presuppose
larger economic relations.   I did not find very helpful
the attempts of ancient historians like Finley to
exclude the notion of social class from the study of
antiquity.   After all, "class" can validly incorporate
an outsider's perspective.   Even the modern ancient
historians cannot escape being outsiders vis-à-vis the
past.

        I will confess to having a lively interest in
the meaning of this study for contemporary social
issues.   I was thoroughly engaged in the subject
matter.   However, I have tried to be as truthful to
history and as clear about my ideological stance as I
am able.   I certainly hope social historians and social
scientists will find something of value here, in
addition to biblical scholars and students of early
Christianity.

        Some issues have come more into focus for me
since I finished writing this book.   It seems almost
self-evident now to say that Jesus need not have been
entirely aware of what he was doing or saying for this
kind of study to have validity.   A good case in point
is the issue of Jesus and patronage.   Obviously, those
who would like to find support for Christian charity as
the quintessential Christian ethic will be attracted to
Jesus as a broker.   Yet I sense very strongly that
Jesus was--consciously or unconsciously--articulating
something deeper.   If he attacked in practice
redistributive institutions like the Jewish Temple or
Roman state, then he certainly opposed in principle
redistributive relationships based upon patronage.

Those current efforts to connect the work of
Jesus to the biblical Jubilee are justified in my
opinion (Hollenbach, 1985; Ringe, 1985). The Old
Testament Jubilee traditions evidently emerged out of
agrarian crises similar to those of Jesus' day. Yet I
did not attempt, except in a very incidental way, to
link Jesus to those traditions. The Jubilee traditions
are not entirely coherent. Their effect could be
expected to be somewhat dilute in the first century.
Furthermore, one does not have to show a direct
influence of the Old Testament tradition upon Jesus to
recognize that he in fact responded to contemporary
agrarian problems in a fairly consistent way. Nor did
Jesus necessarily have a comprehensive program based
upon the Jubilee model. He certainly had a firm
awareness of what he was doing, as his parables and
specific actions in the tradition demonstrate.
Therefore, the present book has argued on other grounds
that Jesus' words and actions articulate a coherent
response to the economic problems and realities of
first-century Palestine. If the Jubilee traditions can
be used to support this picture, so much the better.

One serious question remains in my mind after
completing this study: If Jesus spoke primarily to
peasants, why did that audience not decisively respond
to his message? Why did they ultimately reject his
way? And why were the majority of post-Easter
followers of Jesus artisans like himself? I think an
explanation must be found through sociological
considerations. Jesus attacked the Temple and the
first-century ethos of self-sufficiency. These were at
least two of the basic "props" of the ancient Jewish
peasantry's value system. No matter how much they were
impressed by Jesus as a holy man, the peasantry could

not see much beyond their own narrow self-interest
(even when Jesus was appealing to a larger self-
interest). On the other side of the coin, Jesus'
artisan followers were much better able to appreciate
the mobile character of a God worshiped "in spirit and
in truth." Artisans were also able to see beyond their
immediate self-interest to a community of interest
shared with strangers. For these and other reasons,
early Christianity flourished in cities and could only
in certain limited ways appeal to the countryside.

        I owe many personal debts through the writing of
this book, all of which I am glad to acknowledge. My
interest in the historical Jesus was first awakened
over a decade ago during undergraduate studies with Dr.
George W. E. Nickelsburg at the University of Iowa. I
was encouraged in seminary days and after by Dr. Edgar
Krentz, Dr. Frederick Danker, and Dr. Ralph Klein, all
now at the Lutheran School of Theology in Chicago. Dr.
Everett Kalin and Dr. Robert Smith at Pacific Lutheran
Theological Seminary were kindly advisors in recent
years.
        Dr. Herman Waetjen of San Francisco Theological
Seminary proved to be a helpful director for my
dissertation and a gracious friend. I wish also to
thank my other doctoral advisors: Dr. Marvin Chaney of
San Francisco Theological Seminary, Dr. John H. Elliott
of the University of San Francisco, and Dr. Robert N.
Bellah of the University of California. Their interest
in my work and experience in applying the social
sciences to the humanities have made this a better book
than it might otherwise have been.
        Others also contributed in significant ways:
The Rev. Edward A. Wilson of Ashland, Oregon; Dr.

Gildas Hamel of the University of California, Santa
Cruz; Dr. Mary P. Coote of San Francisco Theological
Seminary; Dr. Paul Hollenbach at Iowa State University
in Ames, Iowa; Michael Crosby O.F.M. Cap. and the Rev.
Gustav Schultz both of Berkeley, California; and the
Rev. Dr. Will L. Herzfeld of Oakland, California.

While I have acquired much of value from these
and other people whom I have not named, I alone must
bear the responsibility for the way in which their
ideas or suggestions have been put to use.

I am grateful to Dr. Herbert Richardson of The
Edwin Mellen Press for his willingness to consider this
book for publication and for the oversight of Dr. Peter
Beyer and Ms. Bonnie L. Jones during its final
production.

My parents, Virgil and Dorothy Oakman, and my
wife's parents, Robert and Anna Sattler, have offered
generous support during numerous years of study. My
sons, Justin and Jonathan, made life joyful with their
presence and frequent distractions during countless
hours of writing.

Last but most importantly, my wife Deborah has
been a special source of strength and love, despite
many deprivations. To her this work is affectionately
dedicated.

                              DOUGLAS E. OAKMAN
Santa Clara University
1 October 1986

INTRODUCTION

A NEW SOCIOLOGICAL AWARENESS AND AN OLD
QUESTION ABOUT THE HISTORICAL JESUS

Recent study of Christian origins has adopted a
distinctly sociological stance. This approach is exem-
plified in the work of many scholars and is evidenced
on an international scale.[1]

These innovative attempts, furthermore, have
demonstrated great diversity in their methodologies and
assumptions regarding the nature of the sociological
task. So, for instance, Miranda (1974) embraces an
uncompromising marxian perspective on the biblical
material. Belo (1981) draws both from French struc-
turalism and marxism. Theissen (1978 and 1982), Malina
(1981), and Elliott (1981) have forged their own socio-
historical perspectives out of broader readings of the
social sciences, while Gager (1975) has simply adapted
specific social-scientific theories, for instance about
millennial movements and their dynamics, to the study
of early Christianity. Meeks (1983) and Malherbe
(1983) shy away from sociological theory in favor of
"social description."[2] Methodological and theoretical
differences notwithstanding, these interdisciplinary
endeavors hold the promise of challenging the dominant
hermeneutical assumptions of biblical students and
broadening the questions brought to the exegetical
task.

The present monograph has grown out of the
author's interest in exploring, from the vantage point
of the new sociological awareness of Christian origins,

the relationship between Jesus' message of the reign of
God and the socio-economic conditions of his original
hearers. As the work progressed, it became clear that
an argument needed to be advanced about the historical
Jesus himself.

The following pages explore the meaning of the
words and activities of Jesus in the light of fundamental economic questions of his day. This investigation presumes two hypotheses. On the one hand, Jesus
was limited and shaped by certain economic factors in
his environment--first of all, by his activity as a
rural artisan, but perhaps more importantly by major
economic problems in early Roman Palestine. This hypothesis acknowledges the formative effects of Jesus'
environment on his words and ministry.[3] On the other
hand, Jesus' words and ministry can be understood in
part as an attempt to articulate new economic values
and a new economic behavior. This represents a creative expression growing partially out of Jesus' vision
of the imminence of God's reign. Jesus' values and
behavior were formulated, therefore, within a unique
set of experiences and aimed to a certain extent at
overcoming the socially destructive effects of maldis-
tributed wealth and differential control over material
goods that existed in early Roman Palestine.

This is by no means an entirely new argument.
The historical Jesus has been the subject of concern
since the Enlightenment. The older liberal study of
Jesus attempted at numerous points to understand his
work in economic and social terms, especially during
the late nineteenth century and the days of the Social
Gospel.[4] Of course, there were always pious objections
to pursuing historical investigations of this type.
Yet the demise of old-style liberalism earlier in the

twentieth century, along with the Social Gospel movement and melioristic views of history, more effectively
ensured a hiatus in such efforts.[5]

Though "Jesus and economics" is an old issue,
the time seems right to reexamine it for several
reasons. First, it is believed that a more informed
and critical assessment of the sources, after a century
of developments in the New Testament discipline, makes
possible better historical reflection about Jesus.[6]

Moreover, the disciplines of sociology and
anthropology, which have also grown and matured during
the twentieth century, have developed comparative tools
that can place the study of Jesus--hitherto within the
province of theology or a narrow understanding of
history--on a different footing.[7] It probably goes too
far to say that the new sociological awareness in
biblical circles permits a completely different
approach to the historical Jesus. The theological
dimension of his work--his preaching about the kingdom
of God--remains central. It is certain, however, that
the social sciences and comparative studies can help
the student of Jesus formulate entirely different kinds
of questions about him and the meaning of his message.
Such an approach can also supply hermeneutically fruitful models and interpretive paradigms to answer historical questions in terms of a broader horizon of
meanings.

The dominant concerns of twentieth-century New
Testament scholarship have not been with the social
dimensions of early Christianity or, more specifically
for this project, with the economic aspect in Jesus'
words and ministry. To some extent, of course, this
trend had an "external" aspect, insofar as scholars
were generally concerned with a scientific analysis of

the sources and not with synthesizing a comprehensive
picture. Yet those attempts that can be characterized
as "synthetic," such as Bultmann's program of existential interpretation or the biblical theology movement, did not have a central social or sociological
concern. It would seem that mainstream New Testament
scholars, especially those in Germany, did not ask the
social or economic questions, because their dominant
"internal" interests were with an existential and
privatized, bourgeois theology. A hermeneutical bias
against seeing the role of socio-economic factors in
the genesis of Christianity made the study of Jesus
seem parochial and irrelevant.[8]

The "antisocial" bias with respect to the
meaning of the Jesus tradition continues today. The
dominant interpretive paradigm at present seems to be a
literary-formalistic one. This paradigm seeks the
meaning of texts and text-units apart from, or in only
partial relation to, their original context.[9] When
John Dominic Crossan, a premier modern interpreter of
Jesus' parables, writes:

> When Jesus gave the Sower parable . . . his first
> hearers and his modern readers would probably all
> agree on one thing: Jesus was not interested in
> agrarian reform in eastern Galilee. Whatever he
> might have meant, one is immediately certain that
> agriculture is <u>not</u> the point of the story. . . .[10]

what are the hermeneutical assumptions involved?
Certainly Jesus is speaking metaphorically. Yet were
the original meanings of the parables radically
disjoined from the agrarian realities depicted or the
material interests of their original audience? To
Jesus' peasant audience, would Crossan's certitude have
been so readily accepted as it seems to be among modern
urban scholars?

This point has been raised with force recently
by the ancient historian G. E. M. de Ste. Croix. He
has written the following words:

> We must begin with the central fact about Christian
> origins, to which theologians and New Testament
> scholars have never (as far as I am aware) given
> anything like the emphasis it deserves: that
> although the earliest surviving Christian documents
> are in Greek and although Christianity spread from
> city to city in the Graeco-Roman world, its Founder
> lived and preached almost entirely outside the area
> of Graeco-Roman civilisation proper. Here we must
> go back to the fundamental distinction . . . be-
> tween the _polis_ (the Greek city) and the _chora_ (the
> countryside) . . . the world in which Jesus was
> active was entirely that of the _chora_ and not at
> all that of the _polis_. . . .[11]

Are modern students of Jesus asking the right
questions to begin with when they find Jesus speaking
in philosophical abstractions about a religious individualism or an existential reign of God? It is precisely in overcoming this hermeneutical deficiency that
the recent renewed interest in the social dimensions of
early Christianity and use of sociological approaches
in New Testament study can have a salutary effect upon
the study of Jesus. Robin Scroggs has written:

> To some it has seemed that too often the discipline
> of the theology of the New Testament (the history
> of _ideas_) operates out of a methodological
> docetism, as if believers had minds and spirits
> unconnected with their individual and corporate
> bodies. Interest in the sociology of early
> Christianity [guards] against a reductionism . . .
> a limitation of the reality of Christianity to an
> inner-spiritual, or objective-cognitive system.[12]

Rural sociology and the study of folklore would seem
more likely aids in getting at the original meaning of
Jesus' speech than philosophical or literary theories
that only serve a modern individualism.[13]

Returning to the purpose of this work, the
exploration of our proposal involves three components.
First, the general features and problems of the economy
of first-century Palestine are spelled out. To insure
sound methodology, this first task largely requires the
use of non-biblical evidence. Secondly, it is necessary to determine whether Jesus in fact responded in
some specific way to the economic situation of his
time. The canonical gospels supply the major eviden-
tial basis. Finally, a connection needs to be established between the character and values of Jesus and
his specific experiences in the economic sphere.

In view of these methodological requirements,
the investigation in the following pages is divided
into two parts. Part One sketches the general
character of production (Chapter 1) and distribution
(Chapter 2) in first-century Palestine. The economic
categories enlisted for organizing the discussion are
admittedly broad. It is believed, however, that
production and distribution can provide foci (with
suitable qualifications) to analyze the economies of
the early Roman period.[14] Part One does not propose to
offer a comprehensive view of the ancient Palestinian
economy, but concentrates on providing a meaningful
framework for looking at the economic and social
realities and problems Jesus encountered in his
environment. Evidence is drawn from a variety of
ancient sources. Several models from peasant studies,
economic anthropology, and so on, are used to organize
and discuss the evidence.[15]

Part Two attempts to assess both how Jesus
responded to the realities and problems perceived
through Part One and how those realities and problems
shaped him. Chapter 3 outlines some different assumptions for getting at the meaning of Jesus' parables
with the help of rural sociology. A detailed treatment
of four parables of growth then asks what they imply
for the conditions of production in Jesus' Palestine.16

The discussion in Chapter 4, however, is
organized topically with reference to Part One. This
allows an examination of a broader selection of
Synoptic material in the light of specific economic
issues.

Chapter 5 explores, on the basis of comparative
evidence and certain features of the Jesus tradition,
economic factors informing the character and activity
of Jesus. The point of view switches away from
ideology and values in the Jesus tradition to an
argument about the personal makeup and social contacts
of Jesus. The chapter looks first into the work Jesus
is likely to have engaged in, as well as the experiences he is likely to have had, as a rural artisan in
the first century. Jesus' social contacts, and the
connection between them and Jesus' occupation, are then
explored. Finally, a heuristic model for the roles
Jesus played both as village artisan and as religious
leader within the agrarian context envisioned is
developed--largely on the basis of comparative study
and social theory, but with a concern to demonstrate
the appropriateness and plausibility of the model.

In general, the exegetical methodology of this
work presumes the standard disciplines of form,
tradition, and redaction criticism. Present-day New
Testament scholarship rests upon "the shoulders of

giants." Bultmann, Jeremias, and Perrin have perhaps
contributed the most in this area. Their work respectively on the Synoptic forms, parables, and teaching of
Jesus, has laid a firm foundation with the help of the
"criterion of dissimilarity." Every modern interpretation of Jesus must begin with the most original and
unique aspects of the Jesus tradition. Perrin's words
identify the starting point:

> We are ourselves convinced that there are three
> aspects of the tradition where the establishment of
> the history of the tradition and the application of
> the criterion of dissimilarity enable us to
> reconstruct major aspects of the teaching of Jesus
> beyond reasonable doubt: the parables, the Kingdom
> of God teaching and the Lord's Prayer tradition.[17]

It is, of course, assumed that any interpretation such as the one presented on the following pages
must cohere with itself and illuminate what is already
known about Jesus from other study (Perrin's "criterion
of coherence"). An "economic interpretation" of Jesus,
moreover, must be reflected in independent parts of the
tradition and not only in a single strand ("criterion
of multiple attestation").[18] Conversely, subsequent
forms of the tradition, if they have obscured or rein-
terpreted an economic meaning, will have to be
carefully distinguished.

The following body of Synoptic tradition,
therefore, has formed the basis, directly or indirectly, for reflection on the economic aspect in Jesus'
words and ministry in Part Two:

> Triple Tradition (cited according to Mark): Mk.
>   4:3-8 (Sower), 24 (Measure), 25 (More Will Be
>   Given), 30-32 (Mustard Seed); 8:36 (Gaining
>   the Whole World); 10:23 (Rich and Kingdom),

28-30 (Receiving a Hundredfold); 12:1-11
(Tenants in the Vineyard), 14-17 (Tribute to
Caesar); 13:28 (Fig Tree); 14:7 (Poor Always
With You).

Double Tradition (cited according to Luke): Lk.
6:38 (Giving Full Measure); 10:2 (Harvest/
Laborers), 7 (Laborers Worthy of Food/Wages);
11:4 (Forgive Us Our Debts); 12:6 (Price of
Sparrows), 22-31 (Anxiety and Subsistence),
42-48a (Faithful Steward/Slave), 48b (Much
Will Be Required), 58f (Settling a Debt);
13:21 (Leaven); 14:15-24 (Great Feast); 15:1-
7 (Lost Sheep); 16.13 (God and Mammon);
19:12-27 (Talents). We place here for the
sake of convenience, Mk. 12:41-44 = Lk. 21:1-
4 (Widow's Mite).

Special Material: Mt. 5:5 (Blessed are the Meek);
6:19-21 (Laying Up Treasure); 13:24-30
(Darnel Among the Wheat), 44-46 (Treasure and
Pearl), 49-50 (Fish Net), 52 (Old and New
Treasure); 17:24-27 (Temple Tax); 18:23-34
(Unmerciful Servant); 20:1-15 (Laborers in
Vineyard); 21:28-32 (Two Sons); Mk. 4:26-29
(Seed Growing Secretly); Lk. 7:41-43 (Two
Debtors); 10:30-35 (Good Samaritan); 11:5-8
(Importune Friend); 12:13f (Dividing Inheri-
tance), 16-20 (Rich Fool), 47f (Discipline of
Servants); 13:6-9 (Fig Tree); 14:7-14 (Invi-
tations and Status), 28-32 (Counting the
Cost); 15:8-9 (Lost Coin), 11-32 (Prodigal
Son); 16:1-8 (Unjust Steward), 9-13 (Loyal
service), 19-31 (Dives and Lazarus); 17:7-10
(Servant's Reward); 19:1-9 (Zacchaeus).

In addition to this material, extra-canonical traditions from early Christianity (e.g. the Gospel of
Thomas), the Old Testament Pseudepigrapha, and materials from ancient historians have served as points of
reference.[19]

On the basis of a renewed sociological awareness, therefore, as well as through the study of the
socio-historical situation of Jesus and the broad early
tradition about him, this monograph proposes to investigate an old question in a new way.

Notes to the Introduction

[1]For accounts of these developments from the viewpoint of mainstream New Testament scholars, see Scroggs (1980); Harrington (1980); Kee (1980); Malina (1981); Schütz in Theissen, (1982) 1-23; and Malherbe (1983). For other views see also Gottwald (1983b).

[2]This bifurcation in the conception of the task and disagreement concerning the appropriateness of the use of sociological theory in the study of early Christianity has also been evidenced of late by the existence of two separate groups, one relating to "Social Sciences and New Testament Interpretation" and the other to the "Social History of Early Christianity," at Society of Biblical Literature meetings. See Elliott (1986) for an up-to-date perspective on various sociological approaches to the Bible.

[3]Theissen, (1978) 31-95 provided the initial inspiration for this conception through his discussion of various social factors operative on earliest Christianity.

[4]One thinks in this vein of Mathews (1897 - 1971) or of Troeltsch (1911 = 1981), of Dickey (1923) or of McCown (1929).

[5]Countryman, (1980) 1-45 has an erudite survey of earlier studies and objections put forward. Hopkins (1940) gives a thorough review of American develop ments. Bammel (1984) gives a detailed survey of past scholarly work on the socio-political dimension. Appendix I chronicles some of the theological currents that led away from a Social Gospel.

[6]In addition to remarks in this introduction, the reader is again referred to Appendix I for general insights into the contribution that the New Testament discipline has made to the present study.

[7]Kaplan and Manners (1972) and Wolf (1974) outline some of these parallel developments.

[8]There were exceptions, of course, like Jeremias. Borg (1984) 1-19 offers a similar critique of twentieth-century New Testament scholarship.

[9]Unhistorical, formalistic, or abstract inter-pretation is particularly evident in recent work on the parables of Jesus: For instance, consult Kissinger,

(1979) 180-187 (Fuchs: "ontological-existential"
interpretation), 209-221 (Via: literary-existential
interpretation), 221-230 (Crossan: literary-structural
interpretation, concerned to some extent with the
historical).

[10]Crossan, (1973) 56.

[11]Ste. Croix, (1981) 427. The only thing in
which Ste. Croix errs is in thinking that this "central
fact" has not received any attention. Recently:
Theissen (1976, 1977, and 1978) and Schottroff and
Stegemann (1981).

[12]Scroggs, (1980) 165-66.

[13]Hollenbach (1983) especially shows the need
for such a critique in historical Jesus studies and
identifies tentative steps toward the kind of study
being advocated here. Recent thought-provoking works
by Rohrbaugh (1978) and Bailey (1976 and 1980) have
drawn attention respectively to the agrarian and
cultural contexts of Jesus' work.

[14]Pearson, (1967) 59; Baron, (1952) 1:250.
Consumption is viewed essentially as a function of
distribution--if you have more, you potentially can eat
more; if you do not have, you cannot eat--and is of
less importance in the investigation. See the remarks
of H. Berr, in Toutain, (1951) xvii n. 2. Of course,
marxist students of ancient society utilize a different
vocabulary--Asiatic or sub-Asiatic modes of production,
forces and relations of production, and so on. Though
the terminology is variant, the same fundamental
realities are in view. See especially the works of
advocates of the "materialist reading" of the Bible:
Clévenot (1985) and Belo (1981). Ste. Croix, (1981)
29, 50-53, 155-157 has a detailed discussion of Marx's
categories, though he questions the usefulness of the
notion "Asiatic mode of production." Gottwald's
remarks in (1983a), contrasting Marx's concept with the
pattern of European feudalism, are well worth
considering here: Strong centralized state, absentee
landlordism (urbanization), and high levels of rent and
tax extraction from the agricultural sector all
characterized the early Roman empire as we shall see.

[15]Mealand (1980) similarly begins with such
considerations. To those who have read his book, the
difference in approach will be apparent.

[16]The four parables are: The Sower, the Seed
Growing Secretly, the Darnel Among the Wheat, and the
Mustard Seed.

[17]Perrin, (1967) 47.

[18]On these criteria, again see Perrin, (1967)
39-46.

[19]Unless otherwise noted, translations of
biblical or other ancient texts are my own.
Abbreviations of talmudic tractates follow Danby
(1933). Abbreviations of apocryphal works from the New
Testament period follow Funk (1985). Citations of
modern works follow the standards of the Catholic
Biblical Quarterly. Special abbreviations are
explained on their first occurrence.

PART ONE

THE ECONOMIC CONTEXT OF THE HISTORICAL JESUS

> "Jesus belonged wholly
> to the <u>chora</u> . . ."
>
> Ste. Croix

CHAPTER 1

THE GENERAL CHARACTER OF PRODUCTION IN

FIRST—CENTURY PALESTINE

Within the past thirty-five or so years, an important discipline has emerged in the human sciences to help us more effectively conceptualize the character of ancient economies. This relatively new discipline of economic anthropology has called attention to important differences and shifts of emphasis between ancient pre-industrial and modern industrial economies.[1]

Economic anthropology, the work of ancient historians, and other comparative studies offer the following general picture: The economies of antiquity, particularly the economies of the early Roman period in view here, were by and large agrarian economies. There were no factories of the modern type. Specialized production of pottery, weapons, and the like, was primarily done through small family concerns (including slaves), especially in the maritime cities of the Mediterranean. "Markets" in the modern sense did not exist in antiquity. The market was restricted for the most part to the privileged with access to surplus funds. Because of the high cost of land transport, trade was restricted to wine, oil, and other easily transportable goods of high value.[2] Cash cropping of wine and oil was possible in areas with easy access to the Mediterranean Sea. Otherwise, most areas had to make sure that certain basic economic goods were available locally.[3]

17

The primary occupation of most people in ancient societies, therefore, was the cultivation of the soil. These people lived at subsistence level and did not have surplus funds to buy luxury goods. Their production was primarily oriented to consumption, except when it was expropriated by a dominating elite.[4]

Furthermore, economic activities in the ancient peasant household or village were "embedded" within the social structure. There were social limits to the accumulation of wealth (besides tax collection), and the household served as the basis for other social and religious activities.[5]

Ancient peasantries had from time immemorial made their own tools and clothing. Specialization in the village was relatively limited. The lack of peasant buying power meant that any "market" in antiquity lacked "depth." Consequently, markets could only expand in breadth, to incorporate new elites.[6] Production in antiquity, therefore, was subject to certain general social and technical constraints.

The following sections will develop in more detail these preliminary generalizations. Modern economists regularly speak of three standard "factors of production," namely, land, labor, and capital.[7] These factors are primarily defined vis-à-vis modern industrial economies based upon capitalist financial institutions. Since in this chapter the discussion centers upon the productive possibilities in ancient Roman Palestine, three ancient analogs to land, labor, and capital receive attention.[8] The agrarian economy of ancient Palestine certainly depended upon <u>land</u> for the growing of food and materials for other products.[9] Something must be said, therefore, about the geographic determinants of agriculture, soil, and so on. Unques-

tionably, <u>labor</u> and its organization played a great
role in the production of antiquity. Unlike modern
economies, those of the past were far more dependent
upon human and animal power. Something must be said
about labor inputs, division of labor, and so forth.
Finally, rather than capital, we can speak about the
<u>technology</u> available to the ancients. This discussion
needs to include both tools and crops.[10]

A. Land and Geographic Determinants of Production

Farming is always adapted to the prevailing
physical conditions. For instance, whether there are
large areas of flat land or mountainous terrain will
determine to some extent the scale, manner of tillage,
layout of the field systems, and settlement patterns.

In Galilee, the homeland of Jesus, a significant
contrast suggested itself to the ancients in the
division between Upper and Lower Galilee.[11] This
distinction was known both to Josephus and the
Mishnah.[12] The Mishnah also added the environs of the
Sea of Galilee to political Galilee.[13] However, it is
a region significantly separated geographically from
both Upper and Lower Galilee.[14] Succinctly stated,
Upper Galilee is fairly rugged and mountainous terrain,
relatively inaccessible, and yet with good opportunities for farming.[15] Lower Galilee, part of which
constitutes the "Shephelah" for Upper Galilee, is a
combination of low, east-west running ridges, fertile
valleys, and the plains of the Esdraelon Valley. In
antiquity, Lower Galilee was extensively and intensively farmed.[16] The lands about the Sea of Galilee
form the northern portion of the Jordan Rift Valley and
were adjudged extremely fertile in antiquity.[17]

Judaea to the south, by contrast, has a rather different aspect than Galilee. The mountainous terrain is oriented north and south. On the east, Judaea slopes dramatically to the arid Jordan Valley. On the west, Judaea encompasses the piedmont, the Shephelah. In the early Roman period, Judaea too was intensively cultivated.

Judaea and Galilee, though distinct from one another, still share major features in common geographically with other Mediterranean lands:

> Geology . . . made a threefold division of Mediterranean soil, the alluvial plain, the Tertiary slopes, and the mountains; and to each ancient agronomists assign its share in agricultural production . . . The Tertiary soils were suited to crops, the thinner higher land to the planted, the lower to the sown; the alluvial lands nourished store beeves.[18]

Geographic realities tended to encourage local, and perhaps regional, specialization. The valleys were best sown to grain, the hills planted with orchards and vineyards. Social organization, especially in view of the need for local and regional self-sufficiency, tended to mitigate geographic determinants somewhat.

In antiquity, as in the present, Galilee received rather more rainfall than Judaea.[19] Nonetheless, the limited rainfall of almost all parts of Palestine compelled the ancient peasantry to practice what is now called dry or dryland farming. An average annual rainfall between 250-500 mm, or less than 20 inches, determines the need for this kind of agriculture.[20] The basic problem of agricultural production becomes the preservation of enough moisture in the soil to sustain crops every other year. This is accom-

plished through careful cultivation and weed control.
As a rule, the semi-arid soils of dryland farming are
fairly fertile. Plowing stubble or green crops under
occasionally, replenishes nitrogen and other nutrients.

The ancient Palestinian peasantry cultivated
their hilly ground in such a way as to hinder soil
erosion and to maximize capture of the meager winter
rains. In Galilee a frequent method, to judge from the
archaeological record, was the cultivation of strip
lynchets, also known from elsewhere in the Mediterranean and Britain. In this type of cultivation the
plow was run obliquely at a shallow angle up and down
the sides of hills and mountains.[21] Enclosed fields
were also constructed. The enclosure walls additionally functioned as a depository for stones taken off
the fields and a fence against animal or human
intrusion.[22]

The prevalent type of enclosure in Judaea, by
contrast, was the terrace. Ron has identified terraces
via a mathematical criterion: A terrace has a field-
width to wall-height ratio less than or equal to 6.
These dimensions imply a slope equal to or greater than
10 degrees. The oldest terraces are found on the north
slopes of the mountains of Judaea. More recent
terraces on the south slopes are less elaborate.[23] The
extensive terraces of Judaea are probably evidence of
the organizing efforts of the period of the Israelite
Monarchy. Yet some of the terraces are certainly
older, going back to the period of earliest settlement
in the mountains.[24]

The prevalent form of settlement in early Roman
Palestine, as it had been in the remoter past, was the
village.[25] This form of settlement was expressive of
the kinship structure of ancient Israel. Furthermore,

as it has long been recognized, village sites were
chosen for reasons of security and proximity to water.
Hamel has recently pointed to another important ingredient in settlement location--the conservation of the
best soil for agriculture.[26] Consequently, many
settlements are to be found on the tops of hills, as in
Galilee. Such locations would also protect villages
from flooding in downpours.

B. Organization of Labor and Labor Inputs

The peasant family supplied the backbone of the
labor force for the ancient agrarian economy. This
work force was supplemented by animals and slaves.
Slavery did not, however, play a great role in the
agricultural production of Palestine. Even in Italy at
the turn of the eras, slavery was beginning to be a
less important source of labor supply for the great
estates. The future trend would be toward more or less
free tenant labor.[27]

Perhaps making this distinction quibbles over
terminology, because both Finley and Ste. Croix from
different perspectives have emphasized the dependent
status of this labor.[28] The eastern provinces of the
Roman empire never did see the type of slave-run
estates that appeared in Italy during the late second-
century B.C.E., nor the servile revolts that resulted.
On the other hand, the eastern peoples experienced an
ever increasing economic burden and loss of local
autonomy under the empire. In this sense, Ste. Croix
has tried to reinvigorate the marxist notion of a
"slave society" as a framework for considering labor
under the empire.[29] Rightly understood, this is a fair
characterization. It became increasingly expedient for

the elites of the empire to think of the tenants/
peasantry as "human cattle," as mere implements or
livestock of the Roman (or private) estate.[30]

The essential division of labor in any peasant
society lays stress on the individual peasant households. Within the household, there are further divisions between what men, women, and children do. At the
village level, there is sharing of common implements
and labor between households on the basis of balanced
reciprocity.[31]

In early Roman Palestine, the peasant male
concerned himself primarily with agricultural tasks
throughout the year. The nature of these tasks would
depend on the type of crops being raised.[32] The female
occupied herself with preparing food, making clothing,
and tending children.[33] Older children and the peasant
wife also contributed their labor to the fields when
needed.[34]

Palestine in the Graeco-Roman period saw a
greater division of labor within village and society
and some marketization. The marketization was probably
encouraged by the expansion of money volume and
increase in money exchanges. There were pressures by
the elites toward cash cropping.[35] These developments
were, nonetheless, subject to the limitations of pre-
industrial economies previously sketched. MacMullen,
for instance, believes that only a small minority of
the rural population of antiquity ever moved beyond
very basic trades or crafts. A few complex but necessary skills were available to the village primarily
through traveling artisans.[36] Greater division of
labor in the rural areas was more likely a function of
underemployment and the demands for labor on large
estates. There were opportunities for craft speciali-

zation in large urban areas, but these were not necessarily secure.[37] It is necessary to inquire carefully,
therefore, how far such tendencies away from subsistence farming and natural economy actually developed in
the Hellenistic-Roman period.[38]

It has been mentioned that intensive cultivation
was the norm in first-century Palestine. It is
possible to get some idea from the ancient Roman
agronomists, and from modern comparative studies, of
the kinds of labor inputs required in the subsistence
agriculture practiced in antiquity. For instance,
Columella gives the following figures on the amount of
work (days per iugerum [= 5/8 acre]) required in
standard agricultural operations:

   Wheat: Plowing, 4; harrowing, 1; first hoeing, 2;
      second hoeing, 1; weeding, 1; reaping, 1 1/2.
   Barley: Plowing, 3; harrowing, 1; hoeing, 1 1/2;
      reaping, 1.
   Beans: Plowing, 2; harrowing, 1 1/2; first hoeing,
      1 1/2; second hoeing, 1; third hoeing, 1;
      reaping, 1.
   Lentils: Plowing, 1 1/2; harrowing, 1; hoeing, 2;
      weeding, 1; reaping, 1.[39]

White supplies a useful table for comparing Columella's
figures on wheat production with other figures gleaned
from various places and periods. Columella's wheat
field required 14 1/2 to 15 1/2 man-days of work per
acre (the difference depending on whether or not
harrowing was required after plowing). English and
French peasants have expended comparable efforts of
around 12 man-days per acre.[40]

The agricultural calendar of antiquity is well
known to us from both Hebrew/Jewish and Roman sources.
The combination of agriculture, viticulture, and

arboriculture in all Mediterranean lands meant that the
work load was fairly evenly distributed throughout the
year.[41]

C. Technology and Crops

The tools of antiquity were relatively simple.
There was little innovation, mostly because there was
no incentive for the primary producer to increase
production. Any increase was typically carried off by
the tax collector or landlord in the Graeco-Roman
period. Only when the farmer was a conqueror and
liable to profit personally from increase, such as in
the cases of the Macedonian soldier-settlers of the
Ptolemaic period or Roman colonists, were agricultural
improvements possible. Such periods did not last long
in antiquity.[42]

The basic plow of the Mediterranean lands has
been called a "scratch plow."[43] It was not the heavy
plow of Europe. In fact, such a heavy plow is not
really suitable for dry farming conditions. Under
these conditions, subsoil disturbance is best kept to a
minimum to maintain the water reservoir.[44] Hoes,
shovels, and other digging and tilling instruments
supplemented the effort of plows.[45] Harnesses were
developed for use with oxen, but the harness for the
horse had not yet been conceived.[46]

Many different crops were cultivated by the
ancient Palestinian farmer. The major subsistence
crops were, of course, wheat and barley, grapes,
olives, and figs. Deuteronomy 8:8 long ago itemized
the major crops of Palestine (cited from the RSV):

A land of wheat and barley, of vines and fig trees
     and pomegranates, a land of olive trees and honey.
In addition to figs and pomegranates, dates were also

domesticated early.[47] The coming of the Greeks and
Romans dramatically expanded the agricultural
repertory.[48] Among these crops notably were various
vegetables like the cabbage and the lentil, and fruit
trees (apricot, peach, citron). The Jewish cultivator
also tended vegetables like leeks, onions, turnips,
cucumbers, and condiments like mustard, cumin,
coriander, chicory, and garlic.[49]

Grain, nonetheless, remained the staple of the
majority of the people in ancient Palestine.[50] The
basic wheat varieties were the related emmer (triticum
dicoccum) and durum wheat (triticum durum). Barleys
came in two-row and six-row varieties (hordeum
distichum and hordeum hexastichum).[51] Wheat requires
at least three months and a minimum of 225 mm of rain
to grow properly. Barley tolerates drier conditions
and soils with a higher salinity.[52]

Three methods of sowing were available to the
ancient farmer: Broadcasting by hand, drilling, and
planting.[53] Broadcasting was the normal procedure
among the ancient Palestinian peasantry.[54] The more
efficient method of drilling was never employed, it
would seem, in ancient Mediterranean agriculture. The
amount of seed sown on a given piece of ground was
determined by the quality of soil. However, the
ancient farmer probably sowed a little on the heavy
side to ensure adequate germination and yield.

To anticipate slightly a topic to be given
detailed treatment in the next chapter, it is known
that average returns in Palestine were around fivefold.
If approximately 2.12 bushels of grain per acre
constituted the normal seeding rate, an average yield
was around 11 bushels per acre.[55]

Applebaum thinks there were three plowings
before sowing.[56] Certainly there was much plowing in
preparation for annual sowing. The major purpose for
summer plowing was to conserve the water in the soil
under the prevalent dry farming conditions.[57] For the
same reason, weeding and cultivation in grain fields
during the growing season were very important. Weeds
are serious competitors with cereals for the limited
water and nutrients in the soil.[58]

In the absence of irrigation, low rainfall
demanded that half of the fields of ancient Palestine
on the average be left fallow in order to replenish the
water reservoir.[59] The Jewish sabbatical year was in
effect a religiously mandated fallow for all fields.[60]

Turning to some of the other major crops, the
fig tree grows well in semi-arid regions and in sandy
or rocky soil. It has a deep root system, so the tree
is fairly hardy. Figs ripen early in the summer and
are available in the summer months.[61]

Columella thought that olive trees were easily
cared for, but that the grapevine demanded much
attention:

> The cultivation of the vine is more complicated
> than that of any other tree, and the olive, the
> queen of trees, requires the least expense of
> all.[62]

Normally, olive groves were divided into two parts to
insure a steady production, because olive trees do not
bear in successive years.[63] The olive tree normally
takes about fifteen years from seed to full production,
and yields about 25-30 liters of oil per crop.[64]
Groves were usually intercropped in our period, as both
Roman and Jewish sources reveal.[65]

All of the Roman agronomists devoted extensive discussion to the care of grapevines, not only because they required more labor and specialized knowledge but because they were favored as a cash crop by the Roman elite. The vine takes about five years to fully develop.[66] According to Columella, an exceptional vineyard of his day produced over 7000 liters of wine per iugerum. The average production was between 518 and 775 liters per iugerum.[67]

Hamel has attempted to estimate the total possible production of ancient Palestine as a means of assessing the maximum population that could be sustained on the land. His results can be briefly summarized here, in order to give a quantitative idea of total production (in grain). Hamel assumes that half of the area available for growing at any given time would lie fallow. He uses the figure 763,000 hectares for the total area available for crops.[68] Thus, 381,000 hectares (half of 763,000) could be cropped.[69] Assuming then a seeding rate of 150 kilograms per hectare and an average yield of fivefold, Hamel obtains 230,000 metric tons available for consumption. His figure needs to be corrected slightly upward to 286,000 metric tons.[70] This amount would maximally sustain about one million people per year.[71]

D. Conclusion

The foregoing gives some indication of the factors, conditions, and extent of production in first-century Palestine. While Josephus thought the productivity of ancient Palestine was exceptional, that productivity could not transcend the limits of ancient technology and agricultural methods. Furthermore, production viewed in this absolute perspective is not adequate to elucidate how much was actually available to various groups in ancient Palestine. Some idea needs to be gained of the distribution of products and of the social structure in Palestine of the early empire. This is the task to which we shall now turn.

Notes to Chapter 1

[1]The book of M. J. Herskovits (1952) provided the name for the discipline. Karl Polanyi and several others (1957) gave impetus to the study of the economies of classical antiquity. T. F. Carney has given an excellent overview of these developments and significant results, in (1975) 137-234. Carney's book contributes in a number of ways to the thinking behind Part One. It should be remarked that anthropologists have been divided over the question of whether there is a substantive difference between modern and pre-modern economies, hence whether it is appropriate to apply modern economic theory to non-industrial economies. As a rule, economic anthropology has endorsed the "substantive difference" viewpoint. On this formal-substantive controversy, see Pearson in Polanyi, et al., (1957) 3-11; Kaplan (1968); Sahlins, (1968) 115.

[2]Discussion of "market": Carney, (1975) 146-152, 201. Cost of transportation: Lenski, (1966) 205.

[3]Carney, (1975) 179; Finley, (1973) 121ff.

[4]In the view of the "organization and production" school (Chayanov, et al.), "The primary aim of the peasant family is to feed itself and somehow manage to make whatever payments are due to the landlord, the moneylender, the merchant, or the state." This school is discussed in Thorner, (1968) 507.

[5]Nash, (1968) 363.

[6]Carney, (1975) 177. See the treatment of "agrarian societies" given by Lenski and Lenski, (1974) 207-262. Cf. M. Finley, (1973) 17-24. More will be said about peasant values and general features of the economy of the Roman empire at subsequent points in our study.

[7]Sloan and Zurcher, (1970) 163, s. v. "Factors of Production": "The various agents, broadly classified, that combine to produce additional wealth." Cf. Pearson, (1967) 59-62.

[8]A comparable discussion of these productive factors, also taking into account the differences between industrial and agrarian economies, may be found in Premnath, (1984) 11-18.

[9]Carney, (1975) 140: "For the last 200 years

[control of production] has involved capital. Throughout antiquity it involved land." See Ibid.: 181 for
another statement of this important distinction.

[10]Nash (1968) has identified four important
dimensions in primitive and peasant societies: 1)
Technology and division of labor, 2) Structure of
productive units, 3) The system and media of exchange,
and 4) The control of wealth and capital. We are
treating Nash's 1) and 2) in this chapter, 3) and 4) in
the next chapter. Premnath, (1984) 2 similarly
distinguishes factors and nature of production from
systems of exchange and distributive systems.

[11]Freyne, (1980a) 3; Meyers, (1976) 95.

[12]Josephus, JW (= Jewish War) 3.35ff; M. Shebi.
9:2.

[13]Freyne, (1980a) 9.

[14]Ibid.: 10.

[15]Ibid.: 13.

[16]Josephus, JW 3.43.

[17]Josephus, JW 3.35-43. See, however, the
comments of Hamel, (1983) 196ff about the tendency of
ancient writers to exaggerate the productivity of the
land.

[18]Postan, (1966) 1:93f. Cf. Columella, Ag
(Agriculture = Res Rustica) 2.2.1: campestre,
collinum, montanum. See also Varro, Ag 1.6.2. Consult
Applebaum, (1976) 638-41 on soils, along with Hamel,
(1983) 207-9.

[19]Consider the "Mean Rainfall" maps at the back
of IDBSup (1976). Cf. Zohary, (1982) 27, 41.

[20]Widtsoe, (1911) 1; Brengle, (1982) 1.

[21]Golomb and Kedar, (1971) 137 and Pl. 29:B.

[22]Ibid.: 137f.

[23]Ron, (1966) 38.

[24]Stager, (1976) 13.

[25]Applebaum, (1976) 641-44.

[26]Hamel, (1983) 219.

[27]White, (1970b) 35, 405. Finley, (1973) 69, 114-15. Ste. Croix, (1981) 215-18; Postan, (1966) 116.

[28]Finley, (1973) 69; Ste. Croix, (1981) 205-75.

[29]Ste. Croix, (1981) 3, 53-4, 209.

[30]White, (1970b) 374; Ste. Croix, (1981) 58, 549 n. 12.

[31]Gregory, (1975) 76.

[32]Hamel, (1983) 220ff has collected a number of rabbinic texts on this subject.

[33]M. Ket. 5:5 lists as basic tasks of women: Grinding flour, baking bread, washing clothes, cooking food, giving suck to children, and working in wool; cited in Hamel, (1983) 222.

[34]More on the agricultural work of women and children in Chapter 3, Section C, 3.

[35]Carney, (1975) 141-52.

[36]MacMullen, (1974) 14.

[37]See Finley, (1973) 134ff.

[38]Kreissig, (1969) 226f discusses these develop- ments. He thinks specialized production had taken hold in a number of areas (Galilee, Jericho), but that grain was still overall the prevalent crop. This picture agrees with our previous generalizations about the economy. J. Klausner, (1925) 177 has gathered evidence on the extent of the division of labor. This subject is taken up again in Chapter 5.

[39]Columella, Ag 2.12.1-4.

[40]White, (1970b) 413. Wolf, (1966) 28. Addi- tional modern figures for comparison can be examined in Clark and Haswell, (1970) 93-130. Richard Duncan-Jones has drawn attention to White's uncritical use of Columella's contradictory statements about labor inputs and has tried to give an independent assessment, in (1982) 327-333.

[41]For Palestine, one thinks especially of the ancient Gezer Calendar; see Wright, (1962) 183 and Galling, (1977) 3. Hamel, (1983) 212 and White, (1970b) 194-195 give conspectuses of agricultural operations on the basis of primary sources. See additionally Hamel, (1983) 219-22.

[42]I am indebted to Professor Marvin Chaney for the insights of this paragraph. See further Hamel, (1983) 223-41.

[43]Wolf, (1966) 32.

[44]Brengle, (1982) 90.

[45]Turkowski, (1968) 20, 31 and (1969) 102, 104, 107, supplies illustrations of these various kinds of agricultural implements.

[46]Postan, (1966) 142, 144.

[47]Stager, (1976) 12; Applebaum, (1976) 655.

[48]Applebaum, (1976) 648ff. The extent of this development is attested by the Zenon papyri (third century B.C.E.) and the talmudic literature especially. See further Hengel, (1974b) 1:44, 47; 2:35 n. 344.

[49]Applebaum, (1976) 653. Turkowski, (1969) 109-112. Zohary (1982) is especially useful.

[50]An incomparable treatment of the crops and diet of the people of early Roman Palestine is given in Hamel, (1983) 67-138. Hamel's study is based upon an extensive knowledge of ancient Greek, Roman, and Jewish, as well as modern, sources. The reader is referred there for more comprehensive information.

[51]Hamel, (1983) 73. Zohary, (1982) 74, 76. Cf. Trever (1962a) and (1962d).

[52]Liphschitz and Waisel, (1973) 35.

[53]White, (1970b) 178.

[54]Cf. Mk. 4:3-9. Sprenger, (1913) 80.

[55]Further discussion on the basis of ancient evidence in Chapter 2, Section B. See Hamel, (1983) 258-60 for a discussion of the amount of seed sown on ancient fields. The computer program in Appendix 2, to

which the reader is also referred, has assisted in
converting available figures on yields in antiquity to
modern equivalents. The commentary on the program
indicates how the numerous equations and their
constants were arrived at.

[56]Applebaum, (1976) 651f.

[57]White, (1970b) 180.

[58]This subject is taken up in some detail in
Chapter 3, Section C.

[59]Applebaum, (1976) 652; White, (1970b) 173.

[60]Applebaum, ibid. See also Hamel, (1983) 124
and 414-15 nn. 354 and 355.

[61]Trever, (1962b) 267; Zohary, (1982) 58f.

[62]Columella, Ag 5.7.1 (LCL translation); on
which consult White, (1970b) 225. General information
in Trever (1962c); Zohary (1982).

[63]White, (1970b) 227.

[64]Therefore, a symbol of peaceful conditions,
Finley, (1973) 31. Also, Frank, (1927) 60; Cowell,
(1967) 63; Jeremias, (1963) 181 n. 36 (citing Dalman).
Hamel, (1983) 73 thinks 50-60 liters, although he does
not give the source for his figures.

[65]White, (1970b) 226. Cf. M. Peah 3:1, 4; 7:2.

[66]Frank, (1927) 60; Cowell, (1967) 63. See also
M. Hengel, (1968) 11 n. 41.

[67]Columella, Ag 3.2, 7. On the volume of the
amphora, see Duncan-Jones, (1982) 373.

[68]Including Israel, the West Bank, and Gaza, on
the basis of the Atlas of Israel: Hamel, (1983) 473 n.
241. Peraea and the Decapolis are left out of
consideration.

[69]Hamel, (1983) 264.

[70]The 150 kilograms per hectare is near the
Jewish seeding rate of one cor per cor's-space and
Roman rate of 5 modii per iugerum. The correction is

urged, because 150 x 5 = 750 kgs/ha = 0.75 metric tons per hectare.   Then, 381,000 x 0.75 = 286,000.

[71]Hamel, (1983) 264.   Further considerations about production, in conjunction with a discussion of Herodian taxation, are taken up below, Chapter 2, Section B.

CHAPTER 2

THE GENERAL CHARACTER OF ECONOMIC DISTRIBUTION
IN THE PALESTINE OF JESUS

While historians frequently describe the productivity of the soil in ancient Palestine in terms
similar to those in the preceding chapter, it is necessary to note that this approach reveals little of how
that produce was distributed, or who consumed what.[1]
Yet it seems essential for an understanding of historical dynamics to know, for instance, that the many in
antiquity who did the work of cultivating the cereals,
logumes, olives, grapes, and so forth, themselves lived
at a bare minimum subsistence, and that their precarious situation could easily deteriorate further.[2]
The absolute productivity of the land in
antiquity cannot be the sole topic of conversation.
One must proceed to discuss the "relative" productivity
of land vis-à-vis various groups of people. One must
also investigate the interrelationship of historical
events and agrarian conditions. The historical and
sociological character of this investigation will be
evident in what follows, as land tenure, subsistence
levels, taxes, rents, and levels of indebtedness are
examined.

A. The Tenure of Land

Land tenure viewed from the perspective of
elites, that is "from above," is usually expressed in
territorial or legal terms. Land tenure viewed from
the vantage point of the peasant proprietor, "from

37

below," probably can best be expressed in terms of
customary right or even a relationship of "kinship."[3]

When one begins to search for a model for land
tenure in first-century Palestine, one must be clear
about whose interests are being served by the concept.
It is not accidental that the elites of antiquity
thought territorially and the small proprietors rela-
tionally. The former realized that territory added to
their possession meant added income. In other words,
the income of the elites stood in direct proportion to
the territory they controlled. One reads in existing
treatments of land tenure in antiquity about "categories" of tenure: Royal lands, settlement lands, city
land.[4] Eventually these categories became sacrosanct
through codifications of law, expressing the rights and
privileges of elites.

On the other hand, the small proprietor was
attached to a plot of land that was considered an
inalienable heritage and acknowledged as such within
the village. Outsiders who "took possession" of the
territory upon which the smallholder resided were
viewed as usurpers who forced themselves upon the
peasantry and demanded an undeserved share of the
land's produce. In this way, the relational aspect of
tenure bifurcates--expressed toward a landlord through
grudgingly-paid tributes, taxes, rents, corvées, and
other obligations and duties, on the one hand, but
toward the family patrimony in land through a feeling
of loyalty and quasi-familial relationship, on the
other.[5]

Unfortunately, the historical and archaeological
data available for clarifying in detail the agrarian
situation in first-century Palestine is not as abundant
as it is, say, for first-century Roman Africa, Egypt,

or Asia Minor.[6] There is a dearth of Graeco-Roman
inscriptional evidence for Palestine. No one apparently has ever collected in one place what does exist.[7]
The Mishnah and the Talmuds offer useful material.[8]
The difficulty with this material, however, lies in
determining when it reflects the agrarian situation in
the first century. Only sporadic hints can be gleaned
from Josephus.[9] These difficulties notwithstanding,
the general details of agrarian relations in the
Graeco-Roman period are fairly well known, particularly
from the vantage point of the elites.[10] For Palestine
in the early Hellenistic period, the Zenon papyri are
of special value for gaining insight into agrarian
conditions.[11]

Palestine received its formative administrative
and economic organization in the Graeco-Roman period
under the third-century B.C.E. kingdom of the
Ptolemies. From the Persians, the Ptolemies acquired
royal lands in the Jordan Valley and in the Esdraelon
Plain. These were worked by "royal peasants."[12] The
Ptolemies recognized some temple lands in Palestine,
like those that sustained the Jerusalem cult. Powerful
native princes, like Tobias, upon whom the Ptolemies
depended to pacify the natives, owned land and
villages. The Greek rulers were compelled to recognize
native patrimonial domain, though they tried whenever
possible to limit hereditary tenure (as in Egypt).
Cities on the coast and in Transjordan were assigned
hinterland to support them.[13]

The Ptolemies also inherited, through Alexander,
the basic Persian administrative organization of
Palestine. The Persian province 'Abar-nahara had been
subdivided into smaller provinces, m^edînan. These in
turn were divided into "districts," p^elekhîn. The

Ptolemies simply renamed these divisions.[14] Unlike
Ptolemaic Egypt, however, the larger unit of administration in Palestine was not the nome, but the
hyparchy. This fact underscores, along with the
cleruchies (land allotments to soldier-colonists), the
military character of Ptolemaic presence in Palestine.
The p^elekhîn became topoi as in Egypt.[15] The village,
as also in Egypt, constituted the basic fiscal and
economic unit in "Syria and Phoenicia," as the Palestinian province of the Ptolemies was called in official
parlance.[16] Villages were governed by native chiefs
(komarchs), but the interests of the central government
were protected by special officials, the kōmomisthōtai.
Letters in the Zenon correspondence indicate that, in
Idumaean Marisa at any rate, officials similar to those
of any Egyptian village were in residence.[17]

     Although they thus retained the basic outlines
of the Persian system, the Ptolemies effected some
significant changes as well. While they kept the
fundamental boundaries of the hyparchies of Judaea,
Samaria, and Galilee, they bequeathed special privileges to the military settlements at Scythopolis and
Samaria.[18] As for the coast, under the Persians it was
within the control of the Phoenician cities. The
Ptolemies left this arrangement alone initially, but by
the time of Philadelphus the coast had been "provin-
cialized," Ptolemais (Acco) was founded as a counter to
the older Phoenician cities, and several other cities
(Jamnia, Azotus-Yam) were given special autonomy.[19]

     In the Transjordan new territorial arrangements
were implemented. A host of new hyparchies, designated
by "-itis," came into being. In the south adjacent to
the Lisan of the Dead Sea was Gabalitis. North of this
was Moabitis. Adjacent Ammanitis was the home of the

famous Tobiads of pre-Hasmonean times.   In the region
formerly designated by the Persians as Karnaim, the
Ptolemies created Gaulanitis, Batanaea, Trachonitis,
and Auranitis. City territories, like those of Gerasa,
Amathus, Pella, Gadara, etc., were established in
addition to the districts.[20]

It is easy to perceive in these administrative
divisions a policy quite consistent with the organization of the Ptolemaic administrative bureaucracy,
namely, the fragmentation of native units and
loyalties. Divide and rule! Just as the bureaucracy
was full of a host of officials jealous or suspicious
of one another and ready to betray a colleague for a
price, so one may imagine the provincial arrangements
were such as to create--through regions, city territories, military colonies, and the like--small political entities both easy to farm for revenues and
jealously guarding their meager privileges and territorial rights over against the others.[21]

The Zenon correspondence also illuminates the
agricultural development of Palestine by the Ptolemies
and their agents. The export of a large variety of
agricultural products from Palestine to Egypt is
documented through receipts in the Zenon archives.[22]
Even more important are the direct documentations of
the agricultural development of the country, especially
references to the finance minister Apollonius's large
estate in Galilee that produced wine comparable to the
best Greek wines.[23]

Agrarian conditions in Palestine during subsequent periods, unfortunately, are not so clear as
during the time of the Ptolemies. The brilliant light
of the Zenon correspondence fades. The social historian is forced to employ less direct evidence and
controlled inference.

Though Antiochus III initially expressed grati-
tude to the Jews in Palestine for their assistance in
the defeat of Ptolemy V (Jos. AJ 12.138ff), Seleucid
agrarian arrangements nonetheless marked the continuation of the aims of Alexander. It was his plan to weld
together out of the former subjects of the Persian
kings a vast Greek empire. This would be accomplished
through the political and cultural hegemony of
poleis.[24] The process, of course, had already begun
under the Ptolemies, but they were less interested in
cultural hegemony and more interested in the revenues
that accrued from Palestine. Political expediency
urged the Ptolemies to respect in many ways native
customs and tradition. For this reason, the Ptolemies
were willing to work with, rather than change, existing
realities.[25]

The growing difficulties of the Seleucid House
in the face of Roman power clearly was a more important
policy consideration than native realities or administrative arrangements inherited from the Ptolemies. The
Seleucids took a different direction: Unite and rule!
The Ptolemaic bureaucracy gave way before a combination
of Seleucid prebendalism and "Greek" urban aristocracies. The monarch depended upon the loyalty and
good-will of the aristocracies, not strictly upon
military occupation. Ptolemaic hyparchies were combined into the larger Seleucid eparchies. Judaea and
Jerusalem, however, were grafted into the eparchy of
Samaria.

The appearance especially of Antiochus IV caused
a crisis of unprecedented proportions for the Jewish
people.[26] The venerable high priesthood in Jerusalem
began to be sold to the highest bidder (Jason,
Menelaus). An aspiring group of Jews attempted to have

the native city founded as a Hellenistic polis. The
abolishment of the customary laws--the Torah--provoked
the uprising of the Maccabees and with them the Jewish
peasantry. Along with strong apocalyptic expectations
(e.g. Daniel), there was perhaps an agrarian aspect to
this revolt:

> Schalit, indeed, accepting the predominance of
> royal land in Judaea under the Seleucids, believes
> that the Maccabees freed the Jewish peasants from
> the oppressive taxation associated with that
> regime, and distributed newly acquired lands among
> them in return for the obligation to military
> service, though part of the lands acquired became
> royal property leased to cultivators in tenancy.[27]

After a long struggle, and the decline of the
Seleucid monarchy, the Jews finally achieved independence under the first Hasmonean rulers. Conditions at
the time of Simon are lauded in 1 Maccabees (14:12):
"Each man sat under his vine and his fig tree, and
there was none to make them afraid." Another passage
notes, "And in his days things prospered in his hands,
so that the Gentiles were put out of the country . . ."
(14:36). This seemed to be a return to an agrarian
monarchy like David's and Solomon's (1 Kgs. 4:25). Yet
the emergence of the Phariseee at the time of John
Hyrcanus, and the literature from Qumran, show that not
all Jews were happy with Hasmonean rule. Paradoxically, the Hasmoneans adopted the model of the
Hellenistic kingdom for their own. Simon declared
himself a military dictator (1 Macc. 14:41-48).
Hyrcanus paid mercenaries out of funds robbed from the
tombs of the Israelite kings (Jos. AJ 7.393). He no
longer found support from the former Hasidim
(Pharisees, Essenes), but aligned himself with the

(presumably) more hellenized and worldly Sadducean
aristocracy. According to Schalit, the conflict
between Jannaeus and the Pharisees also had an agrarian
aspect. That Hasmonean (like a Hellenistic monarch)
may have converted autonomous Jewish land back into
royal land in order to support his many military
campaigns.[28] A Jewish peasantry, loving to enjoy the
fruits of agriculture undisturbed by excessive central
taxation, was alienated from an increasingly "hellenized" and oppressive monarchy.

The coming of the Romans again changed all of
this. The territories previously conquered or acquired
by the Hasmoneans were taken away, along with the
Jewish state. Cities were reestablished, to counter-
balance the native Jewish population.[29] Applebaum
thinks this drastic reorganization disenfranchized many
Jewish proprietors and created a social problem that
lasted until the Jewish War.[30] Pompey, of course,
favored the inept Hyrcanus II as the figurehead ruler.
During this period, though, Antipater and his Idumaean
sons played an increasing role in Jewish political
affairs.

The Senate's approval of Herod as king marked
the beginning of the end for Hasmonean hopes of
restoration. The revolt of Antigonus in 40 B.C.E.
failed, despite Parthian support. Herod prevailed in
37, and managed to retain his crown through the
political vicissitudes leading to Octavian's victory
and the Principate. As a client king, Herod retained
the bureaucratic apparatus typical of the Hellenistic
monarchy. He apparently, however, utilized a dual
system of administration--one system for the native
Jewish population in village territories ("king's-
country"), another system for the more hellenized,

urban territories. In king's-country the village was
the basic administrative unit. A "village scribe" was
responsible for the monarch's interests. Heads of
local families, or "elders," represented the village.
A number of villages and their lands made up a
toparchy. There were no real cities in these
territories.[31]

The administrative picture remained the same for
the time after Herod's death and up until the Jewish
War. The procurators in Judaea simply inherited what
Herod and his predecessors had worked out. The Romans,
in general, were conservative in the Hellenistic East
in terms of administration.[32] They were still willing
to use client kingship after Herod, as the careers of
Agrippa I and II show. However, in the post-70 period
when this was no longer possible, the Romans began to
reorganize Palestine along the lines of the other,
older provinces. The fundamental tenet of this policy
was the attachment or "attribution" of native territories to cities, and their administration thereby, as
well as the fostering of urbanization.[33] "As a result
of the policy of urbanisation most of the non-urban
territories were transformed into cities in the course
of the second and third centuries."[34]

This brief survey of agrarian developments
emphasizes the administrative aspect and is exemplary
of history written "from above," from the perspective
of the rulers and the victors. The discussion that
follows aims at deepening our view of agrarian conditions and the circumstances of land tenure in Palestine
under the early empire. While the use of social scientific tools in this historical work cannot overcome the
deficiencies of the evidence entirely, it can help to
bring out, in a way sympathetic to the subject people,
the effects of Roman domination and exploitation.

In Hellenistic and Roman Palestine the domain of
kings or emperors and their prebends or clients could
usurp (in theory and practice) patrimonial rights of
the native peasantry.[35] This social prerogative of the
powerful received some limitation in Graeco-Roman law,
in the terminology and procedures that effected alienation of land: A distinction is made both among the
Greeks and the Romans between the land itself and use
of it. For the Greeks property is denoted by ktēsis,
use or usufruct by chrēsis.[36] Similarly, Roman law
distinguished dominium from possessio, and land taxes
were assessed against the right to use the land
(possessio).[37]

These juristic distinctions indicate that older
notions of hereditary patrimony were displaced by
private property rights and more fluid conceptions of
land and peasant exploitation. If one only paid for
the right to use land, in other words, then that right
could be taken away through legal means and transferred
to another. In older tribal conceptions of land
ownership, among the Greeks and Romans as among the
Jews, land was the inalienable property of the clan.[38]
Under the ancient oriental monarchies, however, kings
had come to consider the land of their dominion as
personal property or "on loan" to other nobility and
peasantry.[39] Laws notwithstanding, the powerful of
antiquity frequently managed to get control over what
they wanted.[40]

That land tenure involves social perception and
questions of legitimation of ownership, as well as
expresses socio-political realities, is further demonstrated when one looks at the rabbinic material on land
use and ownership. The Mishnah, for instance,
prohibits the lease or sale of land to aliens

("gentiles").[41]   In the second century and later, the
rabbinic literature clearly alludes to legal problems
arising from the alienation of land to foreigners.   In
all stages of the tradition, nonetheless, usury was
prohibited (to protect native land) and transfer of
land was considered robbery.[42]

The question is: To what extent was land being
alienated anyway in Palestine in the early first
century, to Romans or their clients, and by what means
was it accomplished?   A general process of destruction
of the Jewish legal view and the free peasantry in
Roman Palestine must be suspected, in view of the
course of Roman domination both before and after the
Jewish War.   What was the aspect of this process in the
early years of the empire--under Augustus and Tiberius?

It is certainly known that large estates existed
at the turn of the eras.[43]   The Hasmoneans, as we saw
above, held domains inherited from the Hellenistic
kings, while Herod confiscated, accumulated, and
dispersed the properties of his political opponents.[44]
Rostovtzeff long ago wrote:

> Judaea, Samaria, and still more Galilee are studded
> with hundreds of villages inhabited by peasants,
> above whom stands a native aristocracy of large
> landowners, who are patrons of the villages . . .
> Still more opulent are the officials of the kings
> and tetrarchs, and the kings and tetrarchs
> themselves and their families.   Lastly, we find
> estates of the Roman emperor himself and the
> imperial family, and even a Roman military colony
> established by Vespasian at Emmaus after the Jewish
> War.   Such were the conditions of life in
> Palestine, and in later times there was clearly no
> change, except that landed proprietors of other

than Jewish origin, like Libanius, increased in
number.[45]

Herod's finance minister, Ptolemy, owned a
village called Arous. Another man of first-century
Jerusalem, Eleazar b. Ḥarsum, is said to have owned a
thousand villages and a thousand ships.[46] In the view
of both Rostovtzeff and Jeremias, then, the peasantry
of Palestine stood already under (hence, in tenancy to)
a hierarchy of elite groups. The discussions of
agricultural matters in the Mishnah proceed as though
the land is unambiguously under Jewish jurisdiction.
How is the difference in perspective to be understood?

While a comprehensive answer cannot be given
here, some observations are possible. Archaeology
seems to bear out Rostovtzeff's contention, for along
with the many nucleated villages in Palestine there
grew up already in the first century B.C.E. isolated
farms that can only be interpreted as villas, dominating estates sometimes including several villages.[47]
Furthermore, careful attention to the rabbinic terminology for these settlements shows that it also supports
this picture: Ir ('yr) denotes an isolated rural
settlement or farm, exactly translated into English by
"town."[48] Irîm (pl.) then correspond to Latin villae.
ᵃyaroth and kiryoth, by contrast, represent "settlements which stood in a certain relationship to given
centres . . . administratively dependent on a larger
centre . . ."[49] Thus, the Mishnah does not gainsay the
archaeological evidence, but indirectly confirms it.
In addition, if the Mishnah is not more explicit about
the agrarian situation, this may relate to the fundamental ideological conflict alluded to above, between
the Jewish view of what was happening and the Roman
view.

The historical realities of land tenure in
first-century Palestine present, as can be seen, a
rather confusing aspect. It is useful, therefore, to
consider at this point several models, constructed with
the help of the social sciences, in order to clarify
the picture.[50]

Figure 1 represents the elements of a hypothetical peasant freehold, that is, where the peasant
family lives on the land and has control over what it
produces. The basic "loads" on the agricultural output
are of two general sorts, those that are economically
necessary to maintain the peasant household and those
that are due someone else. These loads can be itemized
as follows:

1) It is, of course, necessary for the peasant
and his family to derive subsistence from their plot.
Thus, the first concern of the peasant will be to
secure output for the food requirements of himself and
his family. These requirements can be estimated by
reference to necessary caloric minima: A person in a
modern industrial country requires roughly 2500
calories per day to balance energy expenditures.
Peasantry in modern Third World countries obtain less,
sometimes much less, than 2500 calories.[51] The subsistence output (S) can be defined, therefore, as the
amount of grain or other produce necessary over a given
time to provide the peasant family with a certain
minimum energy/food intake. The fraction of S available for each member of the peasant household varies
inversely with the number of mouths to feed. Much of
this food energy is "plowed back" by the family into
their plot in the form of agricultural labor (L).

2) The second output comprises the fund of seed
for planting and perhaps feed for livestock necessary

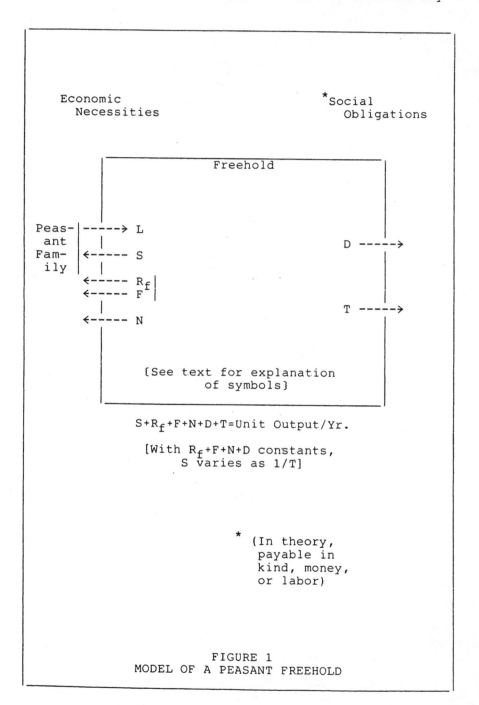

FIGURE 1
MODEL OF A PEASANT FREEHOLD

for the agricultural unit to function during the next
year. The replacement fund (R_f), along with fodder
(F), assures "the upkeep of the instruments of production."[52] Such funds are pretty well fixed from one
year to the next. Wolf gives a medieval example for
such a fund requirement amounting to thirty-three
percent for seed, and over sixty percent for seed and
livestock.[53]

    3) The third output, the needs fund (N), is
reserved for trade or barter, to satisfy household
needs that cannot be met by the peasant family's own
efforts. This output supports the existence of
artisans and other specialists that supply specific
needs.

    4) The dues fund (D) covers expenditures arising
from, or necessitated by, participation in the social
order. These expenditures might cover the costs of a
wedding, a local cultic festival, or other social and
religious obligations. This fund, unlike that for seed
replacement, has a far more variable aspect, because
every group or society will determine differently what
surplus is appropriate or available for ceremonial dues
and how many such obligations are necessary.

    5) Regarding the final charge, Eric Wolf writes:
"It is this production of a fund of rent which critically distinguishes the peasant from the primitive
cultivator."[54] "Rent" is the general term for sur-
pluses extracted from peasantry on the basis of asymmetrical power relations. In Figure 1, however, the
output is designated tax or tribute (T) to distinguish
it from the rent (R) paid additionally to the possessor
of a large estate, to whom the peasant may become
subordinate. In essence, though, rents or taxes are
simply additional burdens alongside the others already

distinguished. Payments of all these social obligations (i.e. dues, rents, or taxes) can be made theoret-
ically in labor, in money, or in kind. In Figure 1
they are expressed by payment in kind.

Turning to Figure 2, the output (R) going to the
private landlord or prebendal official is added to the
picture of Figure 1. It is evident from this way of
looking at the agricultural production of the peasantry
that such outputs could be multiplied in the abstract
ad infinitum, although in practice of course there
would not be enough to go that far. Practically
speaking, all of the outputs have to balance against,
and are limited by, the total unit output per unit
time. Thus, it is further evident that given R_f, F, N,
and D as constants, S varies inversely as T or R + T.
And the more rents and taxes that are demanded, the
more the subsistence level falls. Figures 1 and 2
represent, in summary, the theoretical position of the
peasant "proprietor"--seen from below--both in the
situation of "freeholding" and as part of a larger
estate.

Figure 3 displays in model-form several types of
tenancy. This term can be defined as the condition of
socio-economic subordination expressed in arrangements
of land tenure. Briefly, the four models are:

Figure 3.1 represents in outline how the free
peasant P loses control of his own plot, and becomes a
tenant. His land is incorporated into estate B.

Figure 3.2 shows a situation where the tenant
works the ground of a landlord under agreement to pay a
percentage of the harvest as rent, conversely to
receive a percentage as subsistence.

The situation of 3.3 is that of a tenant who
agrees to pay a fixed rent, either in kind or in money.

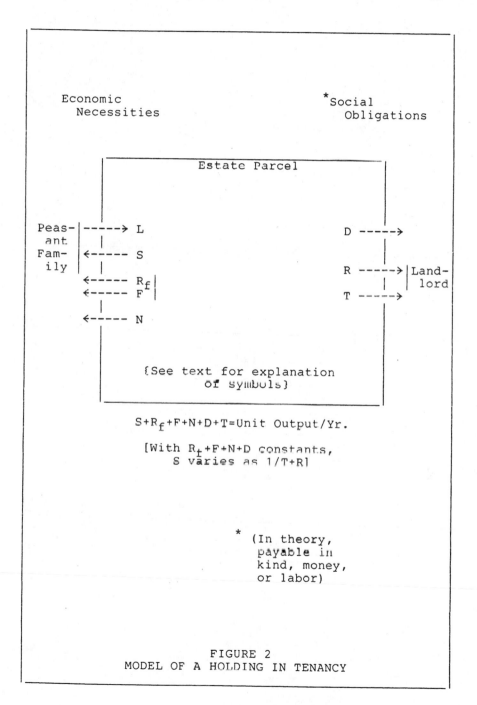

Economic   *Social
   Necessities   Obligations

Estate Parcel

Peas-|------> L   D -----→
  ant |
Fam- |<----- S
  ily | R ----->|Land-
       <----- R_f| | lord
       <----- F | T -----→
        |
       <----- N

{See text for explanation
      of symbols}

$S + R_f + F + N + D + T = $ Unit Output/Yr.

[With $R_t + F + N + D$ constants,
     S varies as $1/T+R$]

* (In theory,
    payable in
    kind, money,
    or labor)

FIGURE 2
MODEL OF A HOLDING IN TENANCY

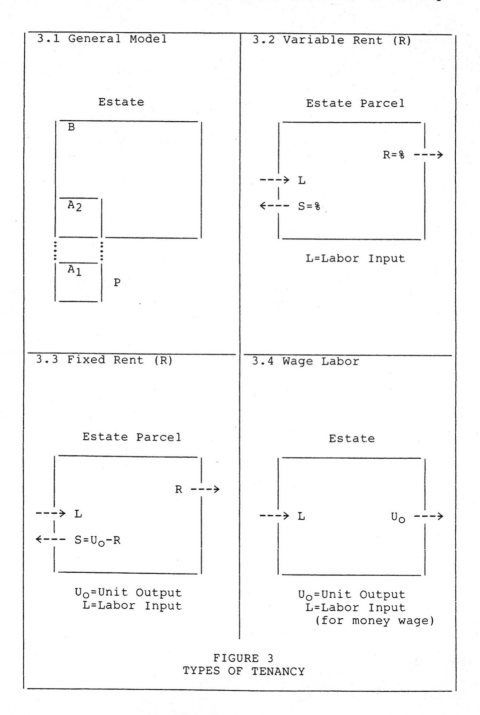

FIGURE 3
TYPES OF TENANCY

Finally, although not dealt with further in this discussion, 3.4 completes the typology by depicting the use of landless wage labor on an estate for required or seasonal work.[55]

Returning to Figure 3.1, the model provides an example of a spatial or territorial representation of estate domain. Figure 3.1 is actually the landlord's view, while 3.2 and 3.3 represent the peasant's. The subsistence from A_1 is no longer adequate for peasant P and his family. Perhaps taxation has become too great, or there has been a bad year and P is forced to borrow R_f from the owner of estate B. Peasant P then has to take S gained from A_1 to repay the loan to B's owner. This is a typical mechanism in the absence of war leading to the establishment of a relationship of dependence.[56]

Thus, an increasingly asymmetrical power relation enters into the life of P, driving him into tenancy. This final step occurs when the peasant's patrimony is alienated to the owner of B, increasing the size of B's estate (A_2). This "transfer" of ownership, however, is not a physical transfer of A_1 like the movement of a puzzle-piece. What is transferred, rather, is control of A_1 into the hands of the owner of B. The peasant family will probably stay on A_2 as tenants of B's owner.

Considering Figure 3 again, 3.2 and 3.3 picture two of the most common forms of tenancy mentioned in the ancient world, types of which have terminological labels extant in Hebrew or Aramaic, Greek, and Latin. While the authorities are not able entirely to agree on the cross-cultural linguistic equivalences, they are in essence:

Figure 3.2: Sharecropper = 'rys = metochos or
geōrgos = partiarius or colonus.[57]

Figure 3.3: Tenant who pays a fixed rent = ḥwkr (in
kind, only in Mishnah) or śwkr (in money, only
in Tosephta) = misthōtēs = conductor.[58]

The type of tenancy in 3.2 allows the risk to be shared
by both tenant and landlord. The type in 3.3, on the
contrary, is characterized essentially by placing the
burden of risk upon the tenant.

G. E. M. de Ste. Croix places ancient tenants
broadly in two classes--those who had written leases
and those who did not. However, Ste. Croix also groups
tenants "according to the nature of the landlord's
return": 1) Tenants who paid a fixed rent in money, 2)
tenants who paid a fixed rent in kind, 3) share-
croppers, and 4) those who provided labor services.[59]
This agrees pretty well with the above schema.
Bernhard Lang, on the basis of modern comparative
studies, has typed agrarian relations in the ancient
Near East in three broad categories: Patronage,
partnership, and exploitation. Tenancies might share
in one or all of these characteristics.[60]

W. W. Tarn has written that the first type (3.2)
was prevalent in Asia (and presumably Palestine), while
the second (3.3) was the dominant form in Egypt:

For while the Egyptian peasant under the Ptolemies
paid a fixed annual sum, the Seleucids continued
the practice, which was immemorial in Asia and had
also obtained in Egypt under the Pharaohs and the
Persians, of taking a tenth of the harvest; they
were thus true partners with the peasantry, sharing
losses in a bad year, a matter of which Antony
boasted when he stressed the beneficence of Rome in
following the Seleucid system of taking a tenth.[61]

In Egypt the so-called royal peasantry on crown lands would enter into a written lease-agreement with the state to pay so-and-so many artabas per aroura of land. The amount of the tax would be fixed each lease period contingent upon the vicissitudes of the Nile flood, which necessitated well-nigh continuous land surveying and affected the times of planting. Because the bureaucracy had gotten the process of registration and assessment down to an exact science, the tax yields could be reasonably predicted in advance. However, as Tarn observes, any misfortune such as pestilence or any destruction of the crop had to be borne by the peasant lessee. The state always got its due as per agreement.[62]

Perhaps the share-rental system can be said to reflect less predictable agrarian conditions and rain agriculture, where the absolute yield of the crop was more uncertain. In this case it would make more sense for the lessor to leave arrangements less exact, yet still with a predetermined share of whatever crop would grow. The share-rental system might appear to be the more humane of the two systems, but in practice the elites extracting rents and taxes always attempted to maximize their take by adding more taxes. This recalls Rostovtzeff's picture of a hierarchy of landlords, each of whom would be sure to exercise his rights over against the limited yield of the land.

B. Level of Subsistence, Taxes, and Rent

It is possible, with the help of the models just outlined and modern comparative studies, to obtain some quantitative notions of the level of subsistence in the ancient Mediterranean world. Moreover, if S varies inversely as T or T + R, then pursuing a quantitative

investigation of taxes and rent levels perhaps can give
a better idea of how great a burden was being placed
upon the ancient resource base and the peasantry.

In order to assess the adequacy of a given level
of subsistence, attention must first be directed to the
caloric content of various ancient Mediterranean foods.
As indicated in the last section, 2500 calories supplies the average daily caloric need for (sedentary)
adult males in modern industrialized nations.[63] This
amount, of course, will vary with age, weight, and sex.
And not all societies have eaten as well as the western
world. Modern figures show a minimum caloric consumption, averaged across all age-groups and sexes, of 2200
for Africa, 2000 for Asia, and 1900 for Latin America.[64]

The 2500 calorie figure, nevertheless, offers a
useful reference point for considering the subsistence
levels of "underdeveloped" nations and ancient peasantries. For example, when the overall daily energy
requirements for adult African males--aged 20-29,
weighing between 50-60 kg, who must also engage in
vigorous physical activity--are considered, a figure of
around 3000 calories emerges! The average energy
figure for heavier, sedentary people in North America
gives a very good indication of the needs of lighter,
more active people in Africa.

From the known properties of grain (assuming
that these have not changed in twenty centuries), the
2500 calorie minimum is satisfied by 794 grams of wheat
or by 756 grams of barley.[65] The weight of wheat is
equivalent to about 0.03, and the weight of barley to
about 0.04, American bushels per person per day. This
works out to around 11 bushels of wheat, or around 15
bushels of barley, per person per year.[66] Clark and
Haswell have given an absolute minimum yearly subsis-

tence requirement, averaged across a whole population, of 210 kg of wheat. This is equivalent to about 8 bushels and supplies 1800 calories daily.[67]

When converting these figures into terms of ancient measures, two problems arise immediately. The first problem is that ancient measures were frequently not standardized and the same unit could vary in capacity from locale to locale.[68] Conversion would be far more accurate by weight, if the ancients had measured grain by weight. The second problem is that the state of the grain (wet, dry, etc.), its density, and the form in which it was measured (bulk, flour, etc.) will variably affect any calculation of energy content on the basis of volume. Approximations necessarily have to enter into the calculation. Fortunately, some ancient data on wheat densities exist that are in good accord with modern experience.[69]

A third problem needs to be mentioned. The ancient peasant diet consisted predominately, but not entirely, of grains. That diet could be, and regularly was, supplemented by other foods. So a strict grain index for subsistence level is not entirely accurate. Taking this problem into account, Clark and Haswell have concluded that an additional 60 kg or so (measured in grain equivalents) rounds out the picture of minimum subsistence, giving a bottom line subsistence reference of 275 kg. This works out to 2400 calories--very near to the previously established 11 bushels of wheat, or 15 bushels of barley, per year.

The investigation proceeds now to a determination of what the ancients thought a suitable subsistence baseline to be.[70] For the period of the Roman republic, Peter Brunt estimates that 144 modii of wheat adequately provided for the needs of a family of

four.[71] This would be equivalent to 35 bushels for
four or about nine bushels for each person per year.
Brunt's estimates are significantly lower, in other
words, than the 11 bushels calculated above to provide
the caloric minimum of 2500 calories. If Brunt's
figures are not in error, the average person in the
republic received a grain minimum that was probably
inadequate for agricultural workers.

A. C. Johnson believes that for Roman Egypt an
"average food consumption of 10 artabae of wheat per
year is probably too high."[72] This would equal 11
bushels of wheat per person per year, a figure in line
with the modern determination of subsistence minima.
The caloric intake in grain for the Egyptian peasantry
living under the empire was either just adequate or
slightly low.

J. Jeremias determines that one-twelfth of a
seah of wheat (i.e. one-twelfth of 13.125 liters or 1.1
liters) per day was the daily minimum meal ration for
the pauper in first-century Palestine. This figure is
corroborated from the gospel accounts of the feeding of
the five thousand, from Revelation 6:6 (assuming the
choinix = 1.02 liters), Cicero, and elsewhere as a
standard ration.[73] Working out the yearly ration from
the 1.1 liter measure, one arrives at 400 liters or
around 11.5 bushels of wheaten meal per year. This
standard was more than adequate, since the density of
meal is greater than that of unmilled grain.

The evidence in the preceding paragraphs
suggests an average baseline for ancient subsistence of
around 10 bushels of wheat per person per year, or 2400
calories daily. The Mishnah allows some additional
inferences concerning the Palestinian situation. M.
Ket. 5:8 details the food allowances for a divorced

woman: 2 qabs of wheat or 4 qabs of barley, 0.5 qab of
pulse, 0.5 log of oil and 1 qab of dried figs per week.
Two qabs (4.4 liters) works out to 228 liters per
year--only 6.5 bushels. With the supplements to the
diet, this represents 2700 calories per day. Taking
the four qabs of barley option, the number of calories
available per day would rise to 3300. Four qabs of
barley was the better deal. This diet must be evaluated in the light of the heavy work load carried by
women in ancient Palestine.[74] Mishnaic law provided
the divorced woman with an adequate diet, if the letter
of the law was met.

These results can be checked by another route.
It is possible to establish the size of a "subsistence
plot." From information supplied by Polybius and Cato
on basic food requirements for the military and for
slaves, it is known that 2 iugera supported one adult
(presumably for a year).[75] A iugerum was 0.63 acres,
so this is a plot roughly 1.3 acres in size. K. D.
White reports on a study by Hopkins corroborating this
result.[76] Hopkins has tentatively concluded that in
ancient Italy between 7 and 8 iugera, or around 4.5
acres, were necessary to meet the food requirements of
3.25 persons. This works out to 1.35 acres/person.

The kinsmen of Jesus in the account of
Hegesippus (in Eusebius EH 3.20.1-2) owned 39 plethra
between two families. Since there is uncertainty as to
whether the plethron corresponded to 0.5 or 1 Roman
iugerum in this period, 39 plethra equalled either 4.9
hectares (12.2 acres) or 10 hectares (24.5 acres).[77]
Each family could have held as little as 6 or as much
as 12 acres apiece. Without taking children into
account, there were 3 to 6 acres per adult. It is
important to remember that these plot-sizes represent

actual peasant holdings, not abstract measurements for
a minimum subsistence plot. Approximately half of each
holding's area needed to be kept fallow every year.
The plots were subject to taxation. And when children
are added into the equation, the amount of each holding
left for the subsistence requirements of one person is
not out of line with the Latin evidence.

A subsistence plot in antiquity was, then, about
1.5 acres. The grain produced on this area in an good
year could feed one adult. How much grain would this
have been? The answer to this question, which would
constitute the check on the results obtained from
nutrition needs, depends upon a knowledge of the
average amount of seed needed to cover 1.5 acres and
the average yields that could be expected. The
discussion will proceed in a moment to a consideration
of this question and a completion of the check.

It is evident, even so (and assuming the
preceding figures are not far off), that the diet of a
typical person in antiquity was barely in line with
modern estimates of minimum subsistence. If external
exactions became too great--the above figures already
assume some exactions--it is also apparent that the
level of subsistence could become too low. It is
necessary, therefore, to make some attempt to assess
the level of exactions, particularly for the period at
the turn of the eras. This can be done in a general
way by considering the other economic necessities and
social obligations (as in Figure 2).

How much would be required for next year's seed?
If the peasant received the seed from the estate owner,
nothing (as in Lang's partnership). In this case,
however, the rent would be higher. If the problem is
viewed from the perspective of a tenant, that is, as a

smallholder from whom a heavy rent is being exacted,
the replacement amount must be taken from whatever
remains after all other dues are paid (Lang's exploitative pattern). It is possible to establish both a
relative and an absolute value for the first-century,
Mediterranean peasant's replacement fund.[78] The Roman
propagandist Columella states that 5 to 10 modii per
iugerum, carelessly sown, produced an average return of
about fourfold in Italy.[79] Brunt gives an estimate of
the average production of a 7 iugera farm, assuming a
yield of fivefold.[80] Cicero reports that 6 modii were
sown per iugerum in Sicily and that yields were roughly
six- to tenfold.[81] In Egypt one artaba of seed was
required for each aroura and yields averaged five- to
tenfold in wheat, seven- to twelvefold in barley.[82]
Egypt and Sicily, it should be noted, were exceptional
agricultural areas.

Obviously, yields were contingent upon the
condition of the soil, water, amount of seed sown, and
variables such as the weather. However, as the
evidence quoted shows, in most Mediterranean lands of
antiquity a yield of about five times would have been
average. So Heichelheim cannot be far off when he
states that the average yield in Palestine was
fivefold.[83] This would imply a replacement fund, on
the average, of one-fifth (not, as Danby suggests, one
forty-fifth) of unit production.[84]

It is possible to specify further the absolute
seed requirements for the average farm in normal years.
Bulk measures in the ancient Near East were not
established arbitrarily, it would seem, but were
defined in such a way as to correlate an area of land
with a specified measure of seed at planting time.[85]
Thus in the Mishnah, area is defined in "cor's-spaces."

A cor's-space is the area one cor of seed would sow.
Alternatively, it would be the amount of grain needed
to sow 75,000 square cubits.[86] Given a cubit = 1.75
ft, and a cor as 11 bushels, a cor's-space would equal
5.27 acres and have a seed requirement of 2.12
bu/acre.[87] Egyptian papyri show that there also a
standard measure was calibrated to a standard area:
One artaba would cover one aroura. It is known that
the artaba measure held the equivalent of 1.1 bushels
and that the aroura indicated an area of approximately
0.68 acres. This translates into 1.8 bushels/acre.
Columella's and Cicero's information (above) give a
range of between 1.8 and 3.6 bu/acre.

     Now the promised check on minimum subsistence
can be carried through. Taking the low end of the
scale for seed requirements (though the poor peasant
was caught between sowing enough to insure adequate
yield and minimizing this to obtain adequate nutrition)
and the average size of the subsistence plot as 1.5
acres, the land could be expected to produce under good
conditions 1.8 x 1.5 x 5 = 13.5 bushels. Recycling 1.8
bushels for next year's seed, gives around 12 bushels
for consumption purposes. This corresponds fairly
closely with the previous result, but assumes no other
exactions from this amount. Furthermore, since the
peasant's parcel of land had to be idled every other
year, the food would have to stretch even farther.[88]

     The Palestinian peasantry certainly had
livestock. Their sustenance had to be provided for
in such a way as not to jeopardize limited resources
available for human consumption. During the summer
fallow, the livestock were allowed to graze upon the
stubble. This assisted the ordinary work of keeping
the weeds down. It also conveniently provided the

manuring necessary for keeping the fields fertile.[89]
During the fall months when the delicate young plants
were just sprouting, livestock were a danger to the
fields and had to be kept penned.[90] Later in the
winter, flocks could be led into the hills or to non-
arable land. At harvest time, animals used in threshing
might be allowed to consume some of the product (Deut.
25:4).

Certainly penned livestock had to be fed some
kind of fodder. Columella gives an idea of some of the
kinds of materials used for fodder in the ancient
Mediterranean world and amounts required per month for
a yoke of oxen:

January–March	Chaff + 6 sextarii of vetch or 0.5 modii of bruised chickpea or 20 modii of leaves; chaff + 20 (Roman) lbs of hay (50 lbs if working)[91]
April	40 lbs of hay
May	"Fodder in abundance" (harvesttime)
June–August	Leaves in abundance or 50 lbs of chaff from bitter vetch
September	Leaves in abundance
October	Foliage of a fig tree
November	Foliage of a fig tree until November 13; then 1 modius of mast (nuts) mixed with chaff + 1 modius of lupins mixed with chaff
December	Dried leaves or chaff + 0.5 modius of bitter vetch soaked in water[92]

It is difficult to determine to what extent the
Palestinian village household or village was self-
sufficient in the first century. It is certainly in
the nature of a peasantry to strive for self-
sufficiency.[93] Since village members were probably

related in an extended family relationship, petty
barter or labor services sufficed to insure mutual
assistance. This kind of mutual aid in the village was
rigorously kept track of in households and has been
called "balanced reciprocity."[94] Yet the extent of
self-sufficiency was not just a village decision. It
also depended on the extent to which the village
economy was peacefully articulated with, or under
compulsion to join, the transregional, or perhaps
larger Mediterranean, economy. This question will be
pursued further below.

For the moment, it can be noted that rabbinic
traditions give unequivocal evidence for the employment
of specialists in the villages.[95] The Palestinian
peasantry, therefore, had to reserve some produce with
which to barter for or buy the services of the outside
craftsmen. For the rural areas of Palestine, these
were most often tanners, potters, carpenters, weavers,
leather workers, and others.[96]

For the peasantry in Palestine, the Jewish
peasantry at any rate, one-tenth of the harvest was due
to the Temple (Deut. 14:22). This tithe can be considered a very minimum estimate of their religious
obligations.[97] If the grain had first to be commuted
into money, which is likely for Jews living at some
distance (Deut. 14:25), price fluctuations added to
hardship. How much went for other village social obligations is not known.

At the very least, then, three-tenths of unit
production went to cover replacement, household, and
religious or ceremonial expenses.

How much might go to rents and taxes?[98]
Starting with taxes, two types are to be distin-
guished--direct and indirect. The former encompassed

taxes levied directly on the land or per capita.[99] The
latter comprised all of the tolls, duties, market
taxes, inheritance taxes, and so forth, that could be
used to extract even more out of the agrarian and
commercial sectors. The difficulty in clarifying the
extent of these burdens should be noted. The Roman
emperors adopted the policy in the East of only grad-
ually reforming the Hellenistic taxation structures.
Since these were on the whole complex and confusing,
the historian often has no more than a superficial idea
of what they were.[100]

It would appear that only after 70 C.E. was the
land formerly under Jewish cultivation in Judaea
considered ager publicus populi Romani, that is,
property of the Roman state and fully "available" for
intensive exploitation.[101] This implies that only then
would the land have been bought and leased by an
increasingly foreign ownership as in the more ruth-
lessly exploited territories of the empire.[102] Previously the Romans had more or less to respect the
Jewish landed arrangements and recognize Jewish views
of patrimony, although the process of expropriation and
exploitation had already started indirectly with Herod
and the procurators. Stated in a different way, pre-70
taxation was not the expression of a direct lease from,
or tenancy to, the Roman state for the Jews.

Probably the ruling families who collected for
the Romans argued that the tax was to insure the Pax
Romana and participation in its benefits:

So taxation was to be viewed not as arbitrary
imposition but as the individual's reasonable sub-
scription to the upkeep of the armed forces . . .
This, from Cicero onwards, was the government's
retort to those who objected to paying their
taxes.[103]

The Jewish peasantry would have had to have a short
memory to believe this. After the initial conquest,
Pompey had laid an exorbitant tax of ten thousand
talents on the Jews. This was reduced by Julius
Caesar.[104] Herod's exactions grew onerous again, and
particularly since he paid tribute to the Romans as
well.[105] Then followed the census under Augustus, as
we learn from Luke 2. How the Zealots felt about
payment of tribute to Rome, is made abundantly clear in
Josephus (e.g. JW 2.117-118). Tacitus tells us that
the provinces of Syria and Judaea petitioned Tiberius
for a reduction of tribute early in his reign.[106]
Undoubtedly the local elites recognized how much
bitterness was being engendered by the tribute.

The concern here is particularly with the taxes
on land and not with other types of tax.[107] If better
quantitative data were available to assess the
magnitude of the Roman tributum soli in early first-
century Palestine, this would facilitate our task.
Julius Caesar's tax reorganization has just been
mentioned. Josephus's reproduction of the rescript of
Caesar to the Jews provides some tantalizing information about the tax situation in the late republic, but
the critical notice concerning the tribute is very
difficult to interpret:

en Sidōni toi deuteroi etei ton phoron apodidōsi,
to tetarton tōn speiromenōn.

In Sidon in the second year, let them pay the
tribute, the fourth part of what was sown.[108]

This part of the decree follows immediately
after Caesar's recognition of the requirements of the
sabbatical year and his exemption of a tax on Jerusalem
in the seventh year. Is the phrase "second year" to be
understood, then, in terms of "second year in the

sabbatic cycle" or simply as "every other year"?[109] If
the latter, then the tribute averaged 12.5% per annum.

Since this question cannot be decided satisfac-
torily, only a rough guess about the level of the
tribute can be ventured. According to data from Cicero
on Sicily during the period of the late republic, the
decuma or tithe was collected from peasants in addition
to the land rent or vectigal paid to the censors for
working ager publicus.[110] The land of the Jewish
peasantry was not considered leased before 70 C.E. The
empire, therefore, could have considered a tithe as
adequate tribute. The whole issue is further complicated by the fact that, at the beginning of the
Principate, taxes in kind were being commuted to money
payments, stipendia (cf. Mk. 12:15). What the total
money amount of the tribute was, is difficult to
assess.[111] It seems reasonable to conclude, nevertheless, that a minimum tribute in kind would probably
have been one-tenth, a maximum one-fourth.

If one tries to estimate the revenues from the
land received annually by Herod the Great, one encounters the problem that the only data to have come down
to us about Herod's revenues are expressed solely in
weight of precious metals.[112] Heichelheim estimates
this income as 1000 to 1300 Tyrian talents.[113]
Jeremias and Applebaum believe it was only around 900
talents.[114] Furthermore, other sources besides the
land supplied Herod's income.[115] The purchasing power
of money did not remain constant, either. If the
difficulties of converting ancient measures of capacity
into modern values of subsistence are imposing, the
task of trying to find the equivalent value of so many
talents in grain or some other commodity appears even
more difficult. Taking M. Shek. 4:9, M. B. M. 5:1, and

B. Taan. 19b as typical, nonetheless, suggests an
average equivalence of one denarius per one seah of
wheat.[116] Since one talent equals six thousand
denarii, it would be approximately equivalent to six
thousand seahs of wheat. A cor is equal to thirty
seahs, so two hundred cors of wheat brought a revenue
of one talent.[117]

Herod required about 1000 talents. Thus, he
needed 200,000 cors of wheat annually. This in turn is
equivalent to 2.2 million bushels. Compare with this,
information from Eupolemus on the amount of grain
imported into Jerusalem (reflecting conditions at the
turn of the eras): The city required 10,000 cors per
month, 120,000 cors per year.[118] Also, during the
famine of 25-24 B.C.E. Herod distributed 80,000 cors
throughout his realm.[119] R. Duncan-Jones has provided
some useful figures for comparison from the Roman
world. According to Duncan-Jones, the two largest
fortunes in private hands in the first century C.E.
(400 million sesterces) had real-term values of between
3/4 and 1 1/2 million metric tons of wheat. A Roman
senator with capital of 8 million sesterces would have
a real worth of 14,000-29,000 metric tons. A senator's
minimum census was worth between 2,100 and 4,300 metric
tons. An equestrian's census had a value somewhere in
the neighborhood of 700 to 1,400 metric tons.[120] By
way of contrast, Herod's income (200,000 cors) had a
comparable value of around 61,000 metric tons of wheat.
Herod, then, was as wealthy as the wealthiest senators
of the early empire.

Herod's territory covered an area of about
1,055,000 hectares. Of this, it is estimated that 65-
70% was cultivated in antiquity.[121] The cropping area
was between 686,000 and 739,000 ha. Assuming that half

of the land lay fallow every year, that only grain was
sown, and that productivity on the average was fivefold
or 11.2 bu/acre, Herod's territory yielded about
10,200,000 bushels or 278,000 metric tons of wheat.[122]
Herod's revenues, by this measure, amounted to 20% of
the annual production.

If Josephus's notices on Herod's revenues do not
add in the Roman tribute, total taxation was well above
the Roman one-tenth to one-fourth base.[123] Let us just
say Herod received--above the Roman land tax and
probably as a quite conservative estimate (cf. Jos. JW
1.524; 2.85f)--one-tenth. This level of land taxation
apparently continued after Herod's death, at least into
the reign of Tiberius.[124] Comparative data from other
agrarian societies corroborates this level of taxation.
Most agrarian states have appropriated between one-
tenth and one-half of agricultural production in
taxes.[125]

What might a typical share-rental agreement have
entailed in terms of a percentage of the harvest? In
the pre-Jewish War setting most of the large landowners
would have been native aristocracy, such as the
Herodians. There were later imperial estates, for
instance, in the Esdraelon Valley and near Jericho.[126]
It might be assumed, however, that whether native
owners or imperial bailiffs stood over the cultivator,
similar rents were asked. Mishnaic law mentions
agreements of one-half, one-third, and one-fourth.[127]
M. B. M. 9:7-10 records rents of 10 cors. Leases from
the time of the Bar Cochba rebellion show rents of 4
and 6 cors. Applebaum thinks these may have been equal
to the amount of seed sown on the land. In that case,
the Jewish cultivator at the time of the rebellion
perhaps paid only one-fifth of the harvest.[128]

For comparison, an inscription from Africa at
the time of Trajan details the public rents established
by the Lex Manciana as follows: "One third of the
wheat from the threshing floor, one third of the barley
from the threshing floor, one fourth of the beans from
the threshing floor, one third of the wine from the
vat, one third of the oil from the press," and so
on.[129] An assumption of one-fourth to one-third of the
produce on Palestinian estates seems reasonable and
conservative.

Totaling up these estimates: On the low side we
have one-tenth (Roman tribute) + one-tenth (Herod,
procurators) + one-fourth (land rent to large
landowners) = one-half (approximate). On the high
side, one-fourth + one-tenth + one-third = two-thirds
(approximate).[130] Adding these to the other social
expenditures and the replacement fund (three-tenths)
and subtracting from unit production leaves one-fifth
of the produce for subsistence with the low estimate,
one-thirtieth of the produce with the high estimate.
The cultivator got at maximum in this period about what
he sowed to the land (assuming a fivefold harvest); he
may have gotten much less.

C. Level of Indebtedness

If a smallholder fell into arrears vis-à-vis any
of the various obligations--or if after taxes, rents,
dues, household, and replacement requirements, there
was not enough for subsistence--the peasant had no
choice but to borrow to meet the deficit.[131] This
obviously required something as surety, part of the
peasant's property, his plot of land, or even himself
or a member of his family.[132]

This raises the inescapable question: To what
extent was the Palestinian peasantry of Jesus' day
being forced to borrow and to mortgage property? It is
essential to note, as background, that debt and
agrarian problems often played a role in Graeco-Roman
historical developments. For this reason, "release
from debts" and "redistribution of land" became
standard demands in the revolutionary movements of
antiquity.[133] An extensive biblical tradition attests
to the corrosive effects of debt on the Jewish side.[134]
The social dynamics leading to tenancy have already
been examined, at least from a theoretical vantage
point. What needs to be clarified now, if possible, is
the extent of mortgaged land and of the appearance of
tenancies in place of freeholdings in early Roman
Palestine.[135]

First-century Palestinian evidence for a debt
problem and the growth of tenancy is for the most part
indirect, and mostly pertinent to Judaea. The
difficult-to-interpret traditions about Hillel's
prosbol and Josephus's narration about the burning of
the debt archives at the beginning of the Jewish War
are the only direct evidences for heavy indebtedness in
the pre-70 C.E. period.[136]

Goodman has argued that the influx of wealth
into Jerusalem from trade and business surrounding the
Temple left much surplus capital in the hands of the
pro-Roman oligarchy, and that this wealth was at hand
to loan to hard-pressed smallholders and petty artisans
or to sink into any land available for purchase.
Goodman goes as far as to say:

     . . . both small independent farmers and the
     craftsmen and urban plebs of Jerusalem fell heavily
     into debt as much because the rich landowners

needed to invest surplus income profitably as
because the poor needed loans to survive.[137]
This view is convincing, but only explains part of the
process. It does not make entirely clear why the
peasantry were being _forced_ to borrow.

Population pressure probably played some role in
the increase of debt. Goodman believes more mouths to
feed led smallholders to borrow in order to purchase
more land.[138] This argument would be more persuasive
if there were evidence for such transactions and if
Goodman could make a convincing case that land was
available to purchase. This just does not seem likely.
Applebaum's assessment is undoubtedly nearer to the
truth: "But overpopulation reduced the Jewish peasant
unit of cultivation and endangered the cultivator's
margin of livelihood."[139]

A debt situation could arise because of lack of
rain or successive poor yields from other causes. Yet
the only severe famines attested in available sources
for Palestine during this period were early in Herod's
reign (25 B.C.E.) and again under Claudius (46
C.E.).[140] Though many of the rural folk in Jesus' day
were living on the edge of economic disaster, human and
not divine causes seem to have played a greater role in
increasing indebtedness.

It is easy to discern from the discussion in the
previous sections that the security of peasant holdings
was being compromised by too many demands placed upon a
limited resource base. Not only was wealth from trade
available to the urban aristocracy to loan, and not
only did they need to invest it, but their demands for
tithes and tributes, combined with demands of the Roman
state, were forcing the peasantry to borrow. This was
perhaps the chief reason for any debt problem. The by-

product of heavy levies against the populace, of
course, was the concentration of property. There is
some evidence that the less scrupulous of the landowning class in Jerusalem used debt contracts as a
means to wrest land from the peasantry.[141] Stegemann
and Kreissig both see a tremendous growth of large-
holdings in early Roman Palestine.[142] The opposite
side of this concentration of holdings, of course, was
a dramatic increase in the numbers of tenant farmers on
the property of others.

Several comparative instances from elsewhere in
the ancient Mediterranean world help to validate this
picture. Ramsay MacMullen has written:

> At two junctures in the empire's history, indeed,
> rural-urban relations do seem to break down into
> actual warfare; once, around the middle of the
> first century in Judaea, a second time in Africa
> three hundred years later. This may not be the
> place to study the story of the Zealots and the
> Circumcellions; but plainly peasants under the name
> and banner of religious fanatics dared to take up
> arms against the wealthy and inflicted a bloody
> revenge on those from whom, in normal times, they
> went cap in hand to borrow money or seed corn.[143]

W. H. C. Frend, in his book The Rise of Christianity,
has provided a convenient translation of a text from
Optatus of Milevis describing the Circumcellion
problem:

> For when men of this sort [were] wandering about in
> every place, . . . no man could rest secure in his
> possessions. Written acknowledgements of indebted-
> ness had lost their value. At that time no
> creditor was free to press his claim, and all were
> terrified by the letters of these fellows . . .

Creditors were hemmed in with perils, so that they
who had a right to be supplicated on account of
that which was due to them, were driven through
fear of death to be themselves the humble
suppliants. Very soon everyone lost what was owing
to him--even to very large amounts, . . .[144]

This sounds very much like the activity of the first-
century bandits and sicarii of Palestine (Jos. JW
2.253, 254; 7.254). One wonders how the messianic
movements and the other social unrest evidenced in
Josephus (e.g. the activities of Judas) might similarly
be understood vis-à-vis the specter of enslavement
through tribute or actual conditions of oppressive
indebtedness.

Carney has alerted us to a potentially important
ingredient in the growth of indebtedness at the turn of
the eras. He writes:

In Gaul, for instance, the imposition of tribute
forced the local notables to seek rents in money
instead of exacting goods and services. They had
also to turn income in kind into money by sending
it to the markets created partly by the buildup of
local towns into administrative centers, partly by
the presence of the Roman armies. The usual social
costs of indebtedness seem to have resulted.[145]

Kreissig also speaks of "marketization" and "monetization" in early first-century Palestine, but Applebaum
warns against carrying these concepts too far.[146]
It has already been mentioned that under the early
empire Palestinian tributes in kind similarly were
being commuted to money (Mk. 12:15; Jos. JW 2.405).

How debtors once in debt stayed in debt is well-
illuminated by a passage from a letter of Pliny the
Younger written under Trajan (107 C.E.):

During the past rent-period (lustrum) despite big
reductions in the rents, the arrears have grown; as
a result most of the tenants have lost all interest
in reducing their debt because they have no hope of
paying off the whole debt; they even seize and
consume the produce in the belief that it will
bring them no gain to keep it.[147]

MacMullen even speaks of debt being inherited in Italy.
The ties of indebtedness for the peasantry were "no
less strong than those of habit and attachment to their
ancestral acres."[148]

During the period between Caesar and Pliny,
pressures to introduce fixed-rent, cash tenancies in
lieu of traditional sharecropping may have been great
because of the need to pay imperial tributes in money.
V. Gordon Childe long ago summarized the dreadful
consequences of the increase of money transactions in
agrarian societies: Money, loans, default, fore-
closure.[149]

A macroeconomic and qualitative argument can be
advanced, therefore, for a clear socio-economic dynamic
in Palestine under the early empire--debt, concentration of land, growth of tenancy.

D. Conclusion

The political and economic conditions of the
early empire encouraged a more intensive exploitation
of the agricultural producer in Palestine and brought
about the concentration of land holdings in fewer
hands. There can be seen here a strong power component
in the actual distribution of economic goods (including
land). The peasantry were pressed to meet many
obligations. The termini of the flow of rents, taxes,
and tithes, as well as the domiciles of the wealthy

landowners, were urban areas like Jerusalem and Rome. This led to "antagonism between town and country."[150]

The work of Karl Polanyi provides some appropriate categories for summarizing this picture. Polanyi has identified three basic types of distribution in pre-industrial economies. He characterizes these types as redistribution through a central institution, distribution on the basis of reciprocal exchange, and distribution through the market.[151]

Redistribution through a central institution adequately describes what is happening when rents, taxes, and tithes from agricultural producers are moved to urban areas, temple complexes, or state coffers, and then redistributed for ends other than meeting the material needs of the cultivators. This process had intensified in Palestine under the early empire, and it engendered other "centralizing" social arrangements-- the growth of big property and numbers of large landowners, as well as the increase of dependent tenants. Thus, redistribution through central institutions accentuated in this period the development of hierarchical and antagonistic class relations.

At the village level, however, reciprocity exchanges, on a more or less horizontal plane, had helped to distribute wealth from ages immemorial. This pattern continued at all times in antiquity. Sahlins has treated reciprocity exchanges against the horizon of primitive tribal interactions and in more detail than Polanyi. Sahlins distinguishes general reciprocity, balanced reciprocity, and negative reciprocity. Negative reciprocity--doing unto others as you would not have them do unto you--is the ethos of hostility and warfare toward non-kin or enemies.

Balanced reciprocity represents exchanges of economic
goods or labor with other households or lineages on a
quid pro quo basis. General reciprocity designates the
giving of gifts without strong expectation of getting
something in return. This type of exchange is reserved
for very close kin or helps to cement good relations
with "ceremonial" kin.[152]

The powerful forces of exploitation that
accompanied the birth of the Roman empire undoubtedly
disturbed village relationships and threatened ancient
economic values through the impoverishment of the
cultivator and expropriation. The "gravitational
effects" of powerful economic centers upon decen-
tralized economic activity were irresistable.
Hollenbach has illuminated how redistribution required
power, which disrupted distribution based upon reciprocity in what were essentially kin relationships.[153]
The result in the village was the growth of a "surviv-
alist" mentality, increased conflict between village
households, and even more rigorous accounting of
exchanges and debts.

Eric Wolf's general observation about the
dilemma of the peasant cultivator seems appropriate as
a general conclusion to this chapter:

> The perennial problem of the peasantry thus
> consists in balancing the demands of the external
> world against the peasants' need to provision their
> households. Yet in meeting this root problem
> peasants may follow two diametrically opposed
> strategies. The first of these is to increase
> production; the second, to curtail consumption.[154]

The peasantry in first-century Palestine, under
pressure from increasingly powerful institutions and
people, were forced either to curtail consumption or to

enter into a hopeless spiral of debt that led to the
loss of the family plot. The only alternative would
have been to increase production by more extensive
cultivation--had the land and the extra food to support
such work been available.[155]

   Applebaum rightly points to lack of cultivable
land as one of the more significant causes of Jewish
unrest before the Jewish War.[156] Expropriation of
peasant lands and increase of surplus peasant children
led in effect to a relative overpopulation in early
first-century Palestine. Jewish peasantry clashed with
gentile settlers in Galilee and in Peraea, because they
perceived a direct threat to their own economic
interests in the gentile "theft of their land." Along
with this struggle, Zealots and bandits increasingly
defied the Romanophile aristocracy who exacted tribute,
distrained on landed securities and, in the eyes of the
rebels, abolished the laws of God. It was in such a
conflicted agrarian situation that Jesus of Nazareth
proclaimed the beginning of the reign of God.

Notes to Chapter 2

[1]For instance, see Avi-Yonah, (1977) 188-211.
See Lenski, (1966) 44 on two "laws" of distribution.

[2]Ste. Croix, (1981) 205ff. The role of
precarious economic circumstances in the social unrest
of first-century Palestine will be explored later in
this chapter.

[3]Freyne, (1980a) 195; Lenski, (1966) 214-216;
Redfield, (1960) 19.

[4]Kornemann (1924b); Rostovtzeff, (1941) 1:276ff;
Toutain, (1951) 109-116, 272-282.

[5]See Barrois, (1962b) 677f.

[6]On this point Frank (1959) offers detailed
evidence in the appropriate volumes.

[7]See Bengtson, (1970) 150; Meyers, (1976) 97.

[8]For agrarian conditions and land tenure:
Mishnah, Order Zeraim. Also M. D. M. 5:8; 9; B. B. 3;
and passim.

[9]Archaeology, particularly settlement surveys,
field studies, and dendroarchaeology, will provide even
more information in the future to be used in the
assessment of the ancient agrarian situation.

[10]Rostovtzeff, (1941) and (1957). Max Weber,
(1976) chs. 5-7. Avi-Yonah, (1977) chs. 1-9. Freyne,
(1980a) ch. 5.

[11]Hengel, (1974b) ch. 1. Tcherikover, (1937) 9-
90. These papyri also offer a good vantage point for
understanding subsequent epochs, because agrarian
societies have tended to be rather conservative in
terms of economic arrangements.

[12]Tcherikover, (1937) 48.

[13]Rostovtzeff, (1941) 1:276ff identifies the
following classes of land in Egypt: Royal land, sacred
land, cleruchic land, gift land (i.e. prebends),
private land. Cf. Weber, (1976) 237.

[14]Avi-Yonah, (1977) 34.

[15]Rostovtzeff, (1941) 1:341.

[16]Hengel, (1974b) 2:3 n. 4.

[17]PCZ 59015 (verso).

[18]Samaria had rebelled against Alexander and had a military colony imposed upon it. Scythopolis was formerly Bethshan: Avi-Yonah, (1977) 36.

[19]Ibid.: 38f.

[20]Ibid.: 50.

[21]For information on Ptolemaic taxation, consult Rostovtzeff, (1941) 1:279, 283, 286, 290, 332ff.

[22]E.g. PCZ 59012.

[23]PSI 554, 594. On all of these developments and for further literature see Hengel, (1974b) 1:35-47. Rostovtzeff, (1941) 1:267ff. Bagnall and Derow (1981).

[24]Avi-Yonah, (1977) 43.

[25]Tcherikover, (1937) 54-56.

[26]The course of this crisis, and the ensuing revolt of the Maccabees, is admirably traced by Tcherikover (1979).

[27]Applebaum, (1976) 635.

[28]Ibid.

[29]Avi-Yonah, (1977) 76, 78.

[30]Applebaum, (1976) 637.

[31]The Hellenistic pattern of administration: Avi-Yonah, (1977) 94.

[32]Rostovtzeff, (1957) 1:514f.

[33]Weber, (1976) 336ff.

[34]Avi-Yonah, (1977) 112.

[35]Lenski, (1966) 214-216.

[36]See LSJ, (1968) 1002, 2006 respectively.

[37]Gil, (1970) 12. See also the excellent account of the agrarian developments hinted at here in Weber, (1976) 301, 309.

[38]For instance, see de Vaux, (1965) 1:166. See Weber, (1976) 270.

[39]Hengel, (1974b) 1:19.

[40]MacMullen, (1974) 6f; Ste. Croix, (1981) passim.

[41]M. A. Zar. 1:8. Cf. Gil, (1970) 14 and n. 13. For some interesting comparative material on social perception of ownership see Wolf, (1969) 190: Access became more important than ownership for the Puerto Ricans.

[42]Gil, (1970) 30f (against usury), 35ff, 38f ("robbery"). Legal problems: Applebaum, (1976) 695.

[43]See Herz (1928); Kreissig (1969); Kornemann (1924a and 1924b).

[44]Applebaum, (1976) 657; Jeremias, (1969a) 91.

[45]Rostovtzeff, (1957) 1:270 and 2:663 n. 32.

[46]Applebaum, (1976) 658; Jeremias, (1969a) 91, 99.

[47]Applebaum, (1976) 641f.

[48]Ibid.

[49]Ibid.: 644. Goodman, (1983) 28 questions these distinctions.

[50]Wolf, (1966) 1-59 has provided the basic framework for looking at peasant economics. Carney, (1975) 285ff suggested the development of "postula-tional models" for land tenure.

[51]Wolf, (1966) 4. See further the discussion below in Section B.

[52]Ibid.: 6.

[53]Ibid. The amount is about 33% lower without livestock to feed.

[54]Ibid.: 10.

[55]These models are an attempt to organize conceptually concrete data on first-century land tenure gathered and discussed by Krauss, (1966) 2:108-111; Heichelheim, (1959) 147f; and Applebaum, (1976) 659.

[56]See further Section C.

[57]Klausner, (1975) 191ff.

[58]Dalman, (1964) 2:15. Billerbeck, (1922) 1:869f. Heichelheim especially emphasizes the linguistic equivalents (see Note 55). A third type of tenant, the "developer" or "entrepreneur" (so Krauss) who is similar to the sharecropper in some respects, received as payment a part of the land he developed for a landlord. This type of tenant is not discussed in the text.

[59]Ste. Croix, (1981) 214.

[60]Lang, (1982) 47-63.

[61]Tarn and Griffith, (1952) 142, cf. 189.

[62]Thorough treatment of this topic is given by Johnson, (1959) 74-145.

[63]The word calorie means the kilocalorie, the current standard measure of energy in human nutrition: Passmore, Nicol, et al., (1974) 6. The word calorie is often capitalized in the technical literature of nutrition, but for convenience the uncapitalized form has been adopted throughout this book. For caloric values of Mediterranean foods see Pellett and Shadarevian (1970).

[64]Clark and Haswell, (1970) 21, though the authors write, "the Latin American figures look improbably low." Cf. Ibid.: 12, 17, and 81.

[65]Caloric equivalences have been calculated with the assistance of the computer program in Appendix 2. In the Middle East, wheat contains about 3.5, barley 3.6, calories/gm according to Pellett and Shadarevian (1970). On the assumptions about properties of grain see also Moritz (1958). Figures are taken from USDA (1971).

[66]The Mishnah (e.g. Peah 8:5) implies a wheat-

to-barley equivalence of 1::2. Hamel, (1983) 412 n.
335a, gives the rule of thumb used by a French colonial
administrator in Egypt as 1::1.5. The ratio adopted in
the computer program of Appendix 2 is 1::1.8.

[67]During the 1985 Ethiopian famine, a relief
worker was quoted on National Public Radio as saying
that 1400 calories was the bare minimum needed to keep
the people alive and that most were actually only
getting 700 calories/day. Additional figures for
comparison in FAO, (1984) 261f.

[68]Hamel, (1983) "Appendix 1: WEIGHTS AND
MEASURES," 499ff. See Sellers, (1962) 828-39.

[69]Modern reference values, adopted in Appendix 2
from USDA (1983), are 27.2 kg/bu of wheat and 21 kg/bu
of barley. Moritz, (1958) 184ff discusses evidence
from Pliny and also provides modern figures for
comparison.

[70]In the discussion, the modern American bushel
is assumed to equal 4.1 Roman modii, 0.9 Hellenistic
artabas, or 0.09 cors. For the value of the cor: Cf.
Sellers, (1962) 834 and Applebaum, (1976) 659. For the
artaba: David and van Groningen, (1965) 38[*]; Duncan-
Jones, (1982) 372. For the modius: Jeremias, (1969a)
122 n. 4; Duncan-Jones, (1982) 371. Values for
converting dry capacities into caloric equivalents are
obtained from Clark and Haswell (1970); USDA (1971);
Pellett and Shadarevian (1970); Moritz (1958).

[71]Brunt, (1971) 35.

[72]Johnson, (1959) 149.

[73]Jeremias, (1969a) 122f.

[74]Hamel, (1983) 222.

[75]Brunt, (1971) 35; cf. Weber, (1976) 278, 285.

[76]White, (1970b) 336; Applebaum, (1976) 657.

[77]Taking the plethron as equal to the Roman
iugerum in the first century: Hamel, (1983) 258 and
471 n. 221; cf. Heichelheim, (1959) 151; Applebaum,
(1976) 657. Other modern scholars believe the plethron
was 0.5 iugerum (= 13,600 ft^2). Bagnall and Derow,
(1981) 261 give a value of 10,000 ft^2 for the
Hellenistic period. Israeli archaeological surveys in

western Samaria have found that 2.5 hectares of land
was a rather standard-sized parcel: Applebaum, (1976)
657. It is interesting to observe that the relatives
of Jesus owned approximately two plots of this size and
that 2.5 ha is about the same as the cor's-space (see
below).

[78]Danby, (1933) 15 n. 1, 363 n. 1 states that
this fund in Palestine was estimated as one forty-fifth
of the average yield. Unfortunately, he neglects to
explain how he arrives at this figure, or what exactly
he means by it. In Wolf's previously cited medieval
example, a third of the crop had to be recycled for the
next years's planting: Wolf, (1966) 5.

[79]Columella, Ag 2.9.1; 3.3.4. Brunt, (1971) 35.
Frank, (1959) 141 and n. 4 observes that by "carelessly" Columella means sown as an intercrop between
vines.

[80]Brunt, (1971) 35.

[81]Scramuzza, (1959) 260.

[82]Johnson, (1959) 59.

[83]Heichelheim, (1959) 128.

[84]Finley, (1973) 83 and 196 n. 67! Also
Klausner, (1925) 180. Cf. Mealand, (1980) 2.

[85]Sperber (1971).

[86]According to Danby, (1933) 798.

[87]See Jeremias, (1969a) 11 n. 12 on the length
of the cubit.

[88]Compare this result with Brunt's calculation,
(1971) 35: "However, if the yield were not to fall
disastrously most land had to be fallowed every other
year. Thus the net average yield per iugerum was not
40, but 20 modii, and a farm of 7 iugera barely
produced enough grain for consumption by the family,
with no fodder for animals, no fruits, no margin for
sales out of which other necessities could be
obtained."

[89]M. Shebi. 3:4; 4:2. Applebaum, (1976) 653,
655.

[90]Applebaum, (1976) 656.

[91]1 sextarius = about 0.5 liter.

[92]Columella, Ag 2.99-101.

[93]Wolf, (1966) 37ff. Shanin, (1973) 67 speaks
of "the low level of institutional specialisation"
among peasantry and of the village community as an
"autonomous society," but admits that villages always
network with other villages.

[94]See a comparative discussion of this in
Gregory, (1975) 76.

[95]An excellent example is provided by Tos. B. M.
9:14, where field-mower, ditch-digger, well-digger and
barber are mentioned, as well as the local master of
the bathhouse and a shipmaster. These take away part
of a landlord's and tenant's harvest in payment for
their own services. See discussion in Kippenberg,
(1978) 148.

[96]Applebaum, (1976) 680ff.

[97]Jeremias, (1969a) 105-108, 134ff. Blackman,
(1964) 1:34-35 n. 5 believes the total was much
higher--about 22%! See Grant, (1926) 94.

[98]Sanders, (1962) 520-22. Heichelheim, (1959)
231ff. Stevenson, (1939) 133ff. Stern, (1974) 330ff.
Freyne, (1980a) 183ff.

[99]Rostovtzeff, (1957) 1:48, 79, 82, etc.

[100]Ibid.: 1:53, 514; 2:561 n. 16, 598 n. 7.

[101]Hamel, (1903) 274-79. But see the somewhat
different views of Isaac, (1984) 80. Stern, (1974)
335. Freyne, (1980a) 167.

[102]Balsdon, (1970) 51ff, however, sees direct
taxation and the census, which had already been
implemented in Judaea after Herod, as characteristic of
the more ruthless administration in the western
provinces.

[103]Balsdon, (1970) 176f. On the responsibility
of indigenous elites for collecting the taxes see
Hamel, (1983) 273, 281.

[104]Freyne, (1980a) 188f.

[105]Stern, (1974) 239f. Applebaum, (1976) 662.
Jeremias, (1969a) 125. Freyne, (1980a) 191. Cf.
Stern, (1975) 81, 92ff, 97, 110, 112f, 115; and
Klausner, (1975) 204.

[106]Tacitus, Annals 2.42.

[107]Josephus, AJ 18.274. Stevenson, (1939) 150f;
Klausner, (1975) 203f; cf. Freyne, (1980a) 178.

[108]Josephus, AJ 14.203. See the discussion in
Kippenberg, (1978) 112.

[109]**Former:** Sanders, (1962) 521. Rostovtzeff,
(1941) 2:1001 and 3:1578 n. 104. **Latter:** Heichelheim,
(1959) 232, 235. Stern, (1974) 331. See also Freyne,
(1980a) 189: A supplement to an annual tax?

[110]Cicero confesses, however, that Sicily
constituted a special administrative case. Stevenson,
(1939) 137. Scramuzza, (1959) 333. On the vectigal in
Africa see Rostovtzeff, (1957) 1:316f.

[111]Hamel, (1983) 271f, 477 n. 6. Duncan-Jones,
(1982) 7. Rostovtzeff, (1957) 1: 208f. Jones, (1974)
162, 164-68, 171-79.

[112]Stern, (1975) 81, 92ff, 97.

[113]Cf. Freyne, (1980a) 181, 191f.

[114]Jeremias, (1969a) 91. Applebaum, (1976) 665.

[115]Ibid.: Jeremias and Applebaum.

[116]Jeremias, (1969a) 122. Freyne, (1980a) 182.

[117]See Belo, (1981) 63.

[118]Holladay, (1983) 123, 146 n. 55. Jeremias,
(1969a) 38-41. Eupolemus's numbers are probably
inflated; cf. Cicero, Verrine Orations 2.3.30.72 on
monthly requirements for Rome: 33,000 medimni/mo =
4401 cor/mo = 52812 cor/yr. Admittedly, this may not
represent all of the grain needs of late republican
Rome.

[119]Jeremias, (1969a) 129.

[120]Duncan-Jones, (1982) 4-5.

[121]Applebaum, (1976) 646.

[122]This compares quite well with the result obtained by Hamel, discussed and slightly corrected above in Chapter 1.

[123]Applebaum, (1976) 662; Stern, (1974) 239.

[124]Safrai, (1975) 330.

[125]Grant, (1926) 105 and (1962) 879 believes that total taxation amounted to about 35-40%, "an intolerable burden." See Lenski, (1966) 267.

[126]Safrai, (1975) 334.

[127]M. Peah 5.5. Cf. Billerbeck, (1922) 1:870.

[128]Applebaum, (1976) 659.

[129]This law originated erlier under Vespasian: See Kornemann, (1924b) 252. Kornemann notes (Ibid.: 253) that the law did not apply to the whole empire. Cf. Haywood, (1959) 93.

[130]Freyne, (1980a) 186, 193, 195. Lenski, (1966) 228 says that the governing class in most agrarian states, comprising the top 2% of the population, have generally appropriated 50-66% of agricultural output. Our figures are in line with this comparative data.

[131]Freyne, (1980a) 179, 182, 195.

[132]Gil, (1970) 36, 44. Jeremias, (1969a) 313 on ex concessu. Consider the train of events in Genesis 47.

[133]Rostovtzeff, (1957) ch. 1. Tarn and Griffith, (1952) 121ff; Ste. Croix, (1981) 215, 298, 608 n. 55; Finley, (1973) 80.

[134]Oakman, (1985) 60. Some of the thoughts in this and subsequent paragraphs parallel or develop those in my article. See also Goodman (1983).

[135]An older, qualitative treatment of similar questions is Grant (1926). See also Lee, (1971) 121-38.

[136]Oakman, (1985) 61, 63-65.

[137]Goodman, (1982) 419, cf. 421 and the excellent model for the dynamics of debt in early first-century Judaea on 427. On the general policy of investing wealth from commerce in land see Rostovtzeff, (1957) 1:57 (the case of Trimalchio). See also the remarks of Finley, (1973) 116.

[138]Goodman, (1982) 423.

[139]Applebaum, (1976) 691.

[140]Jeremias, (1969a) 141. Hamel, (1983) 129ff believes droughts occurred about every twenty years.

[141]Applebaum, (1976) 663. On such practices generally see Ste. Croix, (1981) 225; MacMullen, (1974) 6-15, 38.

[142]Stegemann, (1984) 19; Kreissig, (1969) 239.

[143]MacMullen, (1974) 53.

[144]J. Stevenson translation of Optatus's Donatist Schism 3.4 in Frend, (1984) 572.

[145]Carney, (1975) 145.

[146]Applebaum, (1976) 662f. On marketization and monetization see Carney, (1975) 137.

[147]Translated from Epistle 9.37.2-3 in White, (1970b) 408.

[148]MacMullen, (1974) 25.

[149]Childe, (1954) 166, 202.

[150]The phrase is from Applebaum, (1976) 663. On this general theme in works of students of ancient history see Rostovtzeff, (1957) 1:193ff; MacMullen, (1974) 1-56; Ste. Croix (1981).

[151]Polanyi, (1957) 250-256. Carney provides a useful overview of Polanyi's types in (1975) 140ff.

[152]Sahlins, (1968) 82f, following a typology of E. Service. Carney, (1975) 166ff. Gregory, (1975) 76, 85.

[153]Hollenbach, (1985) 154f.

[154]Wolf, (1966) 15.

[155]A close friend, the Reverend Edward A. Wilson, points out to me that extra work demands extra calories. Since these were not available, this strategy was not really viable.

[156]Applebaum (1975).

PART TWO

AN EXPLORATION OF THE JESUS TRADITION

FROM AN ECONOMIC PERSPECTIVE

"The measure you give
will be the measure
you get . . ."

Mark 4:24

CHAPTER 3

PRODUCTION AND THE REIGN OF GOD

IN THE PARABLES OF GROWTH

The basic character of the economy of early
Roman Palestine, as well as its fundamental tensions
and problems, have hopefully been sketched in the
preceding pages. The investigation turns now to some
of the bedrock of the Jesus tradition, wherein from a
superficial point of view there seems to be concern for
the production of the soil.

The parables of the Sower (Mk. 4:3-8 and par.),
the Seed Growing Secretly (Mk. 4:26-29), the Darnel
Among the Wheat (Mt. 13:24-30), and the Mustard Seed
(Mk. 4:30-32 and par.) have been labeled parables of
growth or contrast.[1] In the twentieth century those
have consistently been interpreted in the light of
Jesus' message about the reign of God. This approach
rightly must be followed by every student of Jesus'
words, as we have already said. The parables of growth
or contrast have further been thought to speak of the
insignificant beginning of the reign of God in Jesus'
ministry and to promise a great harvest when that rule
comes with power.[2] The point of contact between these
parables and the reign of God, then, has been understood in a rather narrow and "theological" way.

What is persistently asked in the following
pages is whether these parables, the central image of
which is the production of the soil, also imply
something about the soil or circumstances of
production. Does probing this material with the

95

sensitivities developed in Part One, in other words,
reveal any inner connection between the imagery of
production in the words of Jesus and the conditions of
production in ancient Palestine? Has Jesus responded
in any way to an economic situation in which production
was constrained by technical and social factors, yet
coupled with heightened exploitation of soil and
humanity?

A. Exegetical and Theological Assumptions About the Parables of Growth

Three of the parables treated in this chapter
are part of an old collection in Mark 4. Jeremias has
given a convincing analysis of the secondary nature of
the narrative framework in Mark 4, which includes the
explanation given for Jesus' use of parabolic discourse
(Mk. 4:10-12 and par.) and the allegorical treatment of
the Sower (Mk. 4:13-20 and par.). Furthermore, the
allegory on the Darnel parable is secondary (Mt. 13:36-
43).[3] Modern scholarship has rightly rejected the
procedure of interpreting the original meaning of these
parables in the light of the allegories. They betray
the nascent church's own theological interests.[4]

How and when exactly the Marcan parables were
brought together is unknown to us. That their linkage
preceded the composition of the Gospel of Mark (during
or shortly after the Jewish War) is fairly certain.[5]
Certainly the centrality of agricultural images in
these parables--seeds, growth, harvest--provides an
adequate justification for their association with one
another. Matthew's chapter, of course, represents a
later, derivative stage of this process. The Darnel
Among the Wheat appears in place of Mark's Seed Growing
Secretly. The sowing of the seed, the sleeping motif,

the growing of the plants, and the lack of cultivation
are present in Mark's and Matthew's respective
parables, but the similarity ends there. That initial
similarity suggests some kind of substitution--perhaps
by Matthew, perhaps by someone earlier in the
tradition.

As far as the actual order of these parables in
the tradition is concerned, there does not seem to be
any cogent reason for saying that Jesus spoke these
parables on a single occasion or in a certain order.
Indeed, comparing the placement of them in the canonical gospels and in the Gospel of Thomas (GThom), it
would seem that Matthew has simply followed Mark, with
the exception of the substitution at 13:24-30, that
Luke has separated the Sower (Lk. 8:5-8) and the Mustard Seed (Lk. 13:19), but kept the Marcan order, and
that Thomas did not know of the close linkage of the
parables in the Synoptic tradition.[6] GThom 9, 20,
(21?), and 57 are widely separated from each other.
GThom 9 and 20, 9 and 57 are in the same relative
order, but 20 and 57 are transposed from the Synoptic
order. The end of GThom 21 has a faint echo of Mark's
Seed Growing Secretly, perhaps not even enough to say
Thomas knew that parable. If Thomas's version is allowed inclusion here, then it can be said that Thomas
knew all of the Synoptic parables under consideration
and arranged them (or received them in his tradition
arranged) chiastically. This observation still does
not clarify why Thomas's parables are so widely separated from each other in contrast to the Synoptic
tradition.

Dodd began his discussion of "Parables of
Growth" with Mk. 4:26-29 (which we shall treat below).[7]
In connection with the Seed Growing Secretly, Dodd

conveniently produced an outline of modern interpretations that can be applied also to the Sower parable.
If we accept with Dodd that the Sower parable is to be
compared somehow with the reign of God (though this is
not expressly stated in the tradition), three major
types of modern interpretation have been advanced: The
reign of God has been compared with the seed, with the
process of growth, or with the harvest.[8] It is noted
here in passing that the "process of growth" interpretation had a particular appeal to nineteenth-century
liberal exegesis, which looked at Jesus' religion
through the lens of evolutionary thought. In contrast,
the harvest emphasis has been particularly attractive
to twentieth-century interpretation, because it has
laid weight upon Jesus' eschatological message and
played down any interpretation which attempted to speak
of a process of the coming of God's reign (especially
if this involved any human effort).[9] Dodd himself
wanted to speak of "realized eschatology," so that he
was willing to see some stages in the kingdom's
advance. In saying this, however, Dodd still did not
allow for human agency in the coming of God's reign.
The work of the Old Testament prophets, John, and
Jesus, was God's work; the harvest, God's harvest.[10]
This viewpoint is consistently held to by Dodd for the
other parables discussed below.

For Jeremias and Perrin, the Sower parable,
along with the Seed Growing Secretly and the Mustard
Seed parables, are to be understood in the context of
Jesus' eschatological message and depict the contrast
between small beginnings and great ends, between the
minuscule effect of Jesus' words and work and the
magnitude of the imminent reign of God. Miraculous
growth or the promise of a rich harvest, then, is the

parabolic sign of God's graciousness and eschatological power.[11] B. T. D. Smith is less certain of the meaning of the Sower, but tentatively concludes that it was "employed by Christ as an encouragement to his disciples to believe that the preaching of the Kingdom would prove fruitful . . ."[12] Rudolf Bultmann classes almost all of the parables considered in the present chapter among those for which the meaning is irrecoverable![13]

Despite Bultmann's doubts, the similarity of content in these parables suggests a substantive connection between them in the actual discourse of Jesus and the possibility of getting at their original meaning. John Crossan has spoken, particularly with regard to the parables of Jesus depicting masters and servants, of theme and variations based upon an "oral," in contrast to a "scribal," sensibility. The latter type denotes a strict attention to the printed word and the priority of syntax. It is the sensibility of the educated. The former type by contrast gives pre-eminence to structure and to the typical. It is the sensibility of popular speech.[14]

Crossan argues that Jesus utilized broad types and structures in the parables; individual examples, then, represent variations on a theme. This typicality is especially evident in similitudes, such as those depicting masters and servants. Some of these display a rather conventional viewpoint about the relations of such people (e.g. Mk. 13:34-35). Other words of Jesus, particularly those traditionally labeled by form critics as parables, relate to a general theme, but illustrate behavior which defies conventional expectations (e.g. Mt. 18:23-34).[15]

It is to be suspected, therefore, in the
parables about to be discussed, that Jesus is toying
with a theme. This is, at any rate, the view
countenanced here.

B. Assumptions About the Agricultural Imagery and Peasant Audience of These Parables

Since the imagery of these parables is agricultural, or has to do with growing plants, it is believed
necessary in evaluating their meaning to devote some
attention to agronomic realities and agricultural
practices in ancient Palestine.[16]

Sociological imagination also informs the work
of this chapter. One of the fundamental premises for
the exegesis is the belief that Jesus' audience
consisted primarily of peasants. This poses the
question of what Jesus' stories and parables signify in
a framework of peasant values. What would peasants
have heard, for instance, when Jesus spoke of the reign
of God?[17] More than this, what would peasants living
in the context sketched in Part One have heard in these
parables?

Anthropologist Eric Wolf, to whom we have had
occasion to refer previously in other connections, has
written about two levels in agrarian religion, the
("higher") level attended to by religious specialists
and the ("lower") level relating immediately to the
peasantry's needs:

> Where peasant religion focuses on the individual
> and his passage through a series of crucial
> episodes such as birth, circumcision, passage to
> adulthood, marriage, death, the higher-order
> interpretations fasten on these events of the life-
> cycle in abstract terms, regarding them as way

stations on the human path through life and fate.
Where peasant religion concerns itself with the
regenerative cycle of cultivation and the protection of the crop against the random attacks of
nature, the higher-order interpretation speaks of
regenerative cycles in general, of the recurrence
of life and death (underlining mine).[18]

A slightly different view of the same reality is
held by Robert Redfield. In his book Peasant Society
and Culture, he writes:

> Let us begin with a recognition, long present in
> discussions of civilizations, of the difference
> between a great tradition and a little tradi-
> tion. . . . In a civilization there is a great
> tradition of the reflective few, and there is a
> little tradition of the largely unreflective many.
> The great tradition is cultivated in schools or
> temples; the little tradition works itself out and
> keeps itself going in the lives of the unlettered
> in their village communities.[19]

This quote might seem to suggest that Redfield sees the
little tradition as derivative, but in fact he does
not. He goes on to say that these two traditions need
to be thought of as currents of thought flowing
dialectically back and forth. One of the examples he
employs to illustrate this process is the Old Testament
tradition.[20]

Redfield contributes some other useful assumptions for the present inquiry. He speaks of the
"peasant view of the good life" centering around three,
interrelated values: A reverent attitude toward the
land, strenuous agricultural work viewed as good (but
commerce as bad), and productive industry considered a
virtue.[21]

What Wolf designates as the higher order of
religious interpretation and Redfield as the great
tradition, I would see as secondary or mediate, an
attempt to express through the words "abstract,"
"philosophical," "spiritual," "theological," and so on.
Conversely, the religious orientation of peasantry
would seem to be primary and immediate, firmly
connected with material realities, and perhaps
expressed through words like "magic," "superstition,"
"ceremony" (especially involving food and drink), and
"reverence" before God who gives rain, sunshine, and
plant growth.

Max Weber long ago contrasted peasant religion
with the "ethical rationalism" of non-privileged
artisans:

> As a general rule the peasantry remained primarily
> involved with weather magic and animistic magic or
> ritualism; insofar as it developed any ethical
> religion, the focus was on a purely formalistic
> ethic of do ut des in relation to both god and
> priests.[22]

What the foregoing discussion tries to provide
warrant for, is a quite different approach to Jesus'
words than is usually encountered in New Testament
scholarship. Jesus spoke his parables within a context
characterized by peasant realities. His words subsequently, through the Christian movement, became a part
of the great tradition of Judaism/Christianity under
the care of religious specialists with somewhat different concerns. Jesus creatively played upon little
traditions; his work was taken up into the great tradition. Our task is to move back, therefore, to his
original intention and context.

One further point needs to be mentioned. The
ministry of Jesus, as we saw previously, took place
during a time of major social stress and change. It
transpired in an occupied country. This fact has not
been overlooked by students of Jesus, but they have
often discussed it in the rather unhelpful terms of the
dilemma--political revolutionary or nonpolitical
reformer.[23] The social sciences may prove ultimately
helpful in sorting out the ways and means whereby
"revolutionary" activities and utterances are subli-
mated, as it were, under other social forms. At any
rate, what needs to be kept in mind when reading the
parables of Jesus is this: Jesus' parables may not be
as direct a discourse as modern theologians think who
have rejected the explanation of them in Mk. 4:10-12.
Jesus lived under the oriental despotism of Antipas, a
client of politically astute Rome. Antipas had John
the Baptizer killed, according to the account of
Josephus, on grounds of political suspicion (AJ
18.116ff). No one who had been affiliated with John's
movement, and who was now trying to carry it on in a
new way, could have missed the significance of the
founder's death in such a manner (cf. Lk. 13:32).
Jesus' speech was, we would argue, deliberately
indirect and multileveled in meaning. Only in this way
could he have conducted his public mission for even a
short time.[24]

C. Exegesis of the Four Parables

1. Mark 4:3-8 = Matthew 13:3b-8 = Luke 8:5-8 = GThom 9

The basic structure of this parable, as it
probably appeared in the speech of Jesus, is apparent
in all four extant versions. The structure is an

excellent example of the "rule of three."[25] The order
of the misfortunes befalling the seed--birds, shallow
soil, thorns--is the same in all versions. Justin
Martyr knew a version almost identical to the
Synoptics', the only difference being the reversal of
the order of rocky ground and thorns.[26] Matthew and
Mark, furthermore, have a threefold description of the
ears of grain produced, although Matthew reverses
Mark's order (by placing a hundredfold first: Mt.
13:8). This basic structure--adverse circumstances,
production of grain--is probably the most important
thing to notice about the Sower parable. It is
certainly more important than the minor divergences
that can be seen to exist between the four versions--to
be explained by reference to translational differences,
traditional divergences (Thomas's "sixtyfold and one
hundred and twentyfold"), or redactional activity
(Luke's hekatontaplasiona in 8:8).[27]

It must be asked, therefore, in the light of
this brief review, whether anything more can be said
about the Sower parable. Many interpretations have
been offered. It is probable that Jesus intended some
meaning in connection with his proclamation of the
imminent reign of God.[28] Although modern scholars have
rejected the tradition's allegorical interpretation of
the parable in principle, it seems they have taken
their cue from it in practice. To identify harvest
with eschaton as many have done, though it has a good
basis in passages like Joel 3:13 (4:13 Hebrew), 4 Ezra
4:28-32, and 2 Baruch 70:2, is somewhat abstract. This
may be the most immediate association to scholars who
have studied the great tradition within which Jesus
stood, but it must seriously be asked, what associa-
tions would have been most immediate to Jesus' original

audience? To answer this obviously involves some
assumptions, such as we attempted to make explicit
previously, but it is believed that the historical task
only progresses through such a circular or dialectical
process.[29]

It is not clear from the parable context whether
the sower is to be thought of as a peasant smallholder
working his own ground or as a laborer who is sowing on
someone else's ground. Each of these possible cases
will be considered in the exegesis. The initial
impression given by the parable is that the sower sows
somewhat carelessly, because so much seed is lost.
From the point of view of the narrative, of course,
this permits the description of the fates of the three
classes of seed. Birds are identified as the first
"natural predator" for the seed. Birds must have been
a familiar problem for farmers throughout the ancient
Near East. Jubilees 11:13, 18, for instance, has
ostensibly recorded the trouble Abraham's neighbors had
with flocks of birds stealing seed. Naturally quite a
bit of energy would have been expended by the peasantry
keeping birds out of the fields.

Vincent Taylor, following C. C. Torrey and
Matthew Black, believes that behind para tēn hodon lies
the Aramaic 'al 'urḥa, "upon the path" (instead of
"alongside").[30] This philological detail would perhaps
strengthen the impression of the sower's carelessness.
Jeremias believes, however, that plowing after sowing
was the normal procedure in ancient Palestine. The
sower covers all ground, knowing that all will be
plowed over.[31] K. D. White has rightly corrected this
view of Jeremias. White points out that the Mediterranean farmer has always known the importance of maintaining a summer fallow.[32] Furthermore, no good farmer

in the past or present would deliberately sow upon
unplowed stubble.[33]   Jeremias and White are nonetheless
in agreement that the parable is not intended to show
bad husbandry on the part of the sower.[34]

      The second threat to the seed, rocky ground, was
equally well known to the Palestinian cultivator. Soil
depths were not uniform, and the extensive terracing of
the land attests to the widespread presence of rocks.
Perhaps this plight of the seed, too, reflects badly on
the sower: Inadequate clearing of the soil could be
suspected. Sometimes, however, underlying rock was not
discovered until plowing was underway.[35] White thinks
the Palestinian peasant would have known where rock
outcroppings were close to the surface of the soil and
protected his plow accordingly. Such outcroppings
frequently could not be removed.[36]

      The appearance of thorns in the story, possibly
acanthus spinosa,[37] might also suggest poor preparation
of the soil in advance of planting. Jeremias has tried
to argue against this inference on the basis of some
rabbinic and Old Testament texts. These texts show, he
believes, that since plowing came after sowing in
Palestine, the sower cannot be considered careless.
Dennis Nineham follows this line of argument as well.[38]
White thinks the presence of the weeds is not to be
understood as typical of the field as a whole. Thorns
could easily appear on the borders of the arable.[39]
There is no need, in White's view, to follow the
erroneous reasoning of Jeremias about sowing before
plowing. We have already seen that the agriculturalist
of Palestine was compelled, by the prevalent dry
farming conditions, to keep summer fields clean
fallowed in order to conserve adequate moisture for the
crops. The presence of thorny weeds on the field at

the time of sowing at least points to the difficulties
the farmer faced. If a small proprietor is here to be
thought of, perhaps there is contemplated the cultivation of very marginal ground. This would place the
sower in a better light, laboring as he is against
formidable enemies.

Despite all the natural factors hostile to the
optimum growth of the plants, the parable ends on an
optimistic note. There are produced individual tillers
with thirty grains, sixty grains, and even one hundred
grains.[40] Taylor reaches this conclusion:

While portions of the seed are lost in various
ways, the rest, perhaps the greater part, yields an
amazing harvest . . . the harvest is the key to the
interpretation of the parable.[41]

We concur with Taylor's judgment. The basic thrust of
the parable seems to be: Despite natural hostility,
nonetheless miraculous growth.

In the light of the peasant attitude sketched
above, how would this parable appear? If poor
practices of cultivation were suspected--stones and
weeds had not been removed, birds were not scared off--
these would be evaluated negatively. If the sower were
perceived as a "hired man," there would perhaps be
thoughts of the evils that have come with the Romans.
Land is no longer under village control, but is worked
by hirelings or tenants who do not care. Otherwise, if
the sower were thought of as a proprietor laboring
under the harsh circumstances of the land, he would
find sympathy.

Despite these negative images, a harvest comes.
Who provides the harvest? Here the peasant audience
would immediately make the connection with God, who
provides despite all that works against the agricul-

tural producer. This "natural theology" is quite in
accord with the views of a peasantry, though it may
perhaps be out of sorts with religious specialists
deeply immersed in the historical traditions of their
religion. The primary producer has an immediate relationship with God. This relationship Jesus capitalizes
on in making the connection between that God and the
imminent reign which he is proclaiming.

What is the nature of this connection? The
great tradition, whether already in the New Testament
itself (Mk. 4:13-20 and par.) or in the modern
scholarship on the parables of growth, has believed the
connection to lie in a view of eschatological events
and/or the success of God's purposes. The above
discussion of the little tradition points, however, in
a different direction. The connection most naturally,
from the point of view of the interests of a peasantry,
lies in God's material providence. God provides a
harvest, despite all of those things inimical to any
crop at all, so that the harvest can be eaten!

It is interesting to observe that 1 Clement 24:5
preserves an extra-canonical parallel to the Sower
bolstering this interpretation:

> The sower went forth and cast into the earth each
> of the seeds, which, when they have fallen into the
> earth dry and naked, are dissolved. Then, out of
> the decay, the sublimity of the Master's providence
> raises them up, and out of the one, much will grow
> and bear fruit.[42]

There is preserved in Papyrus Egerton 2 a tantalizing
story about Jesus taking dust into his hand, planting
seed in it, pouring water over it, and the seed immediately bearing fruit.[43] Furthermore, the Infancy
Gospel of Thomas (InThom) 12:1-2 relates how the child

Jesus reaps one hundredfold (measures?) from a single grain of wheat and feeds the village poor.[44]

These passages imply a rich tradition of sayings and prophetic actions centering around seeds and growth--the point of which seems to be the material importance of the growth and harvest.[45] Clement's tradition expressly links growth with God's providence (pronoia). The Egerton papyrus and the InThom passages point to God's power, funneled through Jesus, to produce growth. While Clement and and the author of the Gospel of John may have been particularly impressed with the symbolism of resurrection in all of this, a land-hungry or hungry and landless peasantry probably would have seen something quite different.

Yet this result must not conceal from us the fact that Jesus is also saying something about peasant values. If the providence of God is so reliable, what must this imply for, say, the peasant values of frugality and strenuous labor? These too may need reconsideration.

2. Mark 4:26-29 (= GThom 21?)

The Seed Growing Secretly is unique to Mark's gospel. The imagery of the parable finds a slight parallel in the vine imagery of 1 Clement 23:4f and 2 Clement 11:3. In a moment, we shall look at a possible connection with GThom 21. The reader is referred to the next subsection of the present chapter for a consideration of the Darnel Among the Wheat, appearing at this point in Matthew's recension of Mark 4. The meaning of the Seed Growing Secretly must be evaluated for the most part upon the basis of internal con- siderations and narrative analysis of this single instance.

Like the Sower, the narrative begins with a man
casting seed upon the ground (Mk. 4:26). While the man
sleeps and rises, the grain tillers and grows long (v.
27b). The earth bears fruit by itself (automatē),
sending out blade of grass (chortos), ear (stachyn),
and grain (v. 28). The ripening of the grain signals
the moment for the harvest (v. 29). These are the
formal elements of the parable that form the basis for
the discussion.

What is immediately surprising here, from the
standpoint of agriculture, is the complete absence of
any mention of cultivation. The man "sleeps and rises
night and day," and the earth brings forth fruit "by
itself." Are we to assume that cultivation will be
carried out anyway, or are these notices in the
narrative really suggesting that the man does not do
anything? The meaning of the parable hinges on this
question, so it will be necessary to devote a little
attention to it.

The summary of a variety of modern interpretations of this parable in Vincent Taylor's commentary
shows that most recent scholarship has neither laid
particular emphasis on the growing of the crop nor on
the detail of the man's idleness.[46] The emphasis upon
growth has often been associated in the past with an
evolutionary view of the progress of the kingdom in
society. The majority view of the twentieth century,
that the emphasis lies on the harvest and supplies
a symbol of God's eschatological rule, can at least
point to Joel 3:13 (4:13 Hebrew), 4 Ezra 4:28-32, or 2
Baruch 70:2, as we have had occasion to mention above.
Dodd finds support for this view in sayings like that
of Lk. 10:2 = Mt. 9:37f.[47]

These interpretations find their cogency in
interests and relationships somewhat removed from those
of Jesus' peasant audience. Where might the interest
of this social class have been in such a parable? What
would a harvest without labor imply for those who
perhaps labored mightily (mostly for others) and for
only a bare subsistence, or for those without access to
land and secure food reserves?

To explore these questions more deeply, a
perhaps-at-first-sight oblique reference is made to the
evidence of Papias. Papias was, in the early second
century, bishop of Hierapolis near Philadelphia in Asia
Minor. He showed special interest in the oral tradition of early Christianity (Eusebius EH 3.39). A
notice from Irenaeus about Papias may explain why.
Irenaeus says Papias heard from "the Elders" what John
the disciple of the Lord relayed about Jesus' message:

> . . . how the Lord taught about those days and
> said: "The days will come, in which vines will be
> produced, each one having a thousand branches, and
> in each branch ten thousand twigs, and on each twig
> ten thousand shoots, and on each shoot ten thousand
> clusters, and in each cluster ten thousand grapes,
> and each grape when pressed will give twenty-five
> metretes of wine . . ." [etc.][48]

Papias's testimony, brief though it is, sheds an
interesting light on the Seed Growing Secretly. In its
present form, the testimony refers clearly to a coming,
and not an already present, existence of such a state
of affairs. It suggests, nonetheless, the framework of
interests and meaning wherein the Seed Growing Secretly
may have found its full resonance--with the stress
falling upon the lack of toil, the material significance of the harvest imagery, and the very-near reality
of the reign of God.

The echo of the conclusion of this Marcan
parable in GThom 21 is not easy to interpret. The
difficulty arises for the most part because the version
in Thomas comprises the end of a conglomerate of
various sayings of Jesus, and not one integrated
saying. So we find there a saying about a thief known
also from the Synoptic gospels, as well as a rather
cryptic saying about the disciples in a field.

The disciples are compared with little children
dwelling in a field that does not belong to them. Does
this mean they are like orphans? If so, then they
perhaps are considered present in the field to be able
to get food. Jewish law provided ample scope for the
poor to glean in fields.[49] In the next image, the
disciples are compared with a thief who breaks in and
steals the householder's goods (lit. vessel). What is
the object of the theft here? Undoubtedly it is a
vessel full of some basic commodity like grain or wine.
Theft is for the purpose of satisfying hunger. In the
final instance, the image is that of the reaper. In
each case, material interest and satisfaction of want
are implicitly in view. If this intention goes back to
Jesus, then there is indirect evidence here for our
reading.

Separated by at least two centuries, but linked
in a substantive way, the traditions in Ethiopian Enoch
and Syriac Baruch offer another dimension to the discussion. 1 Enoch 10 says that the end of time shall be
a time of great blessing and peace. A measure of seed
sown will bear a thousand measures (10:19)! A measure
of olives will yield ten presses of oil. There will be
wine in abundance. 2 Baruch gives a similar picture.
According to 2 Baruch 29:5, the earth will yield ten
thousandfold. Furthermore:

> . . . on each (?) vine there shall be a thousand
> branches, and each branch shall produce a thousand
> clusters, and each cluster produce a thousand
> grapes, and each grape produce a cor of wine. And
> those who have hungered shall rejoice . . .[50]

This is the very prophecy Papias attributed to Jesus.
The similarity of the hopes in 1 Enoch and 2 Baruch
strongly urges the view that such traditions and hopes
persisted all through the period that witnessed the
rise of Christianity.[51]

In addition to 2 Baruch 29:5ff and 1 Enoch 10,
the Sibylline Oracles further attest such beliefs
circulating in the eastern Mediterranean world of the
late first and early second century. For instance,
SibOr 3.619-621 speaks of the win, honey, milk, and
grain of the end time. So also do lines 744-45. Lines
753-54 read: "No war shall there be any more nor
drought throughout the land, no famine nor hail to work
havoc on the crops."[52] These Endzeit hopes counter-
balance the dominant myth about the Urzeit expressed in
places like Genesis 3:17-19 or in Virgil's Georgics
(1.147-159) and Eclogues (4.23, 26). The toil of
farming the ground is a punishment for some primordial
fault in humankind. The Talmud also knows this
belief.[53] The irony of this formulation, apparently
widespread, is that it is brought to expression by
interest groups whose dominant occupations were not of
necessity the labor of agriculture, and whose dominant
ethos was antibanausic and leisured.[54] The hopes of
the agricultural producers undoubtedly gravitated
toward the Endzeit formulation, because that would mean
release from a toil that procured little benefit for
the producer.

Perhaps the most illuminating passage for the
parable under consideration is contained in the New
Testament itself. Rev. 21:4 reads:

And he shall wipe away every tear from their eyes,
and there shall no longer be death, nor mourning,
nor outcry, nor toil, [because] the former things
have passed away (underlining mine).

The underlined words are not to be found in Sinaiticus,
Uncial 2030, and a few others. The words were undoubtedly controversial. Be that as it may, toil is thought
of by some as something that will not be required in
the scheme of the coming aeon.[55]

Would not hearers of Jesus' parable have noticed
the pregnant silence about agricultural work? For
them, the parable spoke volumes about the coming
dispensation of God that would take into account their
physical needs, in contrast to the present dispensation
which did not. In this view, the point of the parable
does lie in the harvest, as modern commentators have
thought, but the meaning of the harvest assumes a
different aspect. The harvest comes to meet material
need. It is a real harvest here thought of, not a
cipher for theologians' speculations about time and
eternity.

3. Mt. 13:24-30 = GThom 57

It is unclear whether Matthew found the Darnel
Among the Wheat in his tradition or himself made the
substitution for Mark's Seed Growing Secretly. Though
Matthew has thoroughly edited it, the authenticity of
the Darnel parable as a parable of Jesus is not
doubted.[56]

As has been said, modern scholarship has
rejected the allegorical interpretation of the parable

in the tradition (Mt. 13:36-43). Most scholars have
followed the lead of Matthew's own theological-
allegorical reading, however--seeing in the householder
a representation of the graciousness and patience of
God, in the weeds a type of sinners, and in the harvest
the final judgment. The parable is, in this view, a
statement about God's prerogative to be merciful.
Jeremias typifies many of these interpretations: "In
the parable of the Darnel, the idea of a premature
separation is expressly rejected, and patience until
the harvest is enjoined."[57]

    While we do not have an alternate tradition of
this parable in the Synoptic tradition, fortunately a
parallel is preserved in Thomas. Saying 57 contains a
slightly shorter version. Events in Thomas's parable
occur in the same order as in Matthew's. His version
lacks, however, the Matthean dialog between the householder and the slaves. It also lacks the express
statement of Matthew that the zizania appeared at the
same time as the wheat grains (v. 26). This event,
however, is implied in Thomas: The man prohibits
weeding, so there must have been a recognition of the
problem. The fact remains, nonetheless, that for
Matthew's version there is a period of time, between
the appearance of weeds and the harvest, when some
response needs to be contemplated; for Thomas, apparently, harvesttime is the only time appropriate to take
action.

    Is there any way, on the basis of these two
versions of the parable, to decide which is the more
original? Wolfgang Schrage, after tradition-critical
analysis, claims that Thomas abbreviated Matthew.[58] I
am inclined to give more originality to Matthew's
version, and the fundamental importance of the slaves'

question to the master about weeding, on the basis of
agronomic considerations.

Most students of biblical flora have identified
the zizania of Matthew's parable with lolium temulentum
or darnel, a noxious weed common in the Levant. The
grains of this annual grass contain a strong toxin.[59]
Therefore, it is not self-evidently wise to harvest
darnel with wheat, because mixing the toxic grains of
darnel with wheat ruins the quality of the grain and
poses a health hazard to anyone eating flour so
adulterated.[60] The weed does not grow above 1000 feet
in altitude.[61] It is typically a weed infesting the
best wheat fields.[62] In wetter than normal years
darnel thrives and successfully competes with the good
crop. Drier years favor the wheat.[63]

The ancients knew darnel well. A common belief
of antiquity held that, through evil agencies, good
seeds changed into degenerate wheat (i.e. darnel).
Theophrastus attests to this belief already in the
fourth century B.C.E.[64] Rabbinic literature, under
similar conceptions, did not consider darnel and wheat
to constitute a mixed kind. A rabbinic etymology did
connect the plague of darnel with the fornication and
evil of Genesis 6.[65] Both Virgil and Pliny had
negative things to say about darnel.[66]

Darnel can infest a field in a number of ways.[67]
If the field is not clean fallowed in the summer after
harvest, weeds of all types grow rapidly and deplete
water reserves. Yet darnel seed, because unsavory to
rodents and birds, is often plowed in with the
stubble.[68] Darnel can also be sown inadvertently with
contaminated wheat seed. This was probably its primary
means of propagation in antiquity. Thus, the phrase
"good seed" of Mt. 13:24 alludes to its purity. In

the days before certified seed, purity was only
attainable by careful examination of the seed before
sowing, and possibly winnowing or sifting out any weed
seed.[69] Furthermore, humans, animals, or wind can
carry weed seed onto a field at any time.[70]

It is often stressed by modern commentators that
wheat and darnel are practically indistinguishable at
the seedling stage.[71] This is true, but less so as the
growing season progresses. As a matter of fact, for a
skilled farmer the developing weeds can be distinguished by the width of their leaves.[72] This would
allow them to be uprooted before they go to seed, if
the farmer were watching the development of the crop
carefully.

Eradication, then, at the earliest possible time
in the growing season, is the treatment of choice for
darnel.[73] Under the prevailing conditions of dry
farming, such weeding has several benefits: It elimi-
nates competition for space, soil nutrients, soil
moisture, and light necessary for the optimum growth of
the crop. Dalman and others have noted that the normal
procedure among Arab peasant cultivators has been to
uproot darnel, repeatedly if necessary.[74]

Conversely, to let darnel grow with the wheat to
harvest without any attempt to weed is an extraordinary
event and undoubtedly poses serious dangers to the
crop. Weed competition will diminish yields. Pliny
tells us that darnel was known to twine around wheat
and strangle the plants.[75] It is plainly not a benign
enemy.

Both Pliny and Virgil attest to the fecundity of
darnel, implying that slovenly farming methods mean
greater problems in coming years.[76] If darnel is
allowed to go to seed, the farmer faces a real crisis.

Weeding after the appearance of grain might pose the
danger of uprooting wheat along with the darnel, but it
possibly can claim to be the lesser of two evils. The
farmer must attempt to prevent propagation, perhaps
accomplished by separating the darnel grains from their
stalks and removing them from the field. Furthermore,
the farmer will try to avoid harvesting the poisonous
darnel along with the wheat, in order to protect the
quality of the harvest.

     If ancient harvesters did bring in wheat and
darnel together to the threshing floor, separating the
grains promised to be a real headache. One option was
to winnow in the hopes that the wind would separate the
two types of grain. Darnel is similar to wheat in size
and appearance, though not in weight.[77] Another option
was to sieve the grains. Only with modern technology
has this alternative become completely effective.[78] So
neither of the ancient methods was likely to gain a
harvest of 100 percent purity.

     The foregoing summary demonstrates the agricul-
tural complexity of the situation envisioned in Mt.
13:24-30. There would have been no absolutely fool-
proof approach to the problem of a darnel-infested
field, but careful weeding offered some hope of
avoiding disaster.

     This brings us back to the question of original
form. Thomas seems to stress unrealistically harvesttime as the time of separating weeds and wheat. On the
other hand, there is reason to wonder about the detail
of the enemy sowing the weed common to both traditions.[79] This detail seems inessential to the point of
the story. The natural introduction of darnel is
easily accomplished (recall the popular belief about
degenerate wheat).[80] There may be here an element of

comedy, seen from the standpoint of the Jesus' rural
audience: The parable perhaps originally lacked v. 25,
but had the reference to an enemy (echthros anthrōpos,
v. 28). From the standpoint of an increasingly alienated rural populace, a landowner is being portrayed in
an unflattering light (see below). Otherwise, this
detail about the enemy could have been introduced under
the influence of early Christian allegorical concerns.
The detail is functional from the standpoint of Mt.
13:39.

It is also difficult to decide whether the
dialog between householder and slaves should be
considered a part of the original parable. I am
inclined to keep at least the final question of the
slaves, along with the householder's response. In any
case, the explicit reason given for the prohibition of
the weeding, in both Thomas and Matthew, is that no
wheat be uprooted and lost to the harvest.

The agronomic and formal considerations laid out
lead me to question whether the point of the Darnel
Among the Wheat really lies in God's merciful fore-
bearance or in an exhortation not to separate out the
bad apples. These interpretations could only come
about by the belief that the householder's decision
reflected good agricultural practice. In the light of
the preceding, would not the point in the discourse of
Jesus rather seem to revolve around the wisdom of the
householder's decision? From this perspective, might
he not be portrayed for us as a negative model?

That this householder deals with slaves would
seem to presuppose some form of landed estate, and
distance the man somewhat from the actual operation of
the farm. The motive for the slaves' suggestions can
be assumed: They are looking out for their own

interests, insofar as they are looking after their
master's. Since they probably were the ones most
directly involved in the agricultural work, they would
have been aware of the seriousness of the problem at
hand.

Whether the householder is to be thought of as a
middleman--a chief slave like a vilicus--or as a large
proprietor, is less clear. The Greek word oikodespotēs
can have both senses, but behind it is the Aramaic
ba'al baytha or Hebrew ba'al habayith. In the Mishnah,
the latter has been understood to be a property owner,
but may in fact be a steward (e.g. Peah 4:1). New
Testament passages like Mk. 14:14 or Mt. 13:52 and
24:45ff also suggest this interpretation.[81] However,
Mt. 13:30b (tēn apothēkēn mou, "my barn") argues
against the vilicus interpretation.

Certainly it can be objected that Matthew's
parable may simply be reflecting the socio-economic
situation of his own community. Oikodespotēs is a word
dear to Matthew (8x), though it also occurs four times
in Luke and once in Mark.[82] Thomas may preserve the
more original form of the parable in lacking this word,
but even in Thomas the man does not do his own weeding.
The division of labor implied in wage-laborers or
slaves who do the harvesting, and possibly the sowing
and weeding, is in conformity with what is known about
Jesus' Palestinian context. For the small peasant, the
division of labor was primarily within the household.
The hard work of weeding was usually assigned to women
and children.[83] Furthermore, that the man in the
parable has the power to plant, that he plants wheat
instead of barley, and that he plants in the best
valley soil points to a man of some wealth and
independent means.[84]

In the light of this discussion, what might have
been the point of the parable when it was originally
uttered? What thought-process would Jesus' peasant
audience go through in evaluating the man's response to
the problem? First, while the man has sown good seed,
no one apparently has watched the development of the
crop carefully to catch any weeds. Only when the grain
has "headed out" (v. 26) is the darnel discovered.
Less than careful agricultural practice is immediately
to be suspected. Second, the man prohibits cultivation
on discovery that the weed has gone to seed. The
reason given is "maximization of yield." The slaves,
however, have recognized an ominous threat to the crop.
Third, the man is going to tell the reapers to do the
separating--but will they be at all as careful as the
situation demands? The end in view is endangered by
the means employed (cf. John 10:12).

An impression of the man's imprudence is
strengthened by two other considerations. In contrast
to the present parable, the previously discussed
parable of the Sower brings out the miracle of
production in the face of all that is hostile to it
(even careless sowing). Such a message would receive a
positive evaluation by poor farmers. The Darnel Among
the Wheat, conversely, depicts the folly of human
presumption unappreciative of the forces arrayed
against it. The man may be sadly disappointed at the
meagerness or quality of the harvest.

A second "vector" in the tradition, then, points
to the Lucan parable of the Rich Fool (Lk. 12:16-20).
There events begin with different assumptions: The
rich harvest comes. What will be done with it? The
man decides to found his future security upon his
storehouse. The foolishness of this decision is

brought out by a general consideration regarding the
insecurity of the foundations of life itself. The
Darnel parable does not have such an explicit conclusion, but the question regarding the wisdom of the
man's response to the situation could have presented
itself to the original audience on the basis of
agronomic considerations about darnel.

An interesting link, in particular, between the
Matthean parable and Luke's Rich Fool is afforded in
the word apothēkē. Granting that behind all of the
Synoptic occurrences of this word there lies an Aramaic
original, it is notable that this Greek word appears in
the Synoptic tradition only six times, four if parallels are taken into account: Four of the occurrences
can be reduced essentially to two, because they appear
in Q sayings (John the Baptizer's speech about eschatological threshing and birds do not gather into barns).
The other two occurrences are in the present parable
and in the Rich Fool.[85]

Matthew has, of course, construed the meaning of
apothēkē here as eschatological. However, looking at
these four independent occurrences, only the Q saying
of John the Baptizer has the eschatological meaning
unequivocally. The other three instances all can have
a quite mundane reference. Such a mundane reference
seems to be implied in this parable in Matthew. It is
interesting, moreover, that the saying about birds not
gathering into barns, as well as the story of the Rich
Fool, are in contexts of statements about God's
providence and subsistence.

In a direct way, then, the parable exposes the
arrogance of human decisions made self-centeredly
without adequate assessment of forces of contingency.
For those who exploit the land only for their own

profit, the impending reign of God is a threat. It is
like the pestilence of weeds, which despite all human
calculations and confidence, thrive and threaten
economic security. Thus, the parable is socio-critical
over against the landowning class. It asks about the
source of sustenance and economic security in the light
of the imminent reign of God. The economic efflores-
cence under the early empire encouraged a kind of
economic self-interest and self-sufficiency that is
criticized in the parable.[86]

4. Mark 4:30-32 = Matthew 13:31-32
= Luke 13:18-19 = GThom 20

With Bultmann, Taylor, and Fitzmyer, we see that
Mark's and Luke's versions of this parable are independent, and Matthew has conflated Mark with Q.[87] B. T.
D. Smith thinks the Q version is more original.[88]
Jeremias points out that probably the Aramaic version
began with the preposition l[e]. This philological
detail is preserved most clearly in the Greek of Mark,
hōs (v. 31), but is also evident in Q, homoia estin.
The editorial work of the evangelists is very clear at
the beginning of this pericope (i.e. Mt. 13:31; Mk.
4:30; Lk. 13:18), but with the actual beginning of the
parable--"(it is) like"--the tradition becomes more
uniform. Thus, it is easier to discern in the parable
itself the basic outline of Jesus' original speech: A
tiny seed is sown, a mustard plant grows into a large
shrub, the birds of the air find shelter in the
branches of the plant.

A number of details need to be explored in order
to approach the meaning of this similitude. To begin
with, one must ask what setting for the sowing is
envisioned in Mk. 4:31 (and par.). As was argued in
previous sections of this chapter, agrarian considera-

tions may prompt the biblical exegete to revise received interpretations of well-read passages. In the
passage under consideration, it is of some import for
the interpretation of the parable to note that mustard
plants have from time immemorial been found as weeds in
grain fields.[89] Yet the standard wisdom on this
parable, even from so sensitive an exegete of the
parables as Jeremias, has never seemed to take cogni-
zance of this fact. Indeed, for most exegetes the
mustard plant is a positive symbol.[90]

     It is interesting to consider the various
settings conceived in the tradition for this parable.
Mark's version rather non-specifically indicates
(temporal relative adverb + subjunctive sparē) that the
seed ends up "upon the earth." Mark's version does not
otherwise make explicit the locale of the final resting
place of the seed. Matthew does make this explicit:
en tōi agrōi ("in [his] field"). Matthew envisions
therefore a cultivated field as the scene of the
parable's action. Luke's version presents a significant difference. For Luke the seed is intentionally
sown in someone's garden (kēpon). Jeremias already
noted this difference, and even recognized in it a
shift to non-Palestinian horticulture. Rabbinic tradition forbade the sowing of mustard in gardens, but not
on fields.[91] However, this change in detail still did
not suggest to Jeremias a different slant on the
meaning of the parable. The GThom version, which
probably represents northern Syrian tradition, agrees
with Matthew in seeing the seed sown upon a cultivated
field.[92] In the light of these observations, there is
good reason to believe that Jesus originally had in
mind a mustard plant growing in or near a field. What
kind of plant and what kind of field were these?

Pliny knew three kinds of mustard plants.[93]   The
Mishnah also distinguishes three kinds of mustard
plants, one wild and two domesticated (laphśân,
hardâl, and hardâl misri respectively).[94] The wild and
either of the domesticated varieties constitute a mixed
kind, according to M. Kil. 1:5. It is the domesticated
varieties that cannot be sown in Palestinian gardens.
Modern botanists have identified these as brassica
nigra and sinapis alba.[95]

The wild mustard, probably charlock (sinapis
arvensis), was unwelcome in any cultivated area. Pliny
says regarding the fecundity of mustard:

It grows entirely wild, though it is improved by
being transplanted: but on the other hand when it
has once been sown it is scarcely possible to get
the place free of it, as the seed when it falls
germinates at once.[96]

In this quality lies the deadliness of mustard as a
noxious weed in grain fields. For as White has noted
about the varieties of rye-grass (including darnel),
plants like these that could quickly reproduce would
outgrow the good grain crops.[97] They were thus
considered weeds and constantly attacked by the farmer
through various methods of cultivation.

Returning then to the question of setting, is
the mustard plant of Jesus' parable actually a cultivated plant or to be considered an unwelcome guest
among the cultivated plants? The Marcan, Matthean, and
Thomas versions of the parable would seem to suggest
that the plant is a wild variety of mustard whose
presence was not anticipated by the cultivator. Only
in Luke is it expressly said that the mustard is sown
for the purpose of raising a condiment. Let us examine
for a moment the other versions on this point. Mark,

as has been noted, refers to the sowing of the plant in
a temporally indefinite manner (subjunctive mood):
"[Mustard seed] which whenever it is sown . . ." Next
in Mark, the smallness of the seed is stressed through
a concessive participial construction. Matthew's
rendition appears to give more of a purposive aspect to
the sowing by using a participle + indicative mood main
verb: "[Mustard seed] which taking, a man sowed . . ."
Then Matthew follows Mark in noting the small size of
this seed. The tradition in Thomas remarks upon the
smallness of the seed's size first. GThom agrees with
Mark about the temporally indefinite time of sowing
(hotan). The GThom version expressly states that this
is a cultivated field.

     While the ambiguities of the three versions
perhaps provide room for the standard interpretation of
the parable, which sees here intentional cultivation of
mustard plants (cf. Mk. 4:32, lachanōn), the versions
more probably indicate that Jesus had in mind an
unintentional sowing and a mustard plant growing as a
weed in a grainfield. The smallness of the mustard
seed and the tallness of the plant carry agronomic
significance. These features point to a wild Galilean
variety of brassica nigra.[98]

     For the Palestinian peasantry, good seed
contaminated by very small mustard seeds will mean a
mustard plant surprisingly and almost mysteriously
appearing at harvesttime. The sower will not be aware
of sowing these seeds, if the good seed has not been
carefully picked or sifted clean by hand. As an
alternative to this view of the situation, Mark and
Thomas (which seem to have the earliest obtainable
level of the parable on this point) may simply have in
mind a plant "sowing" its own seed on the grain field.

In either case, the result is the same. A wild mustard
plant grows up above the grain to contaminate the field
with more seed and to mock the cultivator.

The birds roosting in the branches underscore
this reading of the import of the mustard plant. To my
knowledge, no scholar has ever considered in the
explication of this parable that birds are natural
enemies of the sown.[99] Yet this point is already made
in the Parable of the Sower (Mk. 4:4b and par.)! Most
scholars have immediately made a connection in the
light of the great Jewish tradition between the birds,
the "tree," and Dan. 4:10, 20; Ezek. 17:23; 31:6; Ps.
104:17 [100] In other words, modern scholarship
immediately allegorizes the detail about the birds into
a cipher for the gentiles (Ezek. 31:6). Matthew and
Luke (or Q) already made this leap.

If this reading of the parable is correct, then
its implication is similar to the previously discussed
Matthean parable of the Darnel Among the Wheat. Once
again, the power and surprising appearance of weeds
amidst the grain is brought to expression. Once again,
the hearer of Jesus' parables is asked to reflect upon
the question: How is the reign of God like this
mustard plant?

It is hard to escape the conclusion that Jesus
deliberately likens the rule of God to a weed. In the
indomitable presence of this weed, birds--creatures
completely dependent upon God for sustenance--are able
to take refuge. The presence of the weed allows the
birds to roost and to meet their needs for food in the
grain field. Yet for the cultivator, the weed is no
blessing. The plant promises to spoil the whole field
when it reseeds itself. The birds threaten to make off
with a substantial part of the crop. Does Jesus really

imply that the reign of God will not bring a blessing
to the cultivator without fundamental changes? And if
not to the cultivator, how will the reign of God seem
to the upper classes that live off the toil of the
cultivator? This "weed" stands over against all of the
arrangements of civilization. It threatens the
foundation of the edifice in its threat to the
cultivated field. And yet for the "birds," the weed is
a blessing. Once again, a vector points to God's
providence.[101]

D. Conclusion

This chapter has focused on select parables
concerned with agricultural growth and production in
the Synoptic tradition. The object has been to try to
determine what particular attitude these words of Jesus
display toward human labor and agricultural productivity in the light of the imminent reign of God. The
natural and agrarian significance of the imagery has
been given greater weight than the great tradition in
the interpretation of these parables. The findings
seem to center on three themes:
First, the parables express the theme of
providence and lay emphasis upon the ultimate source of
sustenance in God. Secondly, these words of Jesus
intimate that human labor is devalued, if not
abolished, by the reign of God. There is no evident
concern with innovations in technology or with changing
the means of production. Thirdly, the parables hint in
a number of ways that the rule of God undermines the
current order of production.
Providence appears in the Sower parable in the
fact that the harvest comes despite every natural enemy
of the seed. Mark's Seed Growing Secretly also carries

overtones of God's providential care, in that human
beings are the beneficiaries of the harvest. The birds
of the Mustard Seed parable enjoy the shade of the
plant and their food through the hand of God.

The Darnel Among the Wheat and the Seed Growing
Secretly seem to stand in antithesis concerning the
value of human labor in the light of God's imminent
reign. Are people to keep hoeing or not? Or are the
two parables addressed to different classes of people?
To the peasant, the message of Mark's Seed Growing
Secretly is one of the liberation from work coming with
the rule of God, whereas the Darnel parable indicates
that "more is expected" from the managerial or landlord
class (Lk. 12:48). This is quite possible, since the
two groups stand in different relation to the impending
rule of God and the message of Jesus.

The third theme of the weed suggests a possible
way to resolve these issues. If the reign of God is
like weeds, at least in the last two parables discussed
above, then it stands as a powerful threat against the
social edifice that exists for the benefit of the
landlord class. To those that this class exploits, the
small peasants, tenants, and landless, the fall of the
edifice will be no great sorrow. Jesus is inviting
them to stop hoeing and to wait for God's new edifice.
Yet he must overcome in the peasantry a strong self-
interest and "commonsense" about the need for hard
work. Lack of hoeing brings down the edifice, to be
sure, but also undermines the values of Jesus' peasant
audience. Peasants trust in God's providence and look
forward to rest from their labors in the end time, but
are they willing to put this into practice now? Thus,
Jesus' continual stress upon providence.

On the other side, Jesus is warning the masters
that God's rule will appear with surprising strength--
just as darnel or mustard in grain fields. It will be
hard to eradicate. God's activity in the world is
visible in tangible stages. The work of John, Jesus,
and their disciples is the "heading out" of the
kingdom. The revolution has already begun. Vigorous
action by the masters cannot quash the divinely
instituted movement. Conversely, vigorous action by
the many exploited, in the trust that God will provide,
will bring down the edifice that much faster. Jesus
implicitly advocates a collective agricultural strike
for the sake of the kingdom. A human response to the
coming reign of God is required. This measure is,
moreover, strictly a non-violent action. Its success
depends upon trust in God's providential care and
ultimately his appearance in world affairs. The
providential theme is firmly linked, therefore, to the
revolutionary theme.[102]

If trust in providence and the efficacy of
agricultural strikes appear utopian or unworkable, it
may be recalled that at the time of Jesus there were
several models for the kind of behavior implied here.
Consider again the practice of gleaning by the poor
(GThom 21? M. Peah 8). Furthermore, the fallow of the
seventh year was perhaps observed in Jesus' day.[103]
Certainly the land had to lie fallow at regular
intervals anyway, if only to conserve adequate moisture
in the ground for crops.[104] How could ends be met
under such conditions?

Hamel makes a poignant observation:
. . . one cannot fault the Ancients for not having
created a science of economy as it is now understood. The modern world could afford a theory of

economy only because some of its basic productions
have seen a tremendous increase in the last four or
five centuries. . . . it would have made little
sense to have a "science" of a lack in the ancient
world.[105]

To compensate for lack and hunger, the poor usually
dreamed of Edenic conditions and tightened their belts,
while the rich enjoined one another to charity.

Jesus, however, turns the Edenic dream against
the social edifice. "God will provide" now expresses a
revolutionary vision. In the next chapter, a specific
social mechanism for experiencing God's providential
care, adumbrated in Jesus' words, will be examined.

Notes to Chapter 3

[1]Called parables of **growth**: C. H. Dodd, (1961) 140ff. B. T. D. Smith, (1937) 117ff. Dodd and Smith include the Leaven and other parables under this category. I limit my discussion to agricultural parables. **Contrast:** N. Perrin, (1967) 156. J. Jeremias, (1963) 118ff, 150.

[2]Jeremias, (1963) 150; Bornkamm, (1960) 71-75, 90-95.

[3]Jeremias, (1963) 13-18, 77-79, 81-85.

[4]On the modern rejection of allegory as a key to the parables of Jesus see Dodd, (1961) 2-3, 11; Brown, (1965) 259ff; Jeremias, (1963) 66-89.

[5]Jeremias, (1963) 93f.

[6]Luke has neither the Seed Growing Secretly nor the Darnel parable.

[7]Dodd, (1961) 140ff.

[8]Ibid.: 145.

[9]K. L. Schmidt, (1964) 584f. The most radical statement of this viewpoint, though, was that of J. Weiss, (1971) 73, 84ff.

[10]Dodd, (1961) 142-43.

[11]Jeremias, (1963) 150; Perrin, (1967) 156.

[12]Smith, (1937) 126.

[13]Bultmann, (1963) 199f.

[14]Crossan, (1973) 96-120; (1983) 37ff.

[15]On the distinction between the typical similitude and the atypical or unique parable see also Smith, (1937) 17.

[16]The testimony of the ancients, the work of older scholars like Dalman, modern agronomic science, and comparative studies of peasant agriculture will help in this endeavor.

[17]The inspiration for trying to imagine how a

peasantry might hear these parables comes from Professor Marvin Chaney, who has tried to evaluate the
meaning of the Elisha traditions in the Old Testament
with a similar method.

[18]Wolf, (1966) 101.

[19]Redfield, (1960) 41f.

[20]Ibid.: 42.

[21]Ibid.: 64. The first value has already been
seen in the discussion of land tenure. For me, these
are not abstractions. My grandparents were part of the
great southern European migration to this Land of
Opportunity in the early years of the twentieth
century. When I was growing up, the home of those
sturdy Serbians was for all practical purposes my home.
They lived on the same ground for fifty years,
following the peasant values Redfield has spoken of. I
observed in the home of my grandparents peasant frugality and conservation, hard and constant work, the joy
over growth and harvest, and reverence for the land.
In addition to this, I observed how my grandparents'
agrarian values were firmly linked to their religious
orientation through prayer and ceremony.

[22]Weber's statement specifically applies to the
religion of Iranian peasants, but his remarks in (1978)
468 and 483, along with this quote from 470, make clear
that he views this specific case as typical. It must
be noted that Jesus was far more optimistic about the
peasantry's ability to move outside its typical
interests than Weber. Whether Jesus had any more
success than Zoroaster in bringing a religious-social
transformation among peasants remains to be seen.

[23]On the whole issue see Brandon (1967);
Cullmann (1970); Hengel (1971, 1973, and 1976); Freyne,
(1980d) 216-29; Bammel and Moule (1984).

[24]See the excellent discussion of this question,
in Nineham, (1963) 126, 128. Nineham's two basic
points, that mashal (= parabolē) was not used as a
deliberate means of obscuring the truth and that the
rabbis used parables to clarify their teaching, do not
take into account, it seems, the political context of
Jesus. Furthermore, the rabbinic parables in their
present form reflect a time when Jewish leadership was
struggling to preserve Judaism politically in a hostile
empire. On folktales and other forms of popular speech

as political and social criticism see Coffin, (1983)
328.

[25]Smith, (1937) 35. Crossan, (1973) 43. Balz,
(1972) 134. Delling, (1972) 223.

[26]Dialog with Trypho the Jew 125.1, Greek text
reprinted in Aland, (1973) 175.

[27]On the unimportance of the divergences cf. N.
Perrin, (1967) 155f.

[28]See Taylor's summary of major interpretations
with bibliographic references, in (1953) 250f.

[29]See Bultmann, (1963) 5. The best brief
discussion of the hermeneutical circle(s) that I know
is supplied by Waetjen, (1976) 15-23.

[30]Taylor, (1953) 252. Cf. Jeremias, (1963) 12
n. 4.

[31]Jeremias, (1963) 11.

[32]White, (1964) 301, 304.

[33]Ibid.: 305.

[34]Ibid.: 306.

[35]Nineham, (1963) 135. Jeremias, (1963) 12.

[36]White, (1964) 306.

[37]Bauer, et al., (1979) 29: Ononis spinosa,
cammock. See H. B. Tristram, (1880) 431f; Zohary,
(1982) 165.

[38]Jeremias, (1963) 1. Also Nineham, (1963) 134f.

[39]White, (1964) 301.

[40]White, (1964) 301f correctly argues that this
ending of the parable does not imply an average yield
per unit of field area, but only the production of
individual plants.

[41]Taylor, (1953) 254.

[42]Greek text reprinted in Aland, (1973) 175.
From this passage, of course, Clement is arguing that

God surrounds us with "parables" about the future
resurrection. Similarly in this connection, John 12:24
may be recalled.

[43]The fragment is reprinted in Aland, (1973)
422. A translation is given in Hennecke-Schneemelcher,
(1963) 1:97 [fr. 2^V (60-75)].

[44]Funk, (1985) 1:193. The feeding narratives in
the gospels support this reading.

[45]See also Apocryphon of James 12:20-31 in Funk,
(1985) 1:193.

[46]Taylor, (1953) 265f.

[47]Dodd, (1961) 179.

[48]Quoted from the translation of Against
Heresies in Richardson, (1970) 394f. This quote, as
has long been noted, is paralleled almost verbatim by a
passage in 2 Baruch 29. There is a further parallel in
B. Ketuboth 111b; see Baron, (1952) 1:251. The Elders
and John the Disciple may have handed on to Papias
either a commonplace of Palestinian expectation in the
name of Jesus, or possibly an authentic word of Jesus
now preserved anonymously in Baruch. At any rate,
Papias found in the "abiding voice" a more interesting
and authentic message than in the written sources he
had at hand. It is unfortunate that his book, Exposi-
tions of the Dominical Logia, was not preserved.
Perhaps it could have provided further evidence for
such a literal, millenarian hope leading back to the
early Jesus tradition.

[49]See the measures in M. Peah 8.

[50]2 Baruch 29:5-6a, after the translation of
Charles, (1913) 2:497f. Cf. Charlesworth, (1983)
1:630.

[51]Dickey, (1928) 411ff. Hamel has also noted
stories from a much later time about "Edenic abundance," (1983) 200, 448 n. 8.

[52]Charles, (1913) 2:391f. Cf. Charlesworth,
(1983) 1:378.

[53]Sin led to painful work and poverty, in the
words of Hamel, (1983) 284.

[54]On this ethos see Austin and Vidal-Naquet, (1977) 11, 169.

[55]For further discussion of the labor and end-time hopes of the peasantry see Kreissig, (1969) 230.

[56]A previous version of this subsection was presented as a paper at the March, 1985 Pacific regional meeting of the Society of Biblical Literature at Occidental College, Los Angeles, CA.

[57]Though Jeremias believes this is Jesus' own intention for the parable, Jeremias, (1963) 226. A representative discussion of Matthew's reading of this parable is Kingsbury, (1969) 63-76 or (1977) 64, 71, 74. See Waetjen's critique of Kingsbury on some points, (1976) 154f, although Waetjen limits the inroad of allegorization and sees here an exhortation to inclusiveness and tolerance among the band of Jesus' disciples.

[58]Schrage, (1964) 124.

[59]On this toxin see Moldenke and Moldenke, (1952) 282 n. 130. On darnel generally see Ibid.: 134. Dalman, (1964) 1:407ff; 2:249, 255, 257, 309. Zohary, (1982) 161.

[60]Moldenke and Moldenke, (1952) 134. Holzner and Numata, (1982) 10f.

[61]Salisbury, (1961) 91.

[62]Darnel does not usually affect barley. Cf. Dalman, (1964) 2:249.

[63]Wheat is generally stronger in dry areas than its weed competitors: Pearson, (1967) 326. However, a wetter season allows the darnel to thrive at the expense of the wheat: Dalman, (1964) 2:309 and Thomson, (1882) 2:397.

[64]Löw, (1926) 1:726.

[65]See Billerbeck, (1922) 1:667 (ad Mt. 13:25).

[66]Pliny, NH 18.153: A pestilence of the soil itself. Virgil, Georgics 1.154 speaks of "unfruitful" (infelix) darnel in the same breath as wild oats.

[67]Dalman, (1964) 2:308.

[68]Löw, (1926) 1:726.

[69]Pearson, (1967) 95. Modern seed-cleaning techniques thus have today virtually eliminated darnel as a noxious weed in grain fields; Salisbury, (1961) 30, 32f, 119.

[70]Thomson, (1882) 2:397.

[71]Jeremias, (1963) 224. Cf. Smith, (1937) 196.

[72]Dalman, (1964) 2:325 and Illus. 56. Cf. Moldenke and Moldenke, (1952) Illus. 72.

[73]Dalman, (1964) 2:324. Cf. Turkowski, (1969) 101: Arab peasant women do the weeding in April, but do not eradicate.

[74]Dalman, (1964) 2:323-24.

[75]Pliny, NH 18.155.

[76]Dalman, (1964) 2:310: "Nur gründliches und wiederholtes Pflügen kann dieser Herrschaft ein Ende bereiten." Also Virgil, Georgics 1.147-159; Pliny, NH 18.153; cf. White, (1970b) 137. In addition, compare the English proverb, "One year's seeding is seven years' weeding"; Holzner and Numata, (1982) 65.

[77]Pliny, NH 18.156. Dalman, (1964) 2:248 says 5 x 2 mm is an average size. Cf. Zohary, (1962) 297.

[78]On this matter again see Salisbury, (1961) 119: Modern rotary threshing and screens with 2.8 mm meshes have eliminated darnel as a threat in grain fields.

[79]So also does Smith, (1937) 196. Thomson, (1882) 2:396f.

[80]Dalman, (1964) 2:308.

[81]See Moulton and Milligan, (1980) 441; also Rengstorf, (1964) 49 and Michel, (1967) 149. K. D. White gives details about estate personnel and management, in (1970b) chs. 11 and 12.

[82]Mt. 10:25 (2x); 13:27, 52; 20:1, 11; 21:33; 24:43; Mk. 14:14; Lk. 12:39; 13:25; 14:21; 22:11.

[83]See again Dalman, (1964) 2:324 and Turkowski, (1969) 101.

[84]Recall that darnel does not usually affect barley, nor does it grow outside of Mediterranean valleys.

[85]Mt. 3:12 = Lk. 3:17; Mt. 6:26 = Lk. 12:24; Mt. 13:30; Lk. 12:18.

[86]To this point we shall be returning again in Chapter 4.

[87]Bultmann, (1963) 172. Taylor, (1953) 269. Fitzmyer, (1985) 2:1015. Another version of this subsection was presented as a paper at the March, 1986 Pacific regional meeting of the Society of Biblical Literature at Santa Clara University, Santa Clara, CA.

[88]Smith, (1937) 118.

[89]Pearson, (1967) 162.

[90]Jeremias, (1963) 148 and Perrin, (1967) 157, who see the point of the parable in the contrast between the seed and the grown plant and give no weight to other details of the parable.

[91]Based on M. Kil. 3:2, Jeremias, (1963) 27 and n. 11. Cf. Hunzinger (1971) 288 and Smith, (1937) 117f.

[92]Fitzmyer, (1985) 2:1016 thinks this is allegory.

[93]Pliny, NH 19.171.

[94]Dalman, (1964) 2:293. Billerbeck, (1922) 1:668.

[95]Löw, (1926) 1:516ff; Dalman, (1964) 2:293f; Zohary, (1982) 93.

[96]Pliny, NH 19.170 (LCL translation).

[97]White, (1970b) 137.

[98]Hunzinger, (1971) 289: Brassica nigra averages 725-60 seeds/gm (following Löw). Charlock puts out 1000-4000 seeds per plant, according to Salisbury, (1961) 186.

[99]A somewhat humorous English saying from the early modern period speaks of planting "one [seed] for

the Rook one for the Crow, two to die and one to grow";
Salisbury, (1961) 32. Birds also eat the mustard seeds;
see Billerbeck, (1922) 1:668. Again consider Jubilees
11:13, 18.

[100]Fitzmyer, (1985) 2:1017, note ad loc. Smith,
(1937) 120f.

[101]Mt. 6:25-34 = Lk. 12:22-31 will be treated in
the next chapter.

[102]Cf. Josephus, JW 2.200 on the revolutionary
implications of such agricultural strikes.

[103]Josephus, JW 14.200ff and see again
references in Chapter 2.

[104]Hamel, (1983) 124, 264.

[105]Ibid.: 204f.

CHAPTER 4

THE REALITIES OF ECONOMIC DISTRIBUTION
AND THE WORDS OF JESUS

If, as the results of the last chapter seem to
show, Jesus did not advocate reforms in productive
arrangements or concern himself with innovations in
production, but was rather concerned with God's providential care for those without means and the revolutionary economic implications of the reign of God, this
chapter attempts to explore in economic terms how Jesus
addressed the problem of the maldistribution of, or
differential control over, essential economic goods.

The primary economic good, of course, was land.
Changing forms of tenure and the disruptive effects of
debt, therefore, provide natural points of reference
for the investigation. Other goods, like food,
clothing, shelter, and money, come indirectly under
consideration in the examination of Jesus material
pertinent to wealth and sharing. With an eye to the
earlier treatment of Palestinian economic arrangements,
the discussion proceeds under four main headings: A.
Jesus and the Tenure of Land, B. Debt and Release from
Debt, C. Wealth and Criticism of Wealth, and D. The
Sharing of Economic Goods.

A. Jesus and the Tenure of Land

The attempt was made in Part One to show the
general socio-economic conditions in Palestine under
the early empire. There it was established, at the
very least, that a great conflict arose, with the

coming of the Greeks and Romans, over the "ownership"
of the land of Israel. This battle for ownership, of
course, culminated in the Jewish War. In essence, it
was a battle for the determination of the use of the
land and distribution of its products.

Land, as we have seen, is a primary factor of
production in agrarian societies. Access to land is
crucial for physical survival. Did Jesus formulate any
response to the problem of the loss of indigenous
control over land? If it is possible to apprehend in
the authentic portions of the Jesus tradition Jesus'
own attitude and intentions toward the problem of
ownership, how are his attitude and intentions
regarding this issue to be related to his central
message about the kingdom of God?

Only one passage in the Synoptic tradition
would appear to promise some kind of alternate landed
arrangements in the name of God's reign: Mk. 10:29-30
and par. Bultmann thinks that in its original form,
this saying was strictly an apocalyptic-prophetic word
contrasting losses now and gains in the life to come.[1]
Bultmann believes the original saying ended at the word
hekatontaplasiona (Mk.; Q: pollaplasiona).[2] Certainly
the future tense (lēmpsetai) in Matthew, or the
subjunctive moods in Mark and Luke, would give credence
to a view such as Bultmann's. Moreover, Matthew's
version of the saying, with its coordinate verbs in the
second half, could conceivably be referred to the
eschaton ("shall receive manyfold and inherit eternal
life"--all when that age arrives). Yet Luke has kept
Mark's en tōi kairōi toutōi ("in this age"). And there
is strong textual evidence that Matthew followed Mark's
tradition at the word "hundredfold."

Furthermore, the saying in Bultmann's hypothetical form would not necessarily have to have an otherworldly referent. It could just as readily refer to some future fulfillment of the promise upon earth (as indeed Mark's version makes explicit). This reading finds support from studies of millenarian movements. Such movements have consistently looked for a this-worldly millennium.[3] As the tradition stands, "this age--that age" has a strong claim to authenticity. The transition between the two is thought of as continuous in certain respects. At no point in the history of the tradition does there need to be imagined a version of the saying lacking the "in this age" stipulation.

So the point of the saying as it stands is that "seeking the kingdom" is not "loss now--gain later," but entirely gain (cf. Mt. 6:33). The mechanism by which God's generosity is realized in human affairs is through a new family of the kingdom (v. 30: <u>adelphous</u> <u>kai</u> <u>adelphas</u> <u>kai</u> <u>meteras</u> <u>kai</u> <u>tekna</u>). Note that a father is not gained (but cf. v. 29 and consider the variant readings for v. 30), perhaps because Jesus intends all to have God as father. The point is that material needs will be taken care of through a human support network. However, the notion of a restoration of property in "houses and fields" to individuals or individual families appears to be absent (cf. Mt. 5:5; Mk. 10:21; Acts 2:44f; 5:1-5). There is no indication of how access to these will be provided for. The whole weight of the saying rather falls upon the establishment of new human relations with the coming kingdom.[4]

Several words of Jesus suggest that he viewed the land merely as a cause for contention. He explicitly rejects for himself the role of judge in property disputes (Lk. 12:14). Several parables also focus on troubled landed relations.

The parable that appears in Mk. 12:1-12 and par.
graphically portrays the kind of relationship engendered by landlordism in an agrarian context (if we
resolutely refuse to allegorize the parable as the
Synoptic tradition does). The cultivators become homi-
cidal in their need to acquire ownership. If the
detail in the tradition of GThom 65 goes back to Jesus,
the tenants can no longer even discern the personal
goodness of the owner. This kind of hostility toward
the owning class was typical of first-century Palestinian social relations.[5] Jesus demonstrates no particular sympathy with the tenants' behavior (12:9).

The theme of contention perhaps is in view in a
parable preserved only in Luke's special material (Lk.
13:6-9). A man (apparently an absentee owner) comes
seeking fruit from a fig tree that he has had planted
in his vineyard. Not finding fruit on the tree in the
third year, the man commands the vinedresser to cut
down the tree. Whatever Luke may have understood by
the parable, the crux interpretum seems to revolve
around the datum tria etē aph hou (v. 7). Jeremias
believes this datum shows that six years have elapsed
since the planting of the tree: According to Lev.
19:23, only after the first three years of growth was
the fruit of the tree clean. Therefore in Jeremias's
view, the point of "three years" is that the tree is
utterly barren.[6]

Yet there is really nothing in the story to
suggest that the landowner (tis) is Jewish, to warrant
Jeremias's reading. Taking the "three years" at face
value, its implication could just as easily be that the
tree has not yet reached maturity. Normally such a
tree took about five years.[7] This reading gives the
story a somewhat different flavor. There may even be

some humor involved. The owner of the vineyard, one
who is not directly involved in the working of the land
(i.e. a "city slicker"), does not have the same view of
arboriculture in Palestine as the vinedresser. Perhaps
he does not even understand the rudiments of caring for
the tree.

The fig tree has an extensive and deep root
system. In a dry land like Palestine, this is a
necessity. Fig leaves present a relatively small area
to the atmosphere, hence limiting the ill-effects of
transpiration (evaporation of precious soil moisture
through the leaves).[8] The vinedresser knows, of
course, that to eradicate the tree (ekkopto, v. 7) will
be no easy process. Yet without such labor, the tree
would continue to "use up the ground" and grow, albeit
going to wood. The relatively small investment of
labor to try to save the tree is the wiser course. The
Talmud attests to the reluctance of the later rabbis to
permit cutting down and uprooting trees.[9] If the owner
of the vineyard is going to insist on cutting out the
fig tree, the vinedresser tells him at last: [ei de mē
ge,] ekkopseis autēn ("well then, you shall cut it out
[yourself]!").

The point of the parable indirectly revolves
around who de facto possesses the vineyard. The real
"owner," the one who works the land and cares for the
plantations, is willing to do quite a bit to get
produce out of an unproductive tree (and to avoid
horribly difficult labor!), rather than to have to wait
another three, four, or five years for produce from
another planting. The sympathy of Jesus lies with the
vinedresser. The owner de iure is apparently more
interested in the immediate profit of the vineyard, yet
without apparently understanding what profit will
require.

The owning class manifests other interests as well. In vivid contrast to the plight of the peasantry in the first-century is the picture of the wealthy landowner drawn in Lk. 12:16-20. Here is depicted a man who not only does not need to worry about sufficiency, as do the peasants, but can actually contemplate self-sufficiency (v. 19). Along with this ethic of self-sufficiency goes an attitude of carpe diem. Both of these values were commonplace among the wealthy of the early empire, as the famous story of Trimalchio's Dinner shows.[10]

The tensions and hostilities evident in these parables are not as unrelated as they might at first sight seem. Gordon Childe has supplied an extremely useful framework for evaluating them in his account of the rise of "civilization":

[Each neolithic] village could be self-sufficing. It grew its own food and could make all essential equipment from materials locally available . . . This potential self-sufficiency of the territorial community and the absence of specialization within it may be taken as the differentiae of neolithic barbarism to distinguish it from civilization and the higher barbarisms of the Metal Ages.[11]

The worst contradictions in the neolithic economy were transcended when farmers were persuaded or compelled to wring from the soil a surplus above their own domestic requirements, and when this surplus was made available to support new economic classes not directly engaged in producing their own food (underlining mine).[12]

[There was a tendency in the Roman empire for] capitalist farms to grow into self-sufficing 'households' of the old Oriental pattern . . .

capitalist farms, scientifically run, albeit with
slave labour, and <u>producing</u> <u>for</u> <u>the</u> <u>market</u>, began
to be replaced by, or combined with, estates
exploited by dependent tenants or share-farmers
practising subsistence agriculture . . . The system
offered the new bourgeoisie the opportunity to
'make fortunes out of unspecialized agriculture by
absentee landlords'. It was definitely a step back
towards the Oriental economy of the Bronze Age,
indeed toward neolithic self-sufficiency.[13]

These somewhat lengthy quotations provide yet another
angle on general tensions in the first-century economy
of the Roman empire: On a macroeconomic level, there
was the tension between the so-called natural or
subsistence economy and economic activities that
transcended the locality or were not directly related
to working the soil. On a microeconomic level, there
existed the tension between the desire for economic
self-sufficiency or independence and the necessity for
some type of interdependence.

These tensions were inescapable, because the
civilization and urban culture of the empire rested
upon several general kinds of "interdependence"--
whether in the cities' parasitic extraction of an
economic surplus from the countryside (what Ste. Croix
has called "indirect, collective exploitation") or in
interurban trade--necessary to support the leisured,
the bureaucrats of administration, religious
specialists, craftsmen of various kinds, and all
pursuits not directly concerned with working the
land.[14]

This kind of civilization, by its very nature,
did not distribute equal shares to all its denizens.
Interdependence for the elites meant compulsory cooper-

ation to preserve privilege, as well as dependence on
others for labor and luxuries. Only the privileged few
participated in the benefits of trade relationships
around the Mediterranean basin. With this went a
"peasant-like passion for self-sufficiency" and the
development of self-sufficient large estates.[15] The
have-nots, by contrast, were reduced to the level of
the primordial struggle for sustenance. Interdependence for them meant exploitation from above and
dependence upon mutual aid in the village to get
through hard times. So they also (from quite different
motives) valued, and struggled for, independence and
self-sufficiency.

     Jesus recognizes that the benefits of economic
arrangements under the empire accrue rather one-sidedly
to those who already have (cf. Mk. 4:25 and par.). He
casts a critical eye on existing social relations, as
is apparent from Mk. 12:1-12 and Lk. 12:3-9. He
evidences some sympathy perhaps for the tenant or
laborer in Lk. 13:3-9, but he does not endorse the
actions of the tenants of Mk. 12:1-12.

     The impression established by the tradition is:
Jesus did not advocate a redistribution of landed means
in the revolutionary manner of antiquity. He rejected
the urges of either the wealthy or the peasantry to
establish for themselves arrangements ensuring self-
sufficiency, that is, "property" in land.

     The material we have looked at focuses on the
quality of relations between owners and dispossessed.
It is no accident that the passage in Mk. 10:29-30
points beyond self-sufficiency. The accent of Jesus'
message falls upon a new kind of interdependence.

B. Debt and Release From Debt

Many of Jesus' fellow Jews labored under an increasing load of indebtedness. The problem of debt exacerbated the quality of relations between the owning class of first-century Palestine and those who were forced for one reason or another into tenancy or wage labor. Debt was one of the major mechanisms whereby the rich kept getting richer and the poor, poorer. Through debt, ownership of the patrimonial land of the peasantry could be, and was, wrested from them. The "rights" of the creditor were another manifestation of the insensitive egoism of the empire's elites that demanded security and securities to the detriment of the many disprivileged.

Since debt played a major role in the troubled social relationships of Jesus' day, it is not surprising that he explored the ramifications and opportunities of the problem. In Mt. 18:12-35, set by Matthew in the context of a discussion of moral forgiveness, a Hellenistic monarch is portrayed as a model of the mercifulness required in the act of forgiving. The monarch summons a slave who is to render account for a loan (daneion, v. 27). The debtor, not able to pay, is to be sold into slavery along with his entire family (the normal course in these "executions").[18] Upon the slave's petition the king is moved with pity (splangchnistheis, v. 27) and releases (apolyō) the man from his obligation. This magnanimous gesture is placed in the starkest contrast by the slave's subsequent behavior. When he encounters a fellow-slave owing him a very minor sum (compared with his own previous debt), the man has the other slave thrown into debtor's prison. What callousness! This obviously is the reaction the parable was intended to elicit. The

slave who had the huge debt did not appreciate the
magnanimity and generosity shown to him, at least not
enough to see some claim upon his own conduct. The
rage of the monarch (orgistheis, v. 34) issues in swift
punishment of this callous man.

A positive version of the same parable is
preserved in Lk. 7:41-43. In this case the response of
the "forgiven" is measured by their response of love
toward the merciful creditor. Response is the tertium
comparitionis in both Matthew 18 and Luke 7. The
direction of the response, whether love toward creditor
or mercy toward debtors, should not be allowed to
obscure the underlying point of a response that is
commensurable to the experience of forgiveness or
release ("love," equal generosity shown to others).

Favorable response to generous forgiveness is
also the desideratum of the steward's actions in Lk.
16:1-8. Verse 9 is usually attributed to Luke (cf. the
tale of Zacchaeus, Lk. 19:1ff, where "unjust mammon"
does indeed make friends). As for verse 8, it is
debated whether the kyrios is the wealthy man of v. 1
(cf. v. 3) or Jesus. Jeremias' observation regarding
Lk. 18:6 seems equally decisive here: The Lord is
Jesus in both this parable and that of the Importune
Widow.[17] Jesus himself, in this reading, commends the
behavior of the manager who rips off his master (the
oikonomos is a slave) in order to insure his own future
security.

A comparison of this parable with that of the
Wicked Tenants illustrates the reversal that has taken
place. There (in Mk. 12:1-12) the intermediaries
between owner and tenants (equivalent to Luke's
oikonomos) are abused and even murdered when they try
to collect on the rent. Here the oikonomos circumvents

that normative order and exercises some "enlightened
self-interest." The normal course for a deposed
functionary of the elite is indicated in v. 3: The lot
of the disenfranchised laborer or beggary. Inasmuch as
these intermediaries are the enforcers of an oppressive
agrarian social order, they are hated by the peasantry.

Perhaps the steward's actions are to be understood
as a typical occurrence, when possible. The political
astuteness of the move is, from an agrarian perspective, self-evident. Through the mechanism of releasing
debtors from their obligations, the steward creates
some positive alternatives for himself. Yet it cannot
be overlooked that there is, from the viewpoint of the
dominant culture, adikia involved (cf. v. 8 oikonomon
tēs adikias). Why does Jesus then praise the man? Is
he siding with the oppressed peasantry against the
rich? To do so would not change the dominant ethos of
self-sufficiency. No, the story would seem to be aimed
at the rich themselves (as Luke has well understood).
What is laudable about the steward's behavior is his
generosity (and with others' goods!)--a generosity
certainly motivated by self-interest, but with particularly salutary effects. This is a generosity that not
only mitigates oppressive circumstances, but creates
the basis for a new relationship to the peasantry. To
borrow terminology from Eric Wolf, a singlestranded
relationship between exploitative elite and oppressed
peasantry is modified by the addition of some new
strands.[18] However, the steward will no longer stand
above the peasantry, but will be reduced to their
level--otherwise, lower still!

These passages find resonance with anthropolo-
gical discussions of generalized reciprocity. Sahlins,
following Mauss, had identified generalized reciprocity

as "pure gift," i.e. with "no strings attached."[19]
Gregory's ruminations on what he calls the "expectation
of circumstantially balanced reciprocity" have led him
to modify Sahlin's original typology somewhat.

Gregory believes that in peasant villages where
there are inequities of wealth, there will exist "a
belief that those having much (or more) should share
with those having none (or having less)."[20] Gregory
finds in this quite general expectation a parallel to
the generalized reciprocal exchanges that underwrite
the solidarity of kin groups in the village (e.g. the
sharing of game from the hunt without expectation of an
immediate return). The expectation of circumstantially
balanced reciprocity, however, is not the expectation
of a quid pro quo--not the expectation of balanced
reciprocity. The expectation Gregory has identified is
far less specific and far more fundamental. It holds
the wealthy responsible to the wider social order. If
inequities become too great, the social order will
collapse. Therefore, they must not become too great.

Such considerations prompt Gregory to see
another dimension in Sahlin's general reciprocity. In
addition to giving with no expectation of immediate
reciprocity, or only a vague expectation of a return
sometime, there appears also to be this powerful
expectation to give as a moral obligation to the social
order.[21]

The foregoing stories of Jesus all seem to play
upon such a strong expectation. "Grace" in the stories
does not come without strings attached; rather,
forgiveness paradoxically lays an even greater burden
of responsibility upon the recipients. The recipients,
however, are responsible as to when and how they will
satisfy their new obligation. They are put under a

general, but unconditional, obligation by the
experience of release from debt.[22]

The material significance of debt remission in
the scheme of God's reign is brought out by a central
text of the gospels. The Lord's Prayer has, together
with the parables, been considered bedrock of the Jesus
tradition.[23] The question of original form is, nonetheless, problematic.[24] Luke probably retains the form
closest in length to the original. However, editorial
work of both Matthew and Luke can be detected. Therefore, the original form is not identical with either
extant version. Jeremias writes:

> The Lucan version has preserved the oldest form
> with respect to length, but the Matthaean text is
> more original with regard to wording.[25]

The purpose here is not to reconstruct the
original form of the prayer, but to concentrate on the
petition for forgiveness. It will be necessary in
addition to refer to the petition for daily bread.

Starting with the forgiveness petition first,
how is it to be taken? Underlying the Greek word
aphiēmi and cognates is the notion of both cancellation
of debt and metaphorical forgiveness.[26] The word
aphesis appears in the important text of Deuteronomy
15:2 (LXX). The word is regularly employed in the
Egyptian papyri to denote waiving a debt or releasing
someone from debt.[27] The Aramaic underlying this word
in the petition was perhaps shebōk.[28] Behind
opheilēmata - hamartias (Mt. 6:12 = Lk. 11:4
respectively) probably lies hôbāh. This word had in
Galilean Aramaic the meaning of either sin or debt.[29]

Matthew's understanding of the petition is
indicated by the supplemental condition in v. 15
(paraptōmata). Luke has supplied the word "sins"

instead of "debts." Yet it is significant that Luke
continues with a material application--"as we ourselves
forgive all in debt to us" (11:4b). The Matthean form
of this comparative clause could also formally refer to
actual debtors who are "forgiven" (though the above
consideration argues against Matthew having so understood the clause).

          The basic structure of the Synoptic tradition's
interpretation of this petition--apparent in both
Matthew and Luke--is "forgiveness" requested in the
context of a vertical relationship to God (in line with
the later rabbinic viewpoint), as compared with
"forgiveness" practiced in the context of a horizontal
relationship to the neighbor. In this latter practice,
Matthew seems to metaphorize debt to cover all kinds of
social obligations, while Luke retains the literal
meaning. In the former practice, neither Matthew nor
Luke reads the petition other than as a request for
forgiveness for infractions (debts = trespasses, sins
respectively) against God.

          How did Jesus intend this petition to be
understood? What did it mean within the context of his
ministry? First of all, the parallelism between the
semicola of the forgiveness petition is important. The
parallelism suggests that there must somehow be a
connection (not necessarily causal) between the "small"
forgiveness/release practiced by Jesus' disciples and a
"large" forgiveness/release that only God can wield.
The small forgiveness of the second semicolon is
related to actual debt (as both Matthew's and Luke's
versions reveal), but can probably be extended to moral
debt too. One would suspect that the same logic
originally governed the first half of the petition as
well.

Therefore, rather than release from infractions against God, Jesus primarily asked through this petition for release from the earthly shackles of indebtedness. The problem of debt, oppressing the people of Palestine and controlling their lives, is so vast that only God's power can effectively remove it. Even if one adopts an eschatological hermeneutic framework for this prayer, as for instance does Jeremias, one must still see in such an eschatology this material expectation.[30]

It is important to notice, secondly, a _material_ link between the petition for forgiveness and the preceding petition for daily bread. These two petitions form a synonymous parallelism, if you will. Indebtedness threatens the availability of daily bread. Conversely, the petition for daily bread is at the same time a petition for a social order that will supply such basic human needs in a regular and consistent manner. Thus, the succeeding petition for forgiveness can be seen to address in another way this same concern: Indebtedness disrupts the ability of a social order to supply daily bread. God is petitioned to remove the oppressive power of debt in people's lives.

The suggested interpretation urges itself, finally, on the basis of another consideration. Jesus' ministry appealed particularly to the landless, that is, those forced for one reason or another into beggary, prostitution, tax collection, or other occupations not directly linked to working the land.[31] It may be surmised that many of these people knew the reality of indebtedness. Perhaps they had not been able to get out of debt, and so had been driven from "normal" social ties for this reason. The Lord's Prayer, through the petitions in question, directly addressed such people's needs.

The material parallel between the semicola of
the forgiveness petition, the link between lack of
bread and debt as the "horizon" against which to view
the bread and forgiveness petitions, and sociological
considerations about the religious interests at work in
Jesus' ministry, call into question, therefore, the
"spiritualizing" interpretations of Jesus' prayer
evident already in the Synoptic tradition. These
interpretations could only conceive of the petition to
God for forgiveness in moral terms.

The practice of forgiveness/release on earth is
connected a minori ad maius to the radical forgiveness/
release available with God's kingdom: If Jesus and his
disciples can practice such a release now, how much
more will God's release liberate when it happens.
Jesus advocates release from oppressive economic
burdens, but perceives a moral obligation to a new
social behavior of forgiveness.

A similar behavioral logic, anticipating and at
the same time actualizing God's rule, has been observed
before: First, in Jesus' assurance of God's providence
to idle cultivators and the disenfranchised poor of the
countryside, who are to hope for the weed of the
kingdom; and, secondly, in the abandonment of "houses
and fields" for the new family of the kingdom.

C. Wealth and Criticism of Wealth

The subject of the present section is perhaps
one of the most copiously studied of all that have been
treated in this book. The literature is enormous.
Several recent and representative works have been
chosen to guide the discussion.[32]

David Mealand's book Poverty and Expectation
in the Gospels supplies what is perhaps the best

tradition-critical treatment of the Synoptic material
on this question. His method and results can be
summarized briefly as follows: He starts with an
analysis of the latest stages of the tradition in the
canonical gospels. Matthew and Luke evidently were
writing to or for relatively wealthy Christians or
patrons. Matthew as a result has tended to be uneasy
with some of Mark's strictures against covetousness.[33]
Matthew has probably omitted some of the material in Q
most critical of wealth.[34] Matthew's special material
(M) shows little hostility to wealth. Mark shows much
more hostility than M.[35] Luke is by all accounts the
most hostile to wealth, although Mealand shows that
this accent comes to Luke via the tradition. Luke
simply hands on this emphasis. The harshest of all
material on wealth is contained in Luke's special
material.[36]

Mealand believes that a tendency to sharpen the
criticism of wealth and the wealthy existed in the
earliest Christianity of rural Palestine. This _Tendenz_
received its strongest impetus during the famine under
Claudius, when the mutual aid system of the Palestinian
church was inadequate to the crisis.[37] There is reason
to believe, then, that Jesus may not have been so
critical of the wealthy, or rather that his criticism
did not have the sharp, black-and-white formulation of
some of the material in Q (for instance, Lk. 6:24-26).
Mealand arrives at the view that Jesus and his
disciples gave up all their property for the kingdom
(and invited others to do so too), and that they
embraced the lifestyle of wandering preachers:

> The more formal pattern of wandering Christian
> apostles and communal charity was preceded by this
> simpler and more spontaneous surrender of resources
> and possessions.[38]

This viewpoint is in accord with the previous findings of this chapter, as well as with the opinions of Theissen and Hengel.[39]

Martin Hengel has pointed out the apparent contradiction in the Jesus tradition between a "radical criticism of property" and Jesus' "free attitude to property."[40] Mealand does not seem to attribute this contradiction to Jesus himself, although Mealand believes Jesus was less critical of wealth than the later tradition. Nevertheless, the contradiction appears to belong to early levels of the tradition. Indeed, it is most evident in certain contrasts between sayings (criticism of weath) and narrative material (Jesus' eating and drinking with wealthy tax collectors). There is, however, the reproach against Jesus, the truth of which he does not dispute, that he is a "glutton and drunkard, a friend of tax collectors and sinners" (Lk. 7:34). There is a joy in this "asceticism" that apparently belies its poverty!

While an attempt at explaining this discrepancy must await further study of Jesus' social contacts in the next chapter, two passages suggest how the contradiction might be understood. The Q saying on Mammon (Mt. 6:24 = Lk. 16:13) speaks of the utter untenability of this situation of divided loyalty. The epigrammatic quality of the saying, and its combination in Luke with the parallel about not being able to serve two masters, marks it as an authentic saying of Jesus (though perhaps going back to a proverbial commonplace).

The story of the rich man in Mark (10:17-22) underscores the moral quandary of divided loyalty. Though it is not clear in the end whether the man departs with grief (lypoumenos, v. 22) because he must give up his goods or because he cannot give them up,

nonetheless his wealth places him in a difficult
situation. The man is not free to do what the
righteousness of the reign of God demands. Yet Jesus
is said to have loved, and not hated, this man
(ēgapēsen, v. 21).

There does not seem to be here a philosophical
denigration of material things per se. Rather, what is
criticized is a social arrangement--personal property
or a personal hoard intended to ensure self-sufficiency
(Mt. 6:19-21 = Lk. 12:33-34). Possibly Jesus envisioned the abolition of private property (as was
suggested in the treatment of land tenure). As we have
seen, self-sufficiency was the dominant ethos of the
early empire, and Jesus attacked that ethos in several
distinct ways. The rich man above is invited to give
all of his goods to the poor and to follow Jesus (Mk.
10:21). If the man gives up his goods, how will he
subsist? Apparently this is implied in the "following
Jesus," as we shall see in a moment.

Jesus evinces hostility toward personal wealth,
but not toward the person of the wealthy. He
distinguishes, as some of his followers perhaps did
not, the sin from the sinner. In addition, Jesus does
not denigrate the use of material goods. The goods of
life exist only to be used. So Chester McCown
perceptively wrote, "Jesus was not an ascetic; he
worshiped poverty as little as Mammon."[41] It is in
their hoarding by the few that material goods become
the occasion for evil. What will happen when wealth is
shared by all?

D. The Sharing of Economic Goods

Some of Jesus' words stress dependence upon the providence of God in apparently utopian fashion, without indicating concrete mechanisms for how God will provide. Other words reveal a careful attention devoted to the quality of human relationships-- especially between social classes. Inhuman behavior finds censure (Mk. 12:1-12). Praise is bestowed upon relations wherein conventional expectations are violated with a salutary result (Lk. 16:1-8). This impression is amplified by Synoptic material relating to the sharing of economic goods. Human beings themselves can provide for one another's needs, if only they overcome certain social obstacles.

We begin with Mt. 6:25-34 and par. Bultmann excises Mt. 6:27-28a = Lk. 12:25-26 as intrusive insertion and linking passage respectively.[42] He places this group together with other logia that show Jesus as a teacher of wisdom. The sayings stress the connection between merimnan ("worrying," Mt. 6:25) and oligopistia ("little faith," v. 30). The thrust of the entire group of sayings is, mē merimnate ("stop worrying," vv. 25, 31). At the end is a further, rather the central, admonition: Zēteite tēn basileian autou ("keep seeking his kingdom," v. 33).[43]

"Seeking the kingdom" is not to be understood apocalyptically as waiting passively for God's rule to triumph; rather it is the challenge placed before the disciples to actively take the leap of faith that issues in carefree dependence upon God's beneficence. Otherwise, what is the point of referring to the birds or flowers (krina)? The birds and flowers are the premises for Jesus' syllogism (ou polloi mallon hymas, "[will not God clothe] you so much the more?" v. 30b).

Birds have already been discussed with reference
to the parables of the Sower and Mustard Seed. In
those two instances, birds seemed to be a negative
symbol (over against the sown). Here they function
positively as metaphor of dependence upon God for
sustenance.[44] Yet there may be an echo of the Sower
and the Mustard Seed. Perhaps the flowers, too, are
ambivalent symbols in this context. Flowers often
populate grain fields as weeds.[45]

As we pointed out in Chapter 3, there is an
interesting contrast to the story of the Rich Fool in
v. 26. Birds "do not sow, nor do they reap, nor do
they gather into barns" (apothēkas). In Lk. 12:18 the
rich man, not having room to gather his abundant crops,
is going to "tear down my barns (apothēkas) and I shall
build bigger ones." This contrast is not accidental,
but reflects negatively on the self-centered economic
mentality of Jesus' contemporaries.

If "seeking the kingdom" is an act of faith
leading to dependence upon the generosity of God, that
generosity does not have to be without tangible
mechanism as in the case (to the mind of prescientific
humanity) of the sustenance of birds and flowers. This
point is made strikingly in Mk. 10:29-30 and par., a
passage looked at previously. The new family of God is
the basis for material support.

The converse of this "indicative" of God's
generosity and the creation of a new family of support
is the "imperative" of a human generosity that breaks
down the ancien régime. The essentials of the new
ethos come through in Mt. 7:1-5 = Lk. 6:37-42.
Bultmann's reconstruction of the original form posits a
regular arrangement of parallel statements.[46] There is
here a series of contrasts connecting in a causal way

our actions with the responses of others to us. These
sayings in their Matthean form relate to "judging"
others. Verse 2b is to be understood in a figurative
sense, at least for Matthew. Luke 6:38 gives the
literal sense: Giving should be generous; only then
are returns generous.

Certainly this maxim, affirmed by experience in
the old order, has value for the ethos of self-
sufficiency. Any villager could affirm it as the best
way to keep friends for the hard times when self-
sufficiency would be impossible (cf. Lk. 11:5-8).
Bultmann is surely correct, therefore, in including
this passage in its original sense with wisdom sayings.
Another variant of it in 1 Clement 13:2 links recipro-
cating mercy (eleaō), forgiveness, doing, giving,
judging, showing kindness, and "measuring." These
sayings resonate to exchanges based upon balanced
reciprocity. They reflect the justice of the Golden
Rule (Mt. 7:12 = Lk. 6:31).

The magnates of the Roman republic knew the
political wisdom of public largess and extravagant
benefactions, as well as the great debts that went
along with the political life.[47] Yet generosity could
not be sustained economically by either peasantry or
elite, since persistence in such behavior would lead to
starvation on the one hand or default on the other.
The principle soon reaches the point of diminishing
returns in a class society that idealizes economic
independence.

Nonetheless, Jesus advocates precisely this
strategy as a way into the new age. Trust in the
imminence of God's kingdom leads to increasing, not
diminishing, returns. So Jesus can admonish the
disciples to lend without expecting anything back (Lk.

6:35). Here is brought to expression not balanced, but
again the logic of general, reciprocity. There is a
twist. Loaning to enemies or strangers without the
expectation of repayment goes against village commonsense and is commensurate with the traditions forbid-
ding retaliation and enjoining love for enemies (Mt.
5:38-42 = Lk. 6:29-30; Mt. 5:44 = Lk. 6:27). In these
instances, Jesus presses the meaning of the new ethos
to its utter limits.

Perhaps it is appropriate at this point to
recall the alogon of Jesus preserved in Acts 20:35.
The emphasis is not so much on the receiving (as in the
old order), but on the giving. This giving finds its
basis in that faith in God's generosity already
outlined above. The passive voices in Mt. 7:1-5 = Lk.
6:37-42 are not to be interpreted so much in terms of
the future compensation of the last judgment and the
new age, as in terms of the compensation "now in this
age." That is why it is more blessed to give than to
receive, because of the generosity of the Bestower of
the blessing.

Some of Luke's special material lends particular
emphasis to the theme under consideration. The parable
or example story of the Good Samaritan (Lk. 10:29-37)
well illustrates giving without expecting in return.
While the motives of the Samaritan are not made
explicit--that is, it is not stated that because this
man is devout and believes in the universal care and
providence of God he does what he does--nevertheless
his actions demonstrate a kind of generosity that has
negative economic implications for himself. Those
wealthy landowners, the priest and Levite, who are on
their way to their properties in the Jordan Valley (for
why otherwise would they ever leave the city?), refuse

for whatever reasons to help their fellow Israelite.
The Samaritan, however, not only provides emergency
relief but takes the time to see the other to adequate
shelter and provides two denarii (two full-days' wages)
for any further needs, with the promise to supply any
additional compensation that may be required. By no
cultural standards could the Samaritan's actions seem
selfish, even if he were as a traveler trying to
preserve the age-old custom of hospitality to strangers
through some enlightened self-interest. No, the
Samaritan is simply generous and does not count the
cost, even though he probably will never be repaid.

A commonplace of New Testament scholarship
regarding the Good Samaritan is that he has crossed
over the "dividing wall of hostility" between the Jews
and their northern "neighbors."[48] What is even more
despicable from the standpoint of the dominant mores,
is the generosity he carries to extremes. The
irritation of Jesus' critics at his message about God's
generosity and all of its ramifications can be sensed
directly in the story about the Laborers in the
Vineyard (Mt. 20:1-16). This parable is often taken as
a statement about God's generosity.[49] Certainly it is
a parable about the rule of God, but it need not be
directly about God. As the story stands, it is simply
about a farmowner (oikodespotēs) who violates customary
expectations by treating the short-term laborers on an
equal footing with the long-term laborers.

This story is, from the standpoint of our theme,
filled with ironies. In the first place, the initial
lot of workers are hired for the day's-wage standard at
the turn of the eras (v. 2). Those who are hired later
are simply promised ho ean ēi dikaion. Of course,
whatever is just would by normal expectations be less

than a denarius. The farmer unwittingly (or is it for
show?) instructs the steward to start paying the last-
hired laborers first. Perhaps there is here some
customary order to ensure that everyone gets his due.
At any rate, the first-hired get extremely angry over
being paid the same as their coworkers: "You have made
them our equals, we who bore the scorching heat of the
day" (v. 12). The owner gets equally hot: (To the
spokesman) "Friend, I do you no injustice." You agreed
to this, in other words. And the owner goes on to say
ironically, "Am I not allowed to do what I want with my
goods. Or are you envious (lit. is your eye evil)
because I am generous (lit. good)" (v. 15)?[50] The
generosity of the owner gets him into hot water with
his best workers! Perrin points out that the owner may
have cut his own throat by ruining his reputation with
the labor force (so necessary for the cultivation of
vineyards).[51] Whatever the case, the story points up
the fact that generosity carried too far will have
negative consequences. Generosity undercuts the
prevailing order established on the assumption of a
strict quid pro quo and a self-sufficient household
economy. "Justice" preserves these assumptions; what
destroys them will be perceived as "unjust."[52] This
theme of justice/injustice also permeates Luke's
Dishonest Manager (Lk. 16:1-9).

The story preserved in Mt. 22:1-10 = Lk. 14:15-
24, though evidently marred by much later editorial-
izing and allegorization, continues the line of
argument that generosity (even unwitting, even in
anger) undermines the status quo or breaches the boundaries of respectability. Here a wealthy person,
enraged (Mt. 22:7 = Lk. 14:21) that his invitations
have gone unheeded, gives a feast for all of society's

outcasts, in city and country. The same kind of outcome can be expected here, the gaining of friends in
some quarters, the loss of friends in others. Radical
generosity has social consequences--good and bad--
depending upon your perspective.

If the appropriate response to God's generosity
is a life of generosity, even to the point of violating
the mores of society or of committing outright
injustice, nevertheless this behavior is no do ut des.
The intention of such behavior is not, for the sake of
economic security, to obligate the other. This is the
old order creeping back in. Jesus' intention is--and
here an apocalyptic or eschatological overtone is
evident--to announce the destruction of the old order
and the ushering in of the new. Such generosity aims
to meet the needs of the other, to liberate and
empower. All are obligated now to something bigger
than personal economic security.

If God's generosity and forgiveness disrupt
human standards of justice, so much the more is this
the case with human notions of economics.

We begin with reference to the familiar
similitudes in Matthew (13:44-46; cf. GThom 76, 109)
about the treasure and the pearl. What is to be
observed here is the reckless way that the farmer and
the pearl-merchant unload their property in order to
acquire the hoard or the pearl respectively. One may
grant that the value of the objects in each case
warrants the subsequent behavior of the two characters
of the similitudes, but is it not equally warranted to
question the wisdom of their actions?53 This is
especially true since in each case they dispose of
their means of subsistence (pōlei/pepraken [panta] hosa
echei). If the "gold mine" does not pan out as they

think it will, will they not be in terrible shape
economically? At least, this is the kind of reasoning
one might expect Jesus' hearers to have followed in
their evaluation of the stories. The two men's
behavior must appear to be "uneconomical" in the long
run. However, at least in these similitudes, the
results in the long run are not made manifest.

The value of viewing things from the "long run"
of the kingdom begins to be revealed in the parable of
the Sower (Mk. 4:3-9 and par.). We have argued
previously that for the peasantry, the presumed
original audience, the point must surely have been the
miracle of growth. This point is underscored by 1) the
large loss of precious seed and 2) the marvelous yields
that come forth despite the ineffectual farming methods
of human beings and the natural forces that work
against them. The growth occurs anyway! Admittedly,
there is a contrast here, but it seems that the better
way to put it is, "uneconomical means--economically
viable end." God's generosity will overcome the
stinginess of the soil and the first-century farming
methods by which household economies are supposed to be
sustained.

Uneconomic action is particularly underlined in
the story of the widow who gives her whole livelihood
to the Temple (Mk. 12:41-44 = Lk. 21:1-4). By what
security has this woman been able to do this? Where
will she find material support? From Jesus who notices
her gift?

A story in Luke emphasizes this point about
economic viability in a refreshing way (Lk. 15:8-10).
A peasant woman loses a drachma (= a denarius, about
two-weeks' sustenance for one person).[54] With extreme
care (epimelōs v. 8b), the woman lights her lamp and

sweeps her floor until the precious metal turns up.
Lighting the lamp during the day uses up scarce oil.
Luke apparently adds the touch about celebration after
the coin is found (v. 9; cf. v. 6 and Mt. 18:13; cf.
also Lk. 15:22f). This nonetheless brings out what is
implicit (if not explicit) in Jesus' own message. The
woman's time-consuming effort, her use of scarce oil,
and now her celebration which is bound to cost more
than the lost denarius, profoundly illustrates the
point at issue. Out of the woman's action, which
squanders resources for the all-important aim of maintaining the household's meager economic security and
leads to an even more costly celebration, has come
important solidarity with her friends and neighbors.
Uneconomic actions may, under the care of God, lead to
a different kind of community and a different kind of
economics.

E. Conclusion

In conclusion it must be said again, on the
basis of the words studied, that Jesus held a revolutionary ideology. Though he did not speak of a redistribution of landed property, probably because of his
aversion to self-sufficiency in any form and possibly
because he believed the kingdom of God would abolish
private property, he did advocate the other revolutionary agenda of antiquity--remission of debts.
Jesus' words anticipated in several important respects
the dissolution of material mechanisms of social
stratification and power in his environment.

With the expectation of the near advent of God's
rule came several other constructive agendas. Oppres-
sors could begin to behave toward the oppressed with
generosity and magnanimity (Lk. 16:6-7; Mt. 18:27;

20:9, 15; 22:10 = Lk. 14:23). The oppressed themselves
could find joy again in sharing (Mt. 6:33; Mt. 7:2 =
Lk. 6:38; Lk. 10:29-37; 15:9). Furthermore, a new
kinship (Mk. 10:30) and new moral obligations based
upon a "general reciprocity" (Mt. 5:38-42 = Lk. 6:29-
30; Mt. 5:44 = Lk. 6:27; Mt. 7:2 = Lk. 6:38; Lk. 7:41-
42; 10:35) were coming into being with the proclamation
of the kingdom.

        The political authorities undoubtedly would have
perceived--whether in the public advocacy of debt
remission, the criticism of wealth, or unorthodox
social behavior--a subversive and revolutionary agenda.
Jesus did not have to advocate armed insurrection to be
branded a revolutionary. In fact, he did not advocate
armed insurrection. However, his vision of the
liberation and humanity coming with the reign of God
directly attacked principal elements of the Roman order
in Palestine and attracted a following of people
victimized by that order.

Notes to Chapter 4

[1]Bultmann, (1963) 110.

[2]Note the variant readings in Luke and Matthew for "manyfold." Nestle-Aland[26] has "hundredfold" at Mt. 19:29 and "manyfold" at Lk. 18:30.

[3]See Burridge (1969); Isenberg (1974). On the millenarian character of the Jesus movement consult Gager, (1975) 20-57.

[4]More on these relations in Section D.

[5]As Chapter 2 has already tried to show. See the treatment of Mt. 20:1-20 below in Section D. See especially the article of Hengel, (1968) 1-39.

[6]Jeremias, (1963) 170.

[7]See the legal discussion in M. Maas. Sheni 5:1. Cf. Haywood, (1959) 93.

[8]White, (1970b) 228.

[9]For instance, M. Sheb. 4:4, 10. Cf. Deut. 20:19. See also the evidence collected in Baron, (1952) 1:252.

[10]In Petronius's Satyricon 34, 42, 72, 76. See Rostovtzeff, (1957) 1:57 on this ethic and Pl. VII which illustrates it well. Further, Finley, (1973) 108; Hengel, (1974a) ch. 8.

[11]Childe, (1964) 67.

[12]Ibid.: 77.

[13]Ibid.: 284. On this point see also Rostovtzeff, (1957) 1:59ff, 93, etc.

[14]Ste. Croix, (1981) 205.

[15]Finley, (1973) 108.

[16]See on the execution or praxis Rostovtzeff, (1941) 1:317, 343f; Ste. Croix, (1981) Index, s. v. "Personal Execution."

[17]Jeremias, (1963) 45. Fitzmyer, (1985) 2:1101 thinks the kyrios is identical with the steward's master.

[18]See Wolf, (1966) 81 on single- and manystranded relationships in peasant societies.

[19]Gregory, (1975) 85.

[20]Ibid.: 74.

[21]Ibid.: 83.

[22]Burridge, (1969) 5-6 has spoken of redemptive media as offering periodic satisfaction of debt and millennial redemption as a total discharge of indebtedness leading to a "state of unobligedness." See also Isenberg (1974). I believe Jesus would be able to endorse such millennial freedom only as a transitional state. He is intensely interested in reestablishing grounds for mutual obligation. There is, therefore, in the tradition of Jesus' words a paradoxical formulation of absolute freedom combined with absolute obligation. Other passages in the gospels also play upon the theme of debt or debt remission, but with varied implications. Not treated here is the parable of the Talents, Mt. 25:14-30 = Lk. 19:11-27, which seems no more than a commentary on conventional behavior in the early empire: Finley, (1973) 116. Also not treated: The example story of the Prodigal Son (Lk. 15:11-32) explores the problem of moral debt.

[23]Perrin, (1967) 47. I am once again drawing upon and expanding ideas that first appeared in Oakman (1985).

[24]Jeremias, (1963) 85-94.

[25]Ibid.: 93.

[26]Perrin, (1967) 47, 151.

[27]Moulton and Milligan, (1980) 96.

[28]Dalman, (1930) 1:335. Jeremias, (1963) 94.

[29]Perrin, (1967) 151; Dalman, (1930) 1:334f. Cf. Jeremias, (1967) 92: "Money owed."

[30]Recall again the remarks in the last section about millenarian movements and their material expecta- tions. Jeremias, (1967) 103f does not, in fact, see in this petition a material expectation for the destruc- tion of all earthly debt.

        It must be mentioned that, since "taxation" in
its manifold varieties played a critical role in the
escalation of indebtedness in early Roman Palestine,
Mk. 12:13-17 or Mt. 17:24-27 could be used either to
substantiate or repudiate the view advocated here. The
difficulties in interpreting these passages are evident;
see now the articles by Bruce ("Render to Caesar") and
Horbury ("The Temple tax") in Bammel and Moule, (1984)
249-63, 265-86. Both gospel passages seem deliberately
ambiguous. The political context of Jesus' work would
have warranted this. I think Mt. 17:26b accurately
reflects Jesus' general view on taxation (since he knew
well that the Temple also played a critical role in
Roman taxation). Matthew's redaction (v. 27) reflects
the early church's quietism and accommodation to the
empire.

        31Schottroff and Stegemann, (1981) 15-28;
Stegemann, (1984) 13-21.

        32Mealand (1980); Hengel (1974a); Countryman
(1980). All of these offer additional references to
literature.

        33Mealand, (1980) 14.

        34Ibid.: 34.

        35Ibid.: 22.

        36Ibid.: 27. Countryman fairly much agrees with
this assessment, (1980) 81-89.

        37Mealand, (1980) 39, 90-91.

        38Ibid.: 87.

        39Theissen, (1977) and (1978) 8-16. Hengel,
(1974a) 30.

        40Hengel, (1974a) 23, 26.

        41McCown, (1929) 352.

        42Bultmann, (1963) 80f.

        43Bultmann views "righteousness" as a Matthean
insertion.

        44Hamel, (1983) 284 gives a rabbinic parallel to
birds receiving sustenance without care.

[45]Salisbury, (1961) 34.

[46]Bultmann, (1963) 80.

[47]Finley, (1973) 53ff.

[48]Perrin, (1967) 124.

[49]Ibid.: 118; Jeremias, (1963) 136 (in the chapter "God's Mercy for Sinners").

[50]Jeremias, (1963) 138.

[51]Perrin, (1967) 117.

[52]This direction of thought is inspired by Hengel, (1974a) ch. 3.

[53]One is reminded here a little of fairy tales in our own literature like "Jack and the Beanstalk," George Foster, in a response to Gregory, (1975) 86f, points out the significance of "treasure tales" and "buried treasure" as popular explanations for why peasants get ahead in supposedly "zero-sum" societies. Jesus is apparently playing upon stories that came into currency with new economic opportunities in the early empire.

[54]See Jeremias, (1963) 135: Perhaps part of her dowry. For a similar reading see Bailey, (1980) 152-53.

CHAPTER 5

THE ECONOMIC DIMENSION IN THE MINISTRY OF JESUS

The interests of the gospel writers regarding Jesus have been shown again and again by contemporary New Testament scholarship to be of a different nature than those that motivate modern historical inquiries.[1] To the first Christians, what Jesus did in gaining his livelihood was simply immaterial for an understanding of his mission as a religious figure. To the modern historical view, however, the very opposite holds true. Not to look for interconnections between historical phenomena is incomprehensible. Conditioning factors like occupation, where they can be observed, often prove to shed great light upon apparently independent aspects of historical phenomena.

The dimension that concerns us here has not exactly gone unnoticed. Sixty years ago, Shirley J. Case published his Jesus: A New Biography, in which there is "more than usual emphasis upon the social point of view."[2] Case wanted to move beyond a mere literary, idealistic, or religious appropriation of Jesus to an assessment of his work in its socio-historical context. Because of the breadth of his questions, Case was able to offer some insights into the work and character of Jesus that had not been acquired before. Some of these will be reexamined below.[3]

Following the lead of scholars like Case, what is looked for in the first section (A) are salient

175

features of the everyday world of work Jesus inhabited
that might shed light on the meaning of his religious
activity. The second section (B) explores the social
contacts of Jesus, largely on the basis of the
canonical gospels. Section C, finally, draws upon
comparative studies of patronage, in order to explore
economic aspects of Jesus' networking.

Obviously the evidence called upon here, in view
of the nature of the sources, must be inferential and
circumstantial. However, this does not mean that our
modern interest in this aspect of the historical Jesus
is inappropriate or that attempting to cull the
tradition for hints of what it might tell us on this
subject is futile. As in other aspects of this study,
so here: The proof is in the tasting.

A. Jesus' Occupation

Characteristically, the only direct information
given to us in the gospel records about Jesus' occupational pursuit is incidental and brief. Mark 6:3 tells
how the people of Jesus' hometown Nazareth identified
him by his trade--"the carpenter" (tektōn). They could
not understand how such a man could be teaching in the
manner he was or where he had obtained his wisdom. The
parallel passage in Matthew (13:55) has modified Mark's
formulation to "the son of the carpenter." Redaction-
ally this might be an attempt by Matthew to set Jesus
apart from his working-class origins. This could be
explained if Matthew were writing for a predominately
wealthy audience. By contrast, Mark emphasizes Jesus'
closeness to working people and the poor.[4]

There need not be any bending of historical
truth by these redactional maneuvers. Klausner long
ago pointed out, on the basis of rabbinic evidence,

that trades passed from father to son in ancient
Palestine.[5] There is no reason to doubt that both
Jesus and Joseph plied the same trade. Later traditions, such as those in the Infancy Gospel of Thomas
(InThom 13) and in Justin's Dialog with Trypho (88),
confirm this view. The former source tells that Joseph
was engaged in the making of yokes and plows. The
latter relates the same information about Jesus.

     Two questions suggest themselves in continuing
this line of inquiry: What did an ancient carpenter do
or make? Where might a Palestinian carpenter be
expected to go to ply such a trade?

     McCown published a philological study years ago
attempting to determine what ancient carpenters
occupied themselves with.[6] Tektōnes in the Graeco-
Roman world were, by and large, workers in wood. They
did not work in metal or stone.[7] Of the Semitic
language evidence, McCown writes:

     . . . a careful study of the Tarqums, the Talmud,
     and the Syriac version of the Old Testament will
     show, I believe, that [nagar] was usually applied
     only to a worker in wood.[8]

Admittedly, in both language groups these words could
have a broader sphere of meaning--artisan in general--
but by Jesus' time the division of labor in Palestine
(at least for carpentry) was sufficiently advanced, so
that the specialized meaning could be expected to
apply.[9]

     Some of the tools, and hence the technical
level, of ancient carpentry were already implicit in
Second Isaiah (44:13). Supplementing ancient texts by
archaeology, the following list results: Compass,
pencil, plane, saw, hammer, axe, adze, chisel, plumb
line, drill, file, square, dowels, nails.[10]

The evidence of Justin and the Infancy Gospel of
Thomas have already indicated that Jesus and Joseph
fabricated yokes and plows. This information is in
line with what we might expect a rural carpenter to do.
Nazareth was a tiny village in Jesus' day, so tiny that
neither Josephus nor the Talmud ever mentions it.[11]
Its rural locale not far from the Esdraelon Plain would
offer economic opportunities to carpenters for
supplying the needs of both the local peasantry and
larger estates. The "most important ancient text on
division of labour," preserved in Xenophon's Cyropaedia
(8.2.5), tells us:

> In small towns the same man makes couches, doors,
> ploughs and tables, and often he even builds
> houses, and still he is thankful if only he can
> find enough work to support himself.[12]

This text attests to the "jack-of-all-trades" quality
of rural carpentry--diversification compelled by
economic necessity. The text also reveals the economic
impulse that drove the ancient rural carpenter to seek
work where it could be found.

Klausner, following a suggestion of Joseph
Halevy, claims that Nazareth was a village specializing
in carpentry.[13] This suggestion is supported by a
number of considerations. First, other villages in
Jesus' day seem to have specialized in one craft or
another.[14] Secondly, whole families carried on the
same craft, and the villages of ancient Palestine seem
to have been congregations of related families.
Thirdly, there is a possible etymological link between
the root of the word "Nazareth" and nagar.[15] There are
regularly observed transformations between Aramaic and
Hebrew words involving 'ayin and tsade. 'ayin can have
a gutteral "g" sound; hence, a transformation from g to
ts might not be as remote as it seems.[16]

It cannot be doubted, even if it is granted that Nazareth specialized in carpentry, that most of the residents of the village occupied themselves regularly with subsistence agriculture. Jesus came from peasant stock and without question was socialized early to the routines of farming. Lenski has suggested, from comparative evidence, that surplus peasant children are often driven to seek employment outside the village because of limited land resources.[17] It may be that Jewish villages were driven to specialize in some craft precisely because of the precariousness of subsistence arrangements in the Graeco-Roman period. We may recall the later rabbinic view that if a father did not teach his son a craft, he was teaching him brigandage.[18] There is no way of knowing more precisely, however, about the relationship between the pursuit of a craft and agriculture in these villages.[19]

A village carpenter could be called upon to make any number of agricultural implements. Besides yokes and plows, the carpenter might construct threshing boards, axles for carts, and similar items that the unskilled peasant could not manufacture for himself.[20] A like symbiosis between carpenter and peasant was observable not long ago among modern Palestinian peasantry.[21] For the peasant household, the carpenter contributed benches, beds, or other furniture, as well as cabinets.[22] For the village, the carpenter might be called upon to build coffins, gates, or parts for an oil press.[23] Carpenters were employed on the upper stories of houses, which generally utilized wooden parts.[24] In all of these activities the artisan could normally expect to be paid by the day in money, although sometimes there were barter arrangements.[25]

If economic opportunities were scarce, or when
the local peasantry had nothing left to pay the
artisan, he could be expected to travel to where work
was. As a general rule, the craftsman of antiquity
exported his labor power rather than a product.[26]
Rural craftsmen like Jesus were probably under greater
pressure to travel in order to find work than artisans
of great urban areas. Case notes the proximity of
Nazareth to one such economic center. Sepphoris was
only several miles distant from Nazareth:

> . . . if [the modern traveler] approaches Nazareth
> from the north, by way of the modern village
> marking the site of the ancient Sepphoris, he will
> realize how easily accessible it was to the people
> of Nazareth when travel by foot was the ordinary
> means of locomotion.[27]

Case goes on to suggest that Jesus may have participated in the rebuilding of Sepphoris during the early
years of the first century:

> That a vigorous building enterprise was in progress
> at Sepphoris while Jesus was still a youth, and at
> the same time the main support of a family of at
> least six younger children and a widowed mother,
> suggests the probability that he may have plied his
> carpenter's trade in the city. Very likely
> "carpenter" as applied to Jesus meant not simply a
> worker in wood but one who labored at the building-
> trade in general . . .[28]

The point made in this passage finds some support in
the second-century Protevangelium of James (PJas 13:1),
which records that Joseph built buildings. Case
further believes that laborers employed in Sepphoris
may have moved to Tiberias upon completion of the
former work. On the strength of Josephus AJ 18.35f,

work on Tiberias may have begun at the beginning of
Pilate's procuratorship.[29] This would provide a very
powerful historical motive for Jesus' move from
Nazareth to the Sea of Galilee, although the gospels
never explain this shift in terms of historical
factors. Everything in the gospels is more or less
"telescoped" together, and usually given a religious
explanation. Thus for Matthew, Jesus' move to
Capernaum fulfills Old Testament prophecy (Mt. 4:13-
16). Admittedly the gospels never place Jesus in
Tiberias, nor do they place him in Sepphoris. Since
Mark was written near the time of the throes of the
Jewish War, association of Jesus with these two pro-
Roman centers may have been problematic. Their absence
in the tradition does not necessarily vitiate the view
advanced by Case.

To finish the catalog of work done by the
carpenter, building activity perhaps led to work on
synagogues or the Temple. For most Jews, work on pagan
temples or idols was probably unthinkable. Rabbinic
sources indicate, however, that this was an economic
temptation.[30] Since all of the Herods carried on
extensive building programs of a military nature (for-
tifications, etc.), there may have been opportunities
for the carpenter there. Some carpenters must have
participated in the manufacture of military equipment
requiring woodwork.

Then too, the carpenter offered support to other
crafts. For instance, the carpenter might be called
upon to work on the weaver's shuttle, the baker's
platter, the shoemaker's last, the potter's wheel, and
so on.[31]

One last suggestive item will conclude this
catalog. Ancient carpenters throughout the

Mediterranean world frequently worked upon wooden
boats. Joseph in a later Christian romance was said to
be "in Capernaum occupied by work."[32] Jesus is again
and again associated in the tradition with the Sea of
Galilee and with fishermen (see below). These two
facts led McCown to write: "Perhaps Jesus built the
boats of Peter and Andrew, James and John."[33]

The foregoing begins to indicate the wide
variety of settings an ancient Palestinian carpenter
might have entered to find work. The successful
carpenter was undoubtedly quite versatile in applying
his skill to new situations. The last paragraph
suggests the need now to move into a consideration of
the social contacts of Jesus.

B. Jesus' Social Contacts

The investigation in the preceding chapters has
given some indication of the breadth of interests and
the range of observation preserved in the words of
Jesus. The narrative material of the gospels heightens
this impression of the wide experience of Jesus. An
account is given in what follows, first of all, of the
social contacts Jesus made--as indicated both in the
canonical gospels and in extra-canonical tradition.
Secondly, a suspicion that Jesus' pursuit of a living
in carpentry may have provided the Sitz im Leben for
these social contacts is entertained.

A distinction must be established at the start
between the dimension of the tradition that gives a
religious justification for a particular social contact
and the historical dimension of the tradition that
sometimes hints at a prior ground for a particular
social contact. For instance, the Gospel of Mark gives
no indication that Jesus ever had any prior contact

with John the Baptizer. John simply appears in the
wilderness offering a baptism to "all Judaea" (Mk.
1:4f). Without giving any explanation of motive, the
Evangelist narrates that Jesus too left Nazareth and
was baptized by John (1:9).

The Gospel of Luke (1:36), the Protevangelium of
James (12:2), and Papyrus Cairensis 10 735, know a
tradition that Jesus was a relative of John.[34]
Furthermore, Luke and the later Ebionite tradition know
that John was of priestly lineage.[35] These two bits of
information throw a suggestive light on how Jesus knew
of John's baptism and why he may have gone to John.[36]

Of course, not much is made of these traditions
in later orthodox Christian circles. The tendency was
to dissociate Jesus from John and to show the superi-
ority of Jesus to John (begun already in John 3:30).
There were important reasons for not emphasizing such a
relationship, or even suppressing knowledge of it. For
the modern historian, however, the tradition cannot
hide the fact that Jesus' religious ministry began
under the impetus of John. It is probable that John's
imprisonment by Herod offered the spark that ignited
the activity of Jesus recorded in the gospels.[37]

Jesus' journey to be baptized by John probably
took him through the Jordan Valley. Other traditions
place him there as well (Mk. 10:46; Jn. 1:28; 3:23).
It is not apparent from any of these whether Jesus had
passed that way before his journey to John. Other
considerations suggest that it is probable he had been
in the Jordan Valley, at least in passing, prior to the
events in the gospels.

Matthew and Luke both indicate that Bethlehem
was the ancestral home of Joseph and/or Mary (Mt. 2:1;
Lk. 2:4). John's gospel perhaps implies that Judaea

was considered Jesus' "home country" (Jn. 4:44). There
is in some of these traditions, of course, an obvious
interest in the Davidic descent of Jesus. Nonetheless,
there does not seem to be any reason to doubt the
historical authenticity of them. Relatives of Jesus,
it may be recalled, lived near Bethlehem during the
reign of the emperor Domitian.[38] The alleged connection between the families of Jesus and John, at least
through Mary, supports such a picture. Luke does not
name the village of Zecharias and Elizabeth, but it is
in the "hill country of Judah" (Lk. 1:39). This second
focus of the family of Jesus, then, may have provided
impetus for earlier journeys between Galilee and
Judaea. The Jordan Valley would have been a natural
avenue for such journeys.

Further support for this point can be drawn from
the tradition about Cleopas and the post-resurrection
appearance of Jesus near Emmaus (Lk. 24:18). Eusebius
knew an uncle of Jesus named Clopas (EH 3.11). The son
of Clopas, Simeon, became the second bishop of Jerusalem and a martyr under Trajan (EH 4.22.4, 3.32.3-6
respectively). Origen and a marginal gloss in Codex
Sinaiticus identified the other Emmaus disciple as
Simon. It is likely that Cleopas and the other disciple are identical with this Clopas and Simeon and,
consequently, that Luke preserves a memory of relatives
of Jesus living in Emmaus.[39] Moreover, some scholars
have thought that the same Aramaic proper noun lies
behind Cleopas and Alphaeus.[40] James and Levi (Mk.
2:14; 3:18; etc.) could therefore have been cousins of
Jesus. Jesus' mother and the wife or daughter of
Clopas probably were related (Jn. 19:25).

In this connection, the question must be raised
of journeys by Jesus on religious grounds to Jerusalem.

Luke alone of the Evangelists narrates the story of the
twelve-year old Jesus in the Jerusalem Temple (Lk.
2:42-51). Deuteronomy had enjoined all pious Jewish
males to present themselves before God in the Temple
three times a year (Deut. 16:16). There has been much
debate in modern scholarship regarding the historical
worth of references to Jesus' frequent trips to
Jerusalem in the Gospel of John (within the framework
of a three-year ministry, in contrast to Mark's single
year). If we break with a normative view of the length
of Jesus' activity (as promulgated by modern scholarship on the basis of Mark), John's gospel lends support
to our contention that Jesus traveled to Jerusalem in
the regular course of his life.[41]

Mention of Bethany in the tradition, just east
of Jerusalem, and of Simon the Leper (Mk. 14:3), Mary
and Martha (Lk. 10:38ff), or of Mary, Martha, and
Lazarus (Jn. 11:1ff) supplies additional evidence for
prior social contacts in the Jerusalem area. If Jesus
were just coming to Jerusalem for the first time in his
life, as the Gospel of Mark implies, how then could
Jesus have known these people? The Marcan tradition
presents further difficulties. Jesus sends his
disciples on ahead to prepare to eat the passover (Mk.
14:12-16). The instructions that he gives are very
mysterious, and the passage seems designed to demonstrate his clairvoyance (v. 16: "[they] found it as he
had told them" RSV). Nonetheless, the way that Jesus
identifies himself to the householder in the city--"the
Teacher says, Where is my guest room," etc.--suggests
the householder had had previous contact with Jesus.[42]
A study of the occurrences of this formal title for
Jesus shows that it almost invariably occurs in
traditions of the Judaean ministry. Besides the

householder of Mk. 14:14 and par., Martha and Mary knew
Jesus as the Teacher (Jn. 11:28). Jn. 3:10 and 13:13f
may also be included as evidence. The only exception
to the Judaean setting is the story of Jairus (Mk. 5:35
= Lk. 8:49). However, the designation there (in the
accusative case) does not necessarily have to be
considered a formal title. Jesus characteristically
teaches in the Gospel of Mark (e.g. 1:21). Luke is
simply following Mark, so his evidence in that passage
is not independent. Jesus is also frequently addressed
in the gospels as rabbi (or rabbouni, e.g. Mk. 9:5;
10:51). These are all vocatives, not nominatives.

     If Jesus did journey to the vicinity of
Jerusalem on occasions other than that or those
connected with his ministry and death there, he had in
addition to the Jordan Valley a more direct route
through Samaria. Luke and John preserve traditions
that reflect travel through this area (for instance,
Lk. 9:52 or Jn. 4). Jesus certainly does not evidence
the hostility toward this group manifested in other
Jewish sources of the time (Lk. 10:30ff; 17:16-19).

     This impression of extensive social contacts and
the concomitant freedom of Jesus to move beyond the
narrow confines of his village world is supported
especially by consideration of the traditions surrounding his activity in Galilee. There are again the
curious non sequiturs in the traditions that hint at
longer developments in social relations between Jesus
and others. The accounts of the call of the initial
disciples in Mark are quite abrupt and on the surface
"eschatological" in character (Simon and Andrew, 1:17;
John and James, 1:20; Levi, 2:14). There is no apparent preparation in the narrative for these summonses.
The disciples are simply pulled out of their ordinary

world by the call of Jesus; they thereupon abandon
their normal social ties (Mk. 10:28). The theological
aspect of these call reports is evident. As in the
case of Jesus, the call of the disciples is uncondi-
tioned by any human consideration; the reign of God is
the sole source of the call.

     The modern historian must nonetheless ask, did
Jesus know these people prior to the beginning of his
ministry? A possible answer is supplied through
knowledge of the contacts a carpenter was likely to
make in the pursuit of a living, as we have glimpsed
above. Jesus could easily have found employment
related to the fishing industry. As he had to travel
about somewhat to carry on his business, and as he
possibly carried materials of his trade through toll
points, he would have come to know the man in the toll
collector's booth as well. As in the case of the
Jerusalem tradition, so here: Preexisting conditions
make it likely that Jesus met these people prior to
events recorded in the extant gospels.

     If more could be known about the list of names
that have come down to us as "the Twelve" (Mk. 3:16-19
and par.), it would be possible to make further observations about Jesus' prior social contacts. James (son
of Alphaeus), Simon (the Cananaean), Judas (son of
James, Lk. 6:16), and Judas Iscariot have appellations
or patronymics that might convey additional information. We have already mentioned the possible identity
of Alphaeus and Clopas. Simon would seem to have been
a partisan of something like Josephus's "Fourth Philosophy," the Zealots.[43] The appellation Iscariot, on the
evidence of other such forms in Josephus and the
Septuagint, apparently identifies Judas by his place of
origin. This was perhaps Kerioth south of Hebron, or

Kerioth in Moab.[44] Again, evidence of wide-ranging
contacts is in view.

        In general, many of the people Jesus associated
with were poor. Here can be included references to
sinners (Mk. 2:15). Sometimes members of despised
trades are to be thought of in these references.[45]
Sinners included prostitutes (Lk. 7:37; Mt. 21:32).
Also to be mentioned are references to the sick and
physically impaired, who cannot "carry their own
weight" physically or in an economic sense (Mk. 1:40;
2:3; 10:46).[46] Jesus' reputation as a worker of
wonders naturally would have attracted these types of
people. Jesus demonstrates sympathy toward other
groups of people who were likely to be impoverished at
that time: Here we can mention widows (Mk. 12:42) and
children (Mk. 10:13-16).[47]

        Yet Jesus is rather frequently associated with
wealthy people in the tradition too. Tax collectors
were not necessarily poor. Zacchaeus comes to mind.
People engaged in the fishing trade could make a good
living. Zebedee was able to afford hired servants (Mk.
1:20).[48] Jesus was several times approached by
eminent men: Jairus (Mk. 5:22), the Centurion of
Capernuam (Mt. 8:5), an unnamed rich man (Mk. 10:17 and
par.). In Jerusalem, Jesus is reported to have spoken
with a member of the Sanhedrin, Nicodemus (Jn. 3:1).
Joseph of Arimathea asked Pilate for the body of Jesus
(Mk. 15:43). Mark calls Joseph a "well-to-do
councillor" (euschēmōn bouleutēs). Luke alone reports
that Jesus was supported by some wealthy women, one of
whom was the wife of an official of Herod Antipas (Lk.
8:1-3).

        Jesus' itineracy is evident in Galilee.[49] He
moved from Nazareth to Capernaum, as has been

mentioned. Nevertheless, he still did not entirely
abandon his home town. He preached without success in
the synagogue of Nazareth (Mk. 6:1-6 and par.). The
tradition shows him to have visited surrounding
villages. According to Luke (7:11), Jesus once raised
a dead man in Nain. John remembers a wedding in nearby
Cana (Jn. 2:1) and a subsequent visit (4:46).

Jesus could visit the chōra of Gerasa or Gadara
(Mk. 5:1ff), travel to the vicinity of Caesarea
Philippi and Mt. Hermon (Mk. 8:27), and even go to the
environs of Tyre and Sidon (Mk. 7:24ff).[50] He cursed
Chorazin, Bethsaida, and Capernaum (Mt. 11:21, 23; cf.
Mk. 8:22)--cities of the Plain of Gennesareth where he
had stayed and worked. These cities apparently did not
respond to Jesus' (or the earliest church's) ministry
and preaching.

The picture being developed here would be even
more cohesive if activities in the gospels could be
correlated with known centers of carpentry or building,
or if Jesus' social contacts could be connected with
carpentry. While Jesus cannot be connected with
Sepphoris or Tiberias from the gospel tradition, as the
words in the preceding paragraph indicate, he spent
much time in villages and "cities" around the Sea of
Galilee. Joseph Halevy not only thought that Nazareth
was a village specializing in carpentry; he also
proposed that Gennesareth meant "valley of sawyers."
Jesus perhaps joined many others working in the valley
at various tasks of carpentry.[51]

Jesus' residence in Capernaum, a center of
Galilean fishing, has already been referred to a number
of times. His trip to Caesarea Philippi, taking him up
into the hills and mountains of the Lebanon, would have
placed him in a region with vast timber resources. It

is doubtful that specialization had advanced in first-
century Palestine to the point where the cutting of
timber was a specialty separate from carpentry.[52]
InThom 10:1 narrates how the boy Jesus once healed the
foot of a young man who had been injured by an axe.
Was the young man a woodcutter or simply chopping wood
for the fire? Joseph is depicted in PJas 9:1 as
throwing down his axe when heralds announce the
assembly of the widowers. It may well be that any
distinction between woodcutters and carpenters in the
first two centuries of our era was minimal.

        Jesus says, according to Oxyrhynchus Papyrus 1
(28-31 = GThom 77), "Lift up the stone, and there you
will find me; cleave the wood, and I am there." The
version in GThom merely reverses the two members of the
parallelism. Possessing the two different traditions
of this saying allows us to see that this portion is
not to be interpreted via the companion saying in
either tradition. The two traditions preserve two
different companion sayings. What Jesus says through
this saying is that he is often present where wood is
chopped or stones are lifted--that is, on account of
his being a carpenter. Hennecke-Schneemelcher see an
allusion here to Ecclesiastes 10:9:

    He who quarries stones is hurt by them; and he who
    splits logs is endangered by them.[53]
The parallel is apt, but positing a direct influence
from the Old Testament is not necessary. The natural
connection between wood and stone, carpenters and
masons, in the building enterprises of Palestine was
quite common. Lk. 14:28-30 seems to reflect direct
knowledge of the procedures required in putting up a
guard-tower. Perhaps the interest of the disciples in
the stonework and edifices of Herod's Temple (Mk. 13:1)

does not so much reflect the reaction of country
bumpkins as stem from their actual knowledge of the
tremendous work such buildings would entail.

Certainly the work Jesus engaged in was
dangerous. The Q saying in Mt. 7:5 = Lk. 6:42 reflects
the painful experience of the woodcutter/carpenter.
Jesus also knows the horrors that can befall the
builder in Palestine (Lk. 13:4). Possibly the much-
discussed Lk. 13:1 parallels 13:4 and also contains a
reference to a building accident at the time of Pilate
otherwise unknown to us.

Continuing the previous thread of the discussion, the trip to Caesarea could also have involved the
intention to seek new areas of employment. Philip the
Tetrarch, like his father Herod the Great and brother
Herod Antipas, carried on several building programs.
Philip enlarged Bethsaida and renamed it Julias. He
also renamed the famous Panias after Caesar.[54] Jesus
spent time in or near both of these locales. (Mark
does not say Jesus went into the city of Caesarea.)

A similar intention may have been in view
during Jesus' trips to the regions of Tyre and Sidon
and the Gerasene territory, though a precise motive is
not given in the Synoptic tradition.

The Jerusalem traditions provide some additional
indicators for Jesus' movements. Besides giving
information on visits to the Temple itself, independent
traditions permit the inference that Jesus spent a lot
of time in the northern parts of the city (apparently
outside the second wall).[55] To begin with, John 5:2
locates the healing of a paralytic at the pools in
Bezetha near the Sheep Gate. Bezetha, north of the
Antonia, contained the wool market. Not far to the
northwest of Bezetha was the ancient quarter for

carpenters and the timber market.[56] It is certainly
suggestive to find Jesus in the vicinity of this
quarter.

Mark also seems to place Jesus in the northern
part of the city on his last trip to Jerusalem. The
disciples were sent from Bethany to prepare the
passover meal. They must have crossed the Kidron
Valley and entered one of the northern gates (although
this is not expressly stated). A man carrying a jar of
water was supposed to lead them to the appropriate
place (Mk. 14:13). Was this man taking water from the
Sheep Pools? After the meal, Jesus and three of the
disciples went back across the Kidron Valley to
Gethsemane (Mk. 14:26). These two movements--from
Bethany to the Upper Room and from the Upper Room to
Gethsemane--would most easily and directly have been
accomplished with the "upper room" in a northern
location.[57]

The gospels, as we have already seen, are for
the most part devoid of background information
regarding the people who appear in them. There is some
extra-canonical evidence that shows Jesus' network of
contacts perhaps hinged upon his trade. The Gospel
According to the Nazoreans identifies the man with the
withered hand (Mk. 3:1-6 and par.) as a mason named
Malchus.[58] Carpenters employed in the building trade
worked very closely with masons. The quotations just
given above will confirm this. Jesus possibly knew
this Malchus through connections stemming from his own
occupation. At any rate, he could sympathize with the
man's plea: "I beseech thee, Jesus, to restore to me
my health that I may not with ignominy have to beg for
my bread."[59]

Later Christian symbolism associated a
carpenter's square with Jude and Thomas and a saw with
James (the Less).[60] Carpenters in ancient Palestine
identified their trade to others by wearing a ruler on
their clothes.[61] It is possible that Jude and Thomas
were the same person, since "Thomas" means "Twin."[62]
The Gospel of Thomas (Prologue) identifies the reci-
pient of the secrets as "Didymus Judas Thomas." Compare the passages in John (11:16; 20:24; 21:2). James
and Thomas were apparently fellow-carpenters with
Jesus.

A final consideration stems from a passage in
InThom 13. There Joseph is engaged in making a bed for
a rich patron. It has been shown above that Jesus had
no trouble associating with the wealthy. Admittedly in
the tradition as it stands, these contacts find a basis
in Jesus' ministry, and he is frequently approached as
a healing patron in touch with divine powers
(Centurion, Jairus). Might not Jesus' openness toward
and knowledge of the social circumstances of the
wealthy find a grounding in his previous experiences
with them as a client? Many of the parables that
evidence a detailed knowledge of large estates, the
behavior of slaves and overseers, and so forth,
undoubtedly derive from Jesus' direct experience with
these situations. And the tradition is not equivocal
in stating that Jesus ate with tax collectors and
sinners. Around the meal, Jesus was able to bring
together all of the constituencies--rich and poor--that
he had built up in his many travels.[63]

C. Jesus as Broker Between Patron and Client

The social sciences offer a useful way of
looking at the role Jesus seems to have assumed on many
occasions in the gospel narratives. An entire literature has grown up around the subject of patronage.[64]
Blok defines patronage as:

> . . . a structural principle which underlies
> asymmetric, personal transactions involving
> protection and loyalty between two persons or
> groups of persons.[65]

Eisenstadt and Roniger believe that the best vantage
point for understanding patron-client relations is
given in terms of a model structuring relations between
generalized and specific exchange.[66]

Patronage and clientelism occur prevalently in
societies that are, or have been, characterized by
extensive and extractive economies--having a low level
of internal specialization, little incentive to
technological innovation, and an extra-societal trade
orientation.[67] This means that elite status is
achieved within these societies by means of a limited
number of political strategies--for instance, control
of extensive territory, intensive exploitation of a
zero-sum resource base, or control of strategic trade
routes. Within these societies economic goods might
conceivably flow freely, were it not for this tendency
of individuals or groups to monopolize control of them.
A struggle invariably ensues between individuals or
groups over the control of these resources. In other
words, patrons control access to key social resources
and acquire a supporting network of clients, but such
arrangements are inherently unstable. Other patrons
conceivably can and do usurp control of any access
point when they acquire enough power or influence.

Dissatisfied clients can attach themselves at will to
other patrons. This characterization fits the general
picture of the economy of the early Roman empire that
has been sketched in previous pages.

A special type of patron--one who mediates
between patrons and clients--has been identified under
the label "broker":

> In segmented societies, central authority is firm-
> set but in urban centres rather than throughout the
> countryside. Mediators or brokers are required to
> provide links between these two segments of the
> society.[68]

Jeremy Boissevain offers a more general, theoretical
formulation concerning the role of the broker:

> The resources which a patron controls are of two
> types. The first are those such as land, work,
> scholarship funds, which he controls directly. The
> second are strategic contacts with other people who
> control such resources directly. The former I call
> first order resources; the latter second order
> resources . . . Mayer calls the dispensing of what
> I call first order resources patronage, the
> dispensing of second order resources brokerage
> (underlining his).[69]

Brokers thus stand at key points in social networks.
The patron is more limited in action than the broker,
because the patron must actually deliver. The broker
merely needs to promise to deliver. The broker's
credibility and social standing, however, ultimately
hinge on the ability to establish in fact connections
between client and patron.[70]

The aptness of this perspective for the work of
Jesus is suggested, first of all, by Blok's definition.
Jesus' itineracy and his apparent ability to move

between rural settings and larger population centers, meant he was provided with some of the social skills of the broker.

More generally, one may consider how patronage-brokerage-clientelism structure movements of protest or rebellion in societies similar to that of first-century Palestine. Frequently encountered in such movements are the bandit leader, who is in fact a rebel patron. Another type of rebel patron is "a new type of religious leader carrying a new message of salvation to the downtrodden." This type of religious leader "restructures or organizes his 'clients' into a new solidary community."[71] This latter type brings into focus a number of aspects in Jesus' work and in the Jesus movement.

Jesus played the role of patron-broker in at least two senses. First, he mediated as a healer and holy man between a divine patron and sick or demon-possessed "clients." This aspect of Jesus' ministry has been discussed a great deal lately.[72] Miracle working has not, however, been a major concern in the present study. Only the discussion of the Lord's Prayer in the last chapter indirectly touched upon Jesus' power to mediate between God as liberating patron and indebted clients.

Secondly, Jesus mediated between wealthy patrons in socially stratified, first-century Palestine and an impoverished and hungry clientele. So we would like to understand the phenomenon of eating with "tax collec-tors and sinners." Perhaps Jesus addressed his message of the kingdom of God specifically to acquaintances who were originally patrons in his occupational role as carpenter (e.g. the sons of Zebedee). Otherwise, he improved his skill at brokerage through plying his trade generally.

The sinners were often destitute or economically marginal--prostitutes, practitioners of dispised trades, beggars, those with various diseases, and so on.[73] The tax collectors had some likelihood of being well-to-do, but they were socially ostracized (Levi, Zacchaeus). The ministry of Jesus served as a catalyst for this table fellowship. We cannot help but suspect that the mutual aid symbolized in eating together carried over into other spheres of these peoples' lives as well.

This aspect of the ministry of Jesus was preserved in the "love communism" of the primitive Christian community in Palestine. Scholars have, of course, questioned the historical veracity of the picture preserved in the Acts of the Apostles, but there is certainly a substantive connection between the behavior described and Jesus' message as it can be perceived in the gospels.[74]

One final point needs to be made. That Jesus assumed the role of broker at times, is undeniable. That he intended thereby to endorse patronage as a general system, or to magnify his own role, can seriously be questioned. There are strong indications everywhere in the gospels that Jesus was self-effacing (c.g. Mk. 10:45) and that he expected "brokerage" to be a mark of his disciples and of God's reign (Mk. 0.34-35; 10:43; 14:7; Mt. 5:9; Lk. 6:27-35). Patronage and charity were temporary expedients that were to give way before the egalitarian community of the kingdom of God.

D. Conclusion

Jesus' work as a semi-rural artisan made a strong contribution to the substance of his religious ministry. Jesus' occupation as a carpenter took him

not only to other villages and perhaps to the large
estates in the Esdraelon Plain (experience which manifests itself in his parables), but in all probability
also to major urban centers of Palestine. Itineracy
consequently gave him opportunities for broad social
contacts, taking him far beyond the confines of his
village cultural horizon. Jesus gained experience of
the patronage system through the contracts he landed as
a carpenter. The social contacts Jesus made cut across
social, religious, and economic boundaries. Yet this
very experience simultaneously contributed to under-
mining patronage as a permanent solution to the maldistribution of wealth. Jesus, as we have seen, envisioned a far more radical and egalitarian solution.

There is some reason to suspect that people who
were acquainted with Jesus prior to events related in
the gospels hold prominent positions in that tradition.
The gospels show the continuation of itineracy and the
on-going expansion of social contacts in the ministry
of Jesus. Jesus had an interest in connecting his
previous acquaintances with an ever-larger network of
people under the aegis of the kingdom of God.

This argument, of course, does not constitute a
complete "explanation" for the Jesus movement. The
argument is intended to offer insight into certain
related phenomena of the ministry of Jesus. In this
limited sense, therefore, it seems possible to speak of
a formative economic aspect or factor in the ministry
of Jesus.

Notes to Chapter 5

[1]See Appendix 1.

[2]Case, (1927) vi.

[3]The American scholar Chester McCown also devoted attention to Jesus from a social point of view: McCown (1928) and (1929). The work of Case and McCown was substantially better and more critical than other efforts, for example Mathews (1971). Indirect inspiration for the writing of this chapter has come from Hock (1980).

[4]Waetjen, (1976) 28f supplies this insight. Both Luke and John delete reference to Jesus' occupation as a carpenter. Taylor, (1953) 300 thinks the Matthean formulation was originally in Mark's gospel as well. The aristocratic reproach of men like Celsus in the late second century ("Jesus was a bastard and a mere artisan") may have provided a motive for the creation of a strong MS tradition (including it seems P^{45}) favoring Matthew's formulation in texts of Mark; see Stevenson, (1957) 138.

Though there is a metaphorical use of the word "carpenter" in rabbinic literature (to refer to a "master" of the law), the Jesus tradition only seems to point to a literal meaning of the term for Jesus; cf. Jastrow, 1:876, s. v. nagar.

[5]Klausner, (1925) 177f, 233. See Applebaum, (1976) 684 and EJ (1971) 1042.

[6]McCown (1928).

[7]Ibid.: 176. Cf. Moulton and Milligan, (1980) 628f and Taylor, (1953) 300.

[8]McCown, (1928) 175.

[9]This topic was adumbrated in Chapter 1. On the extent of division of labor, see Klausner, (1925) 177.

[10]Wolf, (1962) 539. Wolf includes photographs of the tools of Egyptian carpenters and tools brought to light by archaeology. Cf. "Holzbearbeitung," in Galling, (1977) 147-49.

[11]Finegan, (1969) 27.

[12]Translated by and cited from Finley, (1973) 135; his characterization of the text.

[13]Klausner, (1925) 178 n. 29: Based upon Halevy's Shemoth 'Arê Eretz Yisrael in Yerushalayim, ed. Luncz, 4:11-20.

[14]Klausner, (1925) 178: Fishermen at Bethsaida, dyers in Transjordanian Magd'la, jarmakers at Kefar Hananya and Kefar Sihin, etc.

[15]This may be the original basis for Halevy's suggestion, mentioned above, though I have not been able to consult the work cited by Klausner. Consider Jastrow, 1:875 (niger = "to saw"), 2:918-19 (nasar and neser = "to saw" and "planed board" respectively), 2:915b (nesôreth = "chips, sawdust").

[16]See Rosenthal, (1961) 14f. On "g" sound of 'ayin compare Hebrew Ebal and Greek (LXX) Gabela; cf. Hebrew forms of Gomorrah, Gaza. Also in the last-mentioned lemma of Note 15 a quote from J. Shabb. 4.1.6[d] [bottom], "we read nesôreth, the teachers of the house of Rabbi read ne'ôreth [i.e. with 'ayin], which shows that both mean the same."

[17]Lenski, (1966) 278.

[18]Jeremias, (1969a) 112; EJ (1971) 1044. This is an urban viewpoint, to be sure, but its wisdom applied also to rural areas.

[19]MacMullen's view, (1974) 14 may be recalled again, viz., that there were few rural specialists in antiquity. Skilled artisans gravitated to the cities. Finley, (1973) 135 agrees.

[20]McCown, (1928) 182. Also Wolf, (1962) 539.

[21]Turkowski, (1968) 30, (1969) 103.

[22]McCown, (1928) 181, 186.

[23]Ibid.: 186. Wolf, (1962) 539.

[24]McCown, (1928) 188.

[25]To repeat what was mentioned earlier, Tos. B. M. 9.14 details how the produce of the threshing floor is to be justly divided to pay first the tax collector and all who have done work for the farmer, lastly the landlord; cited in Kippenberg, (1978) 148.

[26]Childe, (1964) 248, 266, 283. Again Xenophon's observation, Finley, (1973) 135.

[27]Case, (1927) 201.

[28]Ibid.: 205. Compare the views of McCown, (1929) 334.

[29]Case, (1927) 205.

[30]McCown, (1928) 179f; EJ (1971) 1043.

[31]McCown, (1928) 181.

[32]McCown, (1928) 188 cites the Latin text from a (medieval?) Historia Joachim et Anna [out of Thilo's Codex Apocryphus (1832) 1:368, which I have not been able to consult directly].

[33]McCown, (1928) 188 n. 4.

[34]Funk, (1985) xviii, 303, 305. Michaelis, (1971) 740 n. 17.

[35]Lk. 1:5-6, 8. GosEbion 3 in Funk, (1985) 2:366. PJas 8:3 even thinks John's father a high priest!

[36]Was Jesus perhaps referring to John's father in Mt. 23:35 = Lk. 11:51? Cf. PJas 24:2. On attempts to make this identification, see Fitzmyer, (1985) 2:951.

[37]Conzelmann, (1973) 31f. Goguel, (1960) 2:233-252.

[38]Eusebius EH 3.20.1-6. See the discussion in Hennecke-Schneemelcher, (1963) 1:423.

[39]Hennecke-Schneemelcher, (1963) 1:427.

[40]Taylor, (1953) 233. The difficulty with this view is that a "ḥ," rather than "k," would be expected in the transliterated "Clopas."

[41]See the discussion of Caird, (1962) 601-602. Brown, (1966) 1:XLIII, L-LI.

[42]Brown, (1966) 1:XLIII.

[43]Taylor, (1953) 234.

[44]Ibid. I do not accept the view that this appellation identified Judas as a *sicarius*.

[45]Despised trades according to M. Sanh. 3:3 were: Dice player, usurer, pigeon flyer, trafficker in seventh-year produce; according to B. Sanh. 25b and B. B. K. 94b: Shepherd, tax collector, revenue farmer. Some of these, obviously, were not poor, as we shall speak of in a moment. See Jeremias, (1969a) 304, 307; Perrin, (1967) 92-94.

[46]Schottroff and Stegemann, (1981) 24-30.

[47]MacMullen, (1974) 11 documents the general vulnerability of women and children in antiquity.

[48]Wuellner, (1976) 339.

[49]Case, (1927) 268, 276, as far as I know, first observed the importance of itineracy in the study of Jesus. More recently, Theissen (1978) has taken this insight in an entirely different direction.

[50]Taylor, (1953) 278 discusses the variant traditions at Mk. 5:1. Gerasa is the *lectio difficilior*, because Gadara is the city territory closest to the lake. The reference, regardless of the name Mark originally wrote, points to the hinterland of a Transjordanian city.

[51]Cited in Klausner, (1925) 178; cf. (1971) 188. The rabbis thought the word meant "gardens of princes": Klausner, (1925) 262; Jastrow, 1:240a. Of course, many other scholars have traced the word back to the Old Testament "Sea of Chinnereth." Halevy's suggestion is not supported by ancient evidence or most modern etymological discussion, but it is not an impossibility.

[52]Jastrow 2:919a (top) provides evidence for carpenters as woodcutters. See again the list of common craftsmen in Klausner, (1925) 177: Timbercutter is not among them.

[53]Hennecke-Schneemelcher, (1963) 108.

[54]See Reicke, (1968) 126.

[55]The precise location of this wall can only be inferred: Finegan, (1969) 136.

[56]Monson, et al., (1979) Section 14-2.   See Klausner, (1925) 176.

[57]It must be noted that early Christian tradition places the Cenacle, the site of the Last Supper, on Mt. Sion in the southwest corner of the city.   See Finegan, (1969) 151.

[58]Hennecke-Schneemelcher, (1963) 148, 152.

[59]Translated in Hennecke-Sneemelcher (1963).

[60]Wolf, (1962) 539.

[61]EJ (1971) 1044.   Jeremias, (1969a) 112 notes that Shammai was a carpenter and identified by a square (according to B. Shab. 31a).

[62]See the discussion in Blair (1962).

[63]I had arrived at the basic ideas of this section before carefully reading Case's book. I am pleased to find that he had already stressed the importance of Jesus' social contacts and had pointed out that these were very extensive: Case, (1927) 199, 202, 206, 208.

[64]See the extensive bibliographic listing in Eisenstadt and Roniger, (1980) 43-46. A useful anthology, which also includes a bibliographic essay by J. Scott, is in Schmidt (1977).

[65]Blok, (1969) 365.

[66]Eisenstadt and Roniger, (1980) 73.

[67]Ibid.: 62.

[68]Blok, (1969) 369.

[69]Boissevain, (1969) 380.

[70]Ibid.

[71]See the discussion in Eisenstadt and Roniger, (1980) 75-76.

[72]For instance, Vermes (1973); Theissen (1983).

[73]In addition to the references in Notes 45-47 (Section B), see Freyne, (1980b) 161.

[74]Hengel, (1974a) 31-34, 91 (literature). The direct evidence of the Dead Sea Scrolls for the mutual aid practices of the Essenes has more recently strengthened the credibility of the picture in Acts. See Goppelt, (1980) 49 n. 32. The work on the Synoptic tradition by David Mealand (1980) supports this impression from another direction. Chapter 4 sought to show the coherence of Jesus' vision about the redistribution of goods coming with God's reign and the new family of the kingdom.

CONCLUSION

THE ECONOMIC VALUES IN THE WORDS
AND MINISTRY OF JESUS

> It was not so much the curse
> on the ground that needed
> lifting; it was the curse on
> human relationships.[1]

The preceding investigation has endeavored to
show that Jesus responded to certain fundamental economic questions of his day. Given categories appropriate
for looking at the issue in ancient context, it is
believed that such an intention is indeed perceptible
in the words and ministry of the historical Jesus. It
has been possible, moreover, to say something about the
content of "Jesus' economics" in the light of economic
realities and problems in early Roman Palestine.

Before proceeding to a summary of the findings
of this study, reviewing both the economic factors that
shaped Jesus and the economic values he invoked in the
name of God's imminent rule, it is first necessary to
say something about the general relationship between
social power (political realities), distribution of
goods (economic realities), and religion in Jesus'
Palestinian context. In a way, posing the question of
whether social power accrues to control of goods or
control of goods accrues to social power is the
proverbial chicken-and-egg question.

It is our impression that the possession or
control of strategic social or economic locations, and
not the mere possession of goods, is of primary

importance in the development and maintenance of social
stratification and power in agrarian contexts. Robert
Heilbroner's characterization of pre-market societies,
therefore, appears apt for the first-century Roman
empire generally and for Palestine particularly:

> In pre-market societies wealth tends to follow
> power; not until the market society will power tend
> to follow wealth.[2]

Social power in antiquity, in other words, was
evidenced predominately through the control of
"central" political or religious institutions--through
the control of religious media (temples), through
control of the state bureaucracy (emperor and imperial
family, senatorial and equestrian classes), through
control of administrative centers (decurions) or cities
on trade routes (Phoenician cities), through the
control of land by conquest (Rome) or legal. means
(large estates), and so on. This power implied in the
short run being at a strategic social location (whether
achieved or ascribed through birth), but required for
the long run the innate ability to stay in that
strategic location. One thinks, in this latter regard,
of the respective careers of Herod or Augustus. Competition for the relatively limited number of slots meant
only the "survival of the fittest."

We have seen the value, therefore, of talking
about distributive relationships in the ancient economy
by means of language developed in the study of patronage. We also acquired the insight, utilizing the terminology of Karl Polanyi, that central redistributive
institutions and hierarchical relationships were in
first-century Palestine encroaching more and more upon
older, village-based reciprocal types of exchange and
relatively horizontal kin relationships. The growing

problem of indebtedness in early first-century
Palestine was not just one of economics; indebtedness
reflected a situation of exploitation made possible by
the political direction of the Roman empire.

The ministry of Jesus was, then, a bid for
social power--just as was the first-century religious
activity of the Pharisees, Essenes, and Zealots.
Rather than representing the interests of a relatively
small number of religious specialists (Pharisees,
Essenes), Jesus appealed, apparently without strong
moral prerequisites, to the many disenfranchised rural
poor and stood for their interests. However, he did
not a priori exclude the wealthy (even the dishonest
wealthy) from God's rule.[3] Unlike the Zealots, Jesus
did not advocate violent means in the service of the
"end" of the reign of God (Mt. 11:12 = Lk. 16:16). The
means of the "religious ministry" was the only one
available to, or appropriate for, a rural artisan who
blessed peacemakers and cared for outcasts. Yet the
goals of Jesus' ministry were not simply religious, in
the modern sense of the word. Religious and economic
realities were bound up with social power in that
ancient context.[4] The reign of God was, so to speak, a
total social program.

Coming with the reign of God, with this social
vision of Jesus, was a new economic behavior. Jesus
was acutely aware of the harsh economic realities of
first-century Palestine, as his parables demonstrate.
These economic realities incarnated certain economic
values widespread in the early Roman empire. We
referred earlier to the landlord-peasant relationships
identified by Lang.[5] Two of Lang's categories,
"patronage" and "exploitation," are useful at this
point for epitomizing the economic values and behavior

against which Jesus vigorously campaigned in the name
of God's reign. The third category, "partnership"
holds out a model for Jesus' own position.

Patronage establishes a mutual, though unequal,
relationship between patron and client. This relationship is multistranded. The patron protects and feels a
certain responsibility for the peasant and his family.
The peasant pays part of the crop to the patron in
return for these benefits. There is generally some
shared risk in the harvest. The landlord usually lives
on the estate in a villa or castle.

Partnership also involves shared risk in agricultural production. Harvests normally are divided
according to contract, rather than custom, to protect
the rights of both parties involved. Under certain
conditions an "entrepreneur" landlord (perhaps a merchant) supplies the necessary equipment to the peasant
by which he works the land or supplements a strictly
agricultural income (through weaving, for example).
This type of relationship appeared at various times and
places in Mediterranean antiquity, at least with certain forms of commercial agriculture. Because of
unequal power distribution in such relationships,
the normal trend was away from partnership and toward
either patronage or exploitation.

The growth of urbanism, such as can be seen in
the late Hellenistic and early Roman periods, has often
resulted in the crass exploitation of traditional peasantries. The relationship between (a frequently absentee) landlord and peasant is reduced to a singlestrand:
The owner's interest in profitability or the peasant's
obligation to pay the rent. Hence, loyalty or reciprocity are qualities lacking in the relationship. To the
contrary, there will be mutual suspicion (as perhaps in

Lk. 13:6-9) or hostility (Mk. 12:1-12). This exploitative attitude can appear in any strong central economic
institution of an agrarian society. Consequently, the
phenomenon might generally be characterized as the
exploitative pattern or exploitative centralism.

It is necessary to make clear the common set of
assumptions that underlay patronage and the exploitative pattern in antiquity. Despite the recognizable
differences, both types of relationships were under-
girded by the self-sufficient ethos of the household
economy. In the one case, patronage (seen at various
times and under various conditions in the Roman empire)
assumed that the rural household of the patron would
produce just enough surplus to support a natural
economy at that level of social organization. This
economic orientation discouraged specialized farming
and extensive trade relationships. The peasant-
dependents became property of the patron household
socially and economically.

In the other case, exploitative relationships
carried self-sufficiency to the opposite extreme. For
instance, urban exploitation of the agricultural
producer often engendered in bourgeois landlords a
"political" egocentrism and plans for self-
aggrandizement insensitive to the suffering of the
countryside. Under the early Roman empire this
arrangement presupposed, of course, strong trade and
administrative relationships between urban areas. In a
very real sense, the cities were allied against the
countryside. Peasant and urban household were set at
odds, with mutually exclusive interests.

Thus, whereas patronage promoted "soft" relationships of domination and dependence (though peasant
households might have wished to become independent),

the exploitative pattern encouraged a "harsh" domination at the same time as the owning class was striving
for some kind of cultural independence from the low-
life producing class ("boors," "uncultured").[6]

Only in the instance of partnership, at least
ideally, is the interdependence of tenant/food-producer
and landowner/non-agricultural specialist emphasized.
There is potentially the insight of the equal value of
the partners, of agricultural producer and specialist.
It is difficult to say in the abstract how this insight
might be activated, or what types of people might be
the carriers of such an insight.

Lang unfortunately says little about the
"entrepreneurs" involved in partnerships, or about the
historical incidence of their pattern in antiquity. It
can be suspected that the top and bottom social strata
of agrarian societies either are not directly aware of,
or would not appreciate, the notion of partnership.[7]
The notion of partnership would probably be used by the
upper classes either to justify patronage or to
cynically manipulate the lower. We have gotten a
glimpse through Mk. 12:1-12 and Lk. 12:16-21 of how
landlord and peasant might evaluate such a stratified
and conflicted situation. Both elements are trapped in
their class-specific values of self-sufficiency and
drives for independence.

Merchants and artisans, however, seem to be
placed in a unique social position. Merchants are not
well integrated into the dominant mores and have independent means (and so do not entirely appreciate the
aristocrat's or oligarch's need for landed security).
Merchants are well-travelled and have experienced a
broader cultural horizon. Therefore, they can understand the need for mutual dependence. Urban artisans

may not share in this perspective directly, but rural
artisans like Jesus who may have carried their trade
about in order to make ends meet just might. The broad
social contacts of Jesus, we have argued, did play a
significant role in shaping his ethical stance and
socio-religious values.

The historical context of Jesus, therefore,
reflects a social and economic situation in which
exploitative urbanism, powerful redistributive central
institutions like the Roman state and Jewish Temple,
concentration of land holdings in the hands of the few,
rising debt, and disrupted horizontal relations in
society were becoming the norm. This increasingly
oppressive situation can be depicted as in Figure 4 (p. 212).

As the figure shows, patronage relations at
least offered some hope of "balanced" redistribution,
that is, where the appropriation of the peasant's crop
might receive some type of return, say, in the form of
physical protection or material help in hard times.
However, the role urbanism played in maintaining Rome's
imperium, along with the ideal of self-sufficiency
everywhere, encouraged acquisitive attitudes, insensitive exploitation of the agricultural producers, and
the worship of Mammon. Throughout the first century
B.C.E. and the early years of the empire, therefore,
political realities contributed strong pressures toward
the centralization of economic goods and the development of the exploitative pattern. The redistribution
of these goods was essentially unbalanced, going more
to the adornment of urban edifices and fostering of
urban culture than to the betterment of the circumstances of the primary producer.

At the village level, economic and political
pressures disrupted the traditional social fabric.

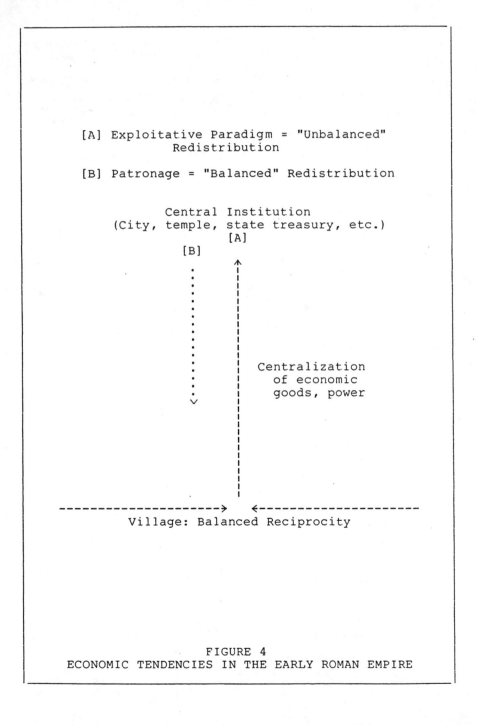

FIGURE 4
ECONOMIC TENDENCIES IN THE EARLY ROMAN EMPIRE

Rigorous accounting of debts and balanced exchanges
became the norm, a fact graphically illustrated in one
of the similitudes of Jesus:

> . . . although he will not give to him . . .
> because he is his friend, on account of his shame-
> less acquisitive desire [anaideian] . . . he will
> give to him . . .[8]

Jesus did not see the economic problems of his
time and place as a function of "too few pies." The
curse, to allude to McCown's poetically satisfying
formulation, was not so much upon the ground. At any
rate, Jesus believed God would provide. The imminence
of God's reign meant that the curse to be struggled
with now, lay more upon human relationships. Future
economic pies would have to be divided differently.

Jesus responded to his economic situation,
therefore, by advocating three apparently interlocking
agendas: First, he called for a reversal of the
centralization of political power and economic goods.
This decentralization would amount to a "general"
redistribution of all goods and evidently the destruction of central politico-economic institutions. Along
with this may have gone the hope for the abolition of
private property (Mammon). Here it needs to be
observed that Jesus probably prophesied against the
Temple and that his prophecy was perhaps the precipi-
tating cause for his crucifixion.[9]

Secondly, Jesus populated his parables with many
"middle" people: Stewards of estates (Lk. 16:1-9),
slaves with responsibility (Mt. 18:23-35), the slaves
and son of the good landowner (Mk. 12:1-12). Jesus
empathized with these middle people. He saw in them a
key ingredient to changing the situation, because they
were neither insensitive and "self-sufficient" as their

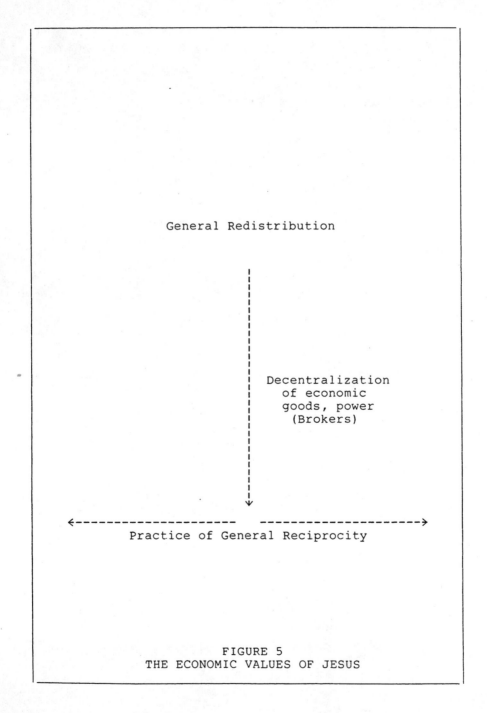

FIGURE 5
THE ECONOMIC VALUES OF JESUS

masters, nor hostile and oriented to survival as the
peasantry. These middle people, whether as brokers or
"outlaws," offered some tangible hope for alternative
behavior that could reverse and change the situation
for the better. Our previous discussion of Jesus and
patronage has shown how he regularly adopted the role
of broker between patron and client. It is clear that
Jesus took to heart the saying: "From everyone to whom
much is given, much will be required" (Lk. 12:48).

These two agendas were only at the threshhold of
the economic reign of God--the achievement of a social
fabric that is not exploitative, that satisfies human
need, that democratizes access to material goods. The
destruction of central institutions and the role of
intermediaries was only an initial step.

The third economic agenda of Jesus showed the
way into, or struggled to actualize, an important
aspect of the reign of God. For its practitioners, at
any rate, here was "realized eschatology." Jesus
advocated as a norm of the kingdom exchanges based upon
general reciprocity (Sahlins)--giving without expecting
in return. The Good Samaritan epitomizes this
behavior. The ruthless accounting of debts and
balanced exchanges are renounced (see Figure 5 (p. 214)
and compare with Figure 4 (p. 212)).

General reciprocity, the giving of gifts, was an
early strategy of the human species designed to
foster the unity of the family and to propitiate the
potential enemy. For Jesus, this practice of general
reciprocity marks a way back toward human solidarity in
an age of insensitive egoism and brutality, back toward
the reestablishment of kinship. This kinship is not,
however, restricted to the narrow horizon of the
village or tribe. There seems to be implied in the

Jesus tradition a genuine quest for universalism. Love
for enemies is an ethical corollary of indiscriminate
economic exchanges based upon general reciprocity (Mt.
5:44 = Lk. 6:35).

Furthermore, the practice of general reciprocity
expresses in a profound way human dependence upon the
graciousness of God, God's willingness and ability to
provide for material human need. Yet this practice
that establishes a community also establishes a human
mechanism for meeting material need. The theme of
God's providence in the Jesus tradition is at the same
time the theme of constructing a society in the image
of God.

The themes traced above in the message and
ministry of Jesus point to a new order based upon
partnership and interdependence (to resume Lang's
terminology). The new economic values envisioned by
Jesus are not, from this perspective, entirely utopian.
His message and behavior emerged out of concrete--even
if fleeting--experiences of partnership. His own
experiences as an artisan-broker supplied a reservoir
of insight. Yet Jesus' attempt to establish through
his ministry truly interclass partnerships--with the
potential to effectively destroy the basis for a class
society--superficially assumes a utopian aspect in the
eyes of the historian because of its "idealistic"
grounding in a message about the kingdom of God.
Otherwise, Jesus' economic views might strike us as a
repristination of "primitive" exchange or a presagement
of marxism.

Of course, Jesus' position is not established upon
historical study or philosophical analysis of relations
of production. He is obviously an acute observer of
"relations" of production, of the class struggle

inherent in his social environment, and so forth. But
his position seems far more to emerge from, in addition
to the socio-economic determinants explored earlier,
the confluence of his reading (or hearing!) of
Scripture, the folk wisdom he makes so much use of, and
his evaluation of the eschatological importance of the
times.

        Gerd Theissen is certainly correct in saying,
"Earliest Christianity began as a renewal movement
within Judaism brought into being through Jesus."[10]
However, the import of Jesus' ministry goes beyond
Jewish Palestine of the first century and beyond
theological issues. Jesus was also addressing problems
endemic to agrarian, indeed all class, societies. Even
if Jesus himself did not perceive his ministry as a
response to a set of conditions that have plagued all
historic societies, comparative social and historical
study can so perceive it.[11]

        It is not at all clear that a reappropriation of
the economic aspect in the Jesus tradition, whether by
the communities that gather in Jesus' name or by
western culture generally, can make a difference in a
world whose economic values no longer take into account
human need and whose debt laden, internationalized
economy is rushing with the inertia of a speeding
locomotive toward disaster. How can the hyper-
exploitative centralism of corporations and govern-
ments, the selfishness and greed that infect the hearts
of individuals, the staggering levels of indebtedness
and the depths of poverty--all compounded by the
callous disregard for human life and rampant military
expenditures--be counteracted? A curse, to be sure,
lies upon human relationships. Perhaps what is not
possible for human beings and institutions is somehow
possible for God (Mk. 10:27).

The twentieth-century world worships Mammon and advocates the survival of the fittest. Jesus points to a community based upon loving service to the least (Mk. 10:44) and worship of God alone (Mk. 12:29-31). The reign of God is at stake in this message, but so also is the survival of the human species.

Notes to the Conclusion

[1]McCown, (1929) 207.

[2]Quoted in Lenski, (1966) 229.

[3]Theissen, (1978) 38 (following H. Braun) speaks of a "lack of principle" in view of the ambivalent attitude of the Jesus movement toward wealth. We have tried to argue in the main chapters of the present work that Jesus himself bequeathed this attitude to the movement and tried to discover reasons for this in Jesus' intermediate social position.

[4]Burridge, (1969) 5 argues that "all religions are basically concerned with power."

[5]Lang, (1982) 50.

[6]See the "Lexicon of Snobbery" (Appendix B), in MacMullen (1974).

[7]Lenski, (1966) 284 is in mind here.

[8]Lk. 11:8. On this meaning of anaideian, see Moulton and Milligan, (1900) 33. We follow Bailey, (1976) 120-125 in seeing the second autou as translating a Semitic pronoun that should be understood reflexively.

[9]Theissen (1976). Cf. Pixley, (1981) 64-87.

[10]Theissen, (1978) 1.

[11]The word "historic" in "historic societies" has somewhat the connotation given to it by Bellah in his treatment of "Religious Evolution," (1970) 32-36. The experience of alienation in societies since about the first millennium B.C.E., and the aspect of world rejection in historic religions, has in part been a function of class antagonisms. The phenomena of "conscience" and the experience of divine transcendence reflect awareness of a tension between what is and what could be. Though modern ideologies have tried to discredit these expressions of historic religion, the modern world is not wholly bereft of them (just as it has not escaped class antagonisms).
While working on the final stages of this monograph, I became aware of similar work by the Scandinavian scholar Halvor Moxnes. Moxnes too has utilized the broad categories of economic anthropology,

especially Sahlins's notions of reciprocity, to
interpret features of the Gospel of Luke. As far as I
am aware, Moxnes is not directly concerned with the
historical Jesus. However, his work provides independent verification of the usefulness of economic
anthropology for the study of the Jesus tradition.

APPENDIX 1

THE NATURE AND DIFFICULTIES OF THE STUDY
OF THE HISTORICAL JESUS

The course of Jesus study in the twentieth
century has been anything but straightforward. As in
the nineteenth century, so in the twentieth, an enormous amount of print has been expended and discussion
offered on the problem of the historical Jesus. This
discussion has been carried on by people of all ideological persuasions--fundamentalists and radical
sceptics, marxists and Jews, Catholics and Protestants,
scholars and popularizers.

In the twentieth-century study of Jesus, German
Protestant scholarship has predominated. Up until
World War II, Roman Catholic scholars were hindered by
papal authority. British study in this area generally
manifested less critical, more traditional concerns.[1]
When modernism prevailed in America, as in the case of
the Chicago School, it entered into a rather static
debate with fundamentalism. American critical scholarship on the whole has had much in common with
nineteenth-century liberalism.[2]

Three central issues have inescapably imposed
themselves upon modern students of the historical
Jesus. The first is, of course, the problem of the
sources: The gospels of the New Testament, the only
extensive sources for the historical Jesus, seem
hopelessly to confuse confession of Jesus with the
truth about him, to substitute a faith-image of Jesus
for the man from Nazareth.[3] Succinctly stated, is it

221

any longer possible to recover the historical Jesus in
view of the nature of the sources?

Secondly and of a similar nature, the modern
historian interested in Jesus is confronted with the
problem of the interrelationship of history and
theology in the interpretation of Jesus. This problem
was raised most strongly at the end of the last century
by two scholars. From the one side, Ernst Troeltsch,
the "dogmatician of the comparative religions
school,"[4] asked whether it is any longer possible for
moderns to take seriously the theological dimension and
still to be true to historical reality. From the other
side, and quite apart from the question of possibility,
Martin Kähler asked whether it is even desirable or
warranted for faith to want to know about the historical Jesus. This radical scepticism about the theological value of Jesus was carried into the twentieth-
century discussion by the work of Rudolf Bultmann.

Still a third issue presents a stumbling block
to the student of Jesus. It also had its first modern
articulation at the end of the nineteenth century by
the proponents of the Social Gospel. This problem
involves the relationship between the religion of Jesus
and his social context. Each of these issues now needs
to be examined in somewhat more detail.

Outside of the New Testament there are only a
few references to Jesus of Nazareth. These references
are generally speaking hostile and colored by attitudes
toward the later Christian church.[5] From the time of
the Enlightenment, it has been generally recognized
that virtually the only historical materials of substance for a treatment of Jesus of Nazareth are those
contained in the New Testament itself. However, the
problems involved in the use of these sources for such

a treatment, that is, their actual value for writing a
history of Jesus' life and work, was not really grasped
for over a century afterward. This painful process of
discovery, traced by Albert Schweitzer in his great
book The Quest for the Historical Jesus, set the stage
for twentieth-century Jesus study.

        The difficulties of "life-of-Jesus" research, of
course, are well known to students of the New
Testament. This research essentially developed in
three phases.[6] The first phase, synchronous with the
German Aufklärung, witnessed the rise of rationalistic
interpretation of Jesus and the gospels over against
orthodox opponents. Thus, Reimarus concluded that
Jesus was a deluded messianic pretender whose
disciples--not wishing to work for a living after
Jesus' death--stole his corpse and founded Christianity. Reimarus did not publish his work during his
own lifetime. Only later did Lessing publish excerpts.
Needless to say, the "Wolfenbüttel Fragments" as they
were called, infuriated the orthodox. Other rationalist interpreters were less uncomplimentary to Jesus
and the disciples, but equally insistent that the
gospels as they stand are in need of an interpretation
that will bring the miraculous into harmony with a
rationalist world view.

        The second phase arrived with the publication in
1835 of David Friedrich Strauss's Life of Jesus,
Critically Examined. Strauss, who neglected to publish
anonymously and whose academic career was ruined
thereby, showed in his massive book that both the
rationalists and the orthodox supernaturalists were
wrong. A convinced Hegelian along with his teacher
F. C. Baur, Strauss utilized Hegel's dialectical and
speculative philosophy to explain the gospels in purely

idealistic terms: The idea of the unity of God and
humanity is the enduring result of Jesus' ministry.   In
this way it was inappropriate for Strauss either to
interpret the gospels as concealing behind the miraculous some actual events (as the rationalists) or to
take them literally (as did the supernaturalists).
These positions merely obscure the central issue.[7]

The third phase of life-of-Jesus research
emerged with liberalism, which reacted to Strauss's
radicalism on the one hand and to the orthodox position
on the other.[8] The liberal lives, which sought to
establish a modern Jesus-religion upon the ethical
principles and teachings of the Great Figure, reacted
equally severely to the dogmas of the church and to the
mythical result of Strauss. The Gospel of John was
excluded from this historical work because of its
manifest theologizing of Jesus' career. On the basis
of the Marcan hypothesis (Mark is the original gospel)
and the Two-source theory (Matthew and Luke used as
sources Mark and a Sayings-source "Q"), the liberal
lives of Jesus proceeded on their search for a
trustworthy authority for modern Christianity.
Schweitzer's book documents the ultimate failure of
this effort.

Why did the Old Quest fail? For Schweitzer the
life-of-Jesus research failed, because it did not
appreciate the historical distance separating Jesus
from modernity. As a result this research manifested a
subjectivism belying its scientific pretensions. The
claim of the liberal lives of Jesus to be scientific,
in other words, was vitiated by the multiplicity of the
pictures of Jesus that resulted. Each "biographer" of
Jesus had his own conception.[9] In Schweitzer's own
view Jesus was influenced by apocalyptic thinking.

Thus the key to Jesus' meteoric, but influential,
career lay in his dogmatic conception of his mission.
Jesus threw himself against the wheel of history--only
to be crushed.[10] Schweitzer acknowledged, nevertheless, that another interpretation was possible. Jesus
research in Schweitzer's time could be summarized in
terms of a dilemma: Either thoroughgoing eschatology
(konsequente Eschatologie) or historical scepticism.[11]

Wilhelm Wrede, a contemporary of Schweitzer,
represented the latter possiblility. Wrede's book Das
Messiasgeheimnis in den Evangelien (1901) formulated
thoroughgoing scepticism. Wrede sought to show that
the Gospel of Mark, the keystone of the liberal
historical quest, was itself founded upon a dogmatic
conception, namely the messianic secret. Wrede argued
that if one refuses to read anything into Mark's
account, one is compelled to admit that certain central
features of the gospel, crucial to its value as
historical source, can only come from Mark himself.
These features, like the incomprehension of the
disciples and the secrecy motif, are rooted in the fact
that Jesus' actual ministry was devoid of messianic
pretension. After the message of the resurrected
Christ began to be proclaimed, some way had to be found
to explain why Jesus was not known as such earlier.
This need the Marcan secrecy motif supplied. To see
this, however, is to see that Mark is no longer viable
as a historical source along the lines that the liberal
lives wanted to use it.[12] The work of Julius
Wellhausen also contributed to this sceptical result.
Wellhausen in many respects anticipated the work of the
later form criticism by suggesting that behind the
gospels lay oral tradition and a good deal of
redactional effort.[13]

Another blow was struck simultaneously at the
liberal lives. They had found their raison d'être in
the attempt to establish a modern religious ethic upon
the reconstructed biography of Jesus. The history-of-
religions scholars Albert Eichhorn, Wilhelm Heitmüller,
Richard Reitzenstein, Otto Pfleiderer, and Wilhelm
Bousset at the turn of the century began to show that
primitive Christianity was much more hellenized,
syncretistic, and cult-oriented than previously known.
These scholars also opposed the modernizing tendencies
of liberal theology and located the center of early
Christianity in the religious, not the ethical
sphere.[14] The Kyrios cult was oriented to a heavenly
Lord, not to an ethical authority in the past. The
Jewish Jesus of history began to look very parochial
indeed. Furthermore, comparative religious study
seemed to undermine the uniqueness and authority of the
New Testament when it documented many connections with
the contemporary religious world. New Testament
theology could be viewed as an aspect of first-century
religion.

Again whereas liberals like Harnack and Ritschl
conceived of the kingdom of God in a fashion quite
commensurate with liberal purposes, Johannes Weiss
pointed out, even before Schweitzer, that Jesus'
proclamation of the kingdom was really eschatological
and not adaptable to a bourgeois ethic. Schweitzer
himself came to speak of an interim ethic vis-à-vis
Jesus' moral demands--something that was only to apply
between Jesus and the coming of the end of the world.
In this way the intellectual basis of the nineteenth-
century quest for the Jesus of history, entwined as it
was with all sorts of romantic aims, eroded away.

The results of the nineteenth-century quest for
Jesus were the beginning point for twentienth-century
studies. It seemed as if an unmitigated scepticism
would hold the field, especially since some were
proposing theological reasons for abandoning the quest
(see below). After World War I the appearance of
dialectical theology and form criticism heralded future
developments. Karl Barth, of course, is invariably
mentioned as the person who opened once again the
question of bibilical hermeneutics for the modern age.
His Epistle to the Romans (first published in 1918), a
modern midrash on Paul's great text, threw down the
gauntlet to biblical scholars to find more of contemporary significance in the New Testament than had
liberalism. Although the theological "establishment"
reacted negatively to Barth's efforts, a young scholar
named Rudolf Bultmann gave a very positive assessment
of Barth's treatment of Paul's "subject matter" (though
Bultmann felt that Barth might have been too loyal to
Paul's expression of the subject matter).

     Bultmann belonged to a trio of important
scholars who opened the era of form-critical studies in
the gospels. Karl L. Schmidt showed in Der Rahmen der
Geschichte Jesu (1919) that the spatio-temporal framework of the gospels was a construct designed as a sort
of setting for the precious stones of the church's
traditional pericopes. Martin Dibelius and Bultmann at
about the same time brought out works that revealed how
these traditional pericopes had circulated for a while
free of any larger literary setting. They were the
arrows for missionary preaching, church discipline, and
the like, in the primitive community's traditional
quiver. Dibelius started his study in Die Form-
geschichte des Evangeliums (1919) from the vantage

point of the early church's missionary need for sermon
material and traced its forms down to their inclusion
in the first gospels. Bultmann, in the classic Die
Geschichte der synoptischen Tradition (1921), worked
back from the gospels to presumed Sitze im Leben, and
understood these in a broader way than Dibelius (cate-
chesis, church discipline, in addition to preaching).[15]

The convergence of thinking in these three
scholars was impressive. They seemed to demonstrate
not only that, but also why, the gospels were unreli-
able for writing a life of Jesus. The early Christian
community was not initially all that interested in
"Christ after the flesh" (a frequently cited text was 2
Cor. 5:16). The church's initial impulse was the
proclamation of the significance of the events, particularly the death and resurrection, related to the
person of Jesus, who is now the Christ. Only later,
perhaps after the death of the eyewitnesses or for
other reasons as we shall see below, was a need felt to
crystalize the Jesus tradition in the gospels. These
were, however, not biographies or history in the modern
sense, but kerygmatic accretions of tradition.

It may seem surprising, in view of the sceptical
climate prevailing in German biblical studies of the
first half of the twentieth century, that all of these
leading form critics wrote books on Jesus. All were
willing to grant that something could be known of Jesus
and his teaching. All, however, sifted through the
traditions critically. Bultmann set out as his own
agenda the encounter or dialog with the oldest Jesus
tradition in the Synoptic gospels.[16] In this, Bultmann
was interested characteristically in Jesus' self-
understanding or understanding of existence. Schmidt,
in his article in the second edition of Religion in

Geschichte und Gegenwart, and Dibelius, in his book
Jesus, as historians paid more attention to what can be
known about actions and events in the life of Jesus.
Thus, for instance, Schmidt discusses (where Bultmann
does not) questions of chronology, the historical
reality behind the tradition about Jesus' miracles, his
purifying of the Temple, and so on.[17]

The next logical step in gospel studies came
after World War II. Form critics of the gospels
characterized their authors as tradents or mere editors
of tradition. Yet it had been clear since the work of
Wrede that there was a creative ("dogmatic") tendency
in the treatment of the Jesus tradition. To whom was
this to be attributed? Form criticism laid the
emphasis upon the oral preaching stage of the Jesus
tradition, when the material was creatively applied to
various life-situations in the church. Now in the
post-war years, a new emphasis emerged as critics
perceived that the Evangelists themselves were authors
and creative theologians in their handling of
tradition. In this connection the names of Günther
Bornkamm, Hans Conzelmann, and Willi Marxsen play a
prominent role. Bornkamm's work on Matthew,
Conzelmann's study of Luke, and Marxsen's attention to
Mark brought the discipline of redaction criticism to
full flower. The English scholar Robert H. Lightfoot
had already some years before pointed in this
direction.[18] It required this new generation of
students on the Continent, however, to move gospel
studies forward from the fruitful, but incomplete, form
criticism.

Redaction criticism itself is, in hindsight,
simply a larger application of form-critical or
tradition-critical work--extended to the gospel genre.

Norman Perrin has written on this point:

> The views that we are here presenting as to the
> nature of the gospel tradition are the results of
> what may loosely be called 'form criticism',
> although technically one would have to use a whole
> array of German words to describe the various
> aspects of the work: Formgeschichte, Redaktions-
> geschichte, Redaktionstheologie, Traditions-
> geschichte, etc. We will . . . refer to them as
> 'form-critical' views.[19]

The final development that needs to be noted in
this connection is the post-Bultmannian "New Quest for
the historical Jesus."[20] Inasmuch as this is leading
us more and more into our second issue of history and
theology, we now turn to a consideration of that
problem.

If the nature of the New Testament sources,
particularly their "dogmatic conceptions" (Wrede), have
complicated any effort to use them for a historical
presentation of the words, actions, and aims of Jesus,
it is not surprising that so much of the twentieth-
century debate surrounding this problem has centered on
the relationship between history and theology.

Ernst Troeltsch is often credited with clearly
articulating in his article "Über historische und
dogmatische Methode in der Theologie" (1898) the aims
of nineteenth-century, "scientific" historiography.
Troeltsch identified three criteria operative in the
historian's presuppositions of the day that rendered
theological work along traditional lines problematic to
say the least. He wrote:

> Once the historical method is applied to Biblical
> science and church history, it is a leaven that
> alters everything and, finally, bursts apart the

entire structure of theological methods employed
until the present.[21]
The three criteria Troeltsch identified are those of
criticism, analogy, and correlation.[22]

The first criterion established that the
historian is compelled to make judgments about the
probability or possibility of causes and events, about
whether something really happened the way it is said to
have happened. The introduction of critical judgment
into thinking about the past and its claims (for
Christians, its claims upon us), seemed to have
challenged the basis for a trustworthy relationship to
the past and the validity of all tradition. For the
Christian community, this criterion seemed to have
annulled the basis for faith itself.

The second criterion challenged the assumption
of some that the work of the historian is concerned
with an utterly unique subject matter. For how then,
argued Troeltsch, could moderns have any basis for
understanding or relating to the past? The work of the
historian would seem to require some commonality, some
shared experience with his subject matter, to enable
comprehension at all. This is why analogy is so
important, to foster genuine understanding. For some
in the Christian fold, this principle of analogy
threatened a naive faith in miracles and even the tenet
of Jesus' resurrection itself. We no longer experience
miracles as people of the first century did. Furthermore, since no one else with critical acumen has ever
met a resurrected man, it is unlikely that the Easter
reports of the gospels are, in this view, to be interpreted literally.

For the more philosophically minded, however, a
different issue is at stake. The principle of analogy

is really an attempt to overcome the relativistic
impasse of historicism: How can there be any truth of
universal applicability in human experience, if there
is no common ground? How can there be understanding at
all without universality of experience? This is the
issue of particularist history versus comparativist
theory. It is not only an issue that confronts
historians, but one that social scientists have
wrestled with as well in trying to find a philosophical
basis for social theory other than some kind of
philosophical "imperialism." Without analogy, history
and human culture are consigned to the chaos of total
relativism. Without analogy, theology too must
question the validity of its own truth claims. Surprisingly then, Troeltsch's criterion is not without
relevance to faith, even if in some respects it has
been negative in its impact.

Yet the third criterion would seem to totally
rule out the validity of theology as a discipline. If
all historical events form a space-time continuum, if
all historical "parts" are related to the "whole" of an
epoch, and if there are no historical causes that
themselves do not have historical causes--as this
principle of correlation demands--then the notion of
God intervening in the historical matrix of causes and
events would appear to be utterly incompatible with a
modern historical world view. God is relegated to the
province of pre-critical, pre-scientific myth, as
indeed he has been by many modern students of religion.

If Troeltsch set an unmitigated negative tone
for twentieth-century theology, his contemporary Martin
Kähler set forth the positive agenda by discussing the
fundamental difference between the historical Jesus and
the historic Christ.[23] Kähler developed his ideas over

against the subjectivist theologies of J. C. K. von
Hofmann and ultimately Friedrich Schleiermacher.24
Kähler also distanced himself from the objectivism of
the historicist quest for the real Jesus. Kähler's
contemporary Wilhelm Herrmann, who stood within the
Ritschl--Schleiermacher camp, had said that the Jesus
of history was the ground of faith, the Christ of faith
the content. Herrmann attempted to mitigate the tension between the modern (historicist) conscience and
faith by giving to each its proper due and proper
sphere. The believer participated in the inner life of
Jesus as discovered by modern historiography.25 ' Kähler
by contrast argued that if the Jesus of history was the
ground of faith, then faith became subservient to the
results gained by expert historians (a prospect not
relished by a Protestant who placed high value in the
Reformation's sola fide). Furthermore, the basis for
faith became uncertain, because with each new picture
of Jesus drawn by the historians, faith would also have
to change. Thus, Kähler denied that the historical
Jesus had any relevance to faith. Only the picture of
Jesus in the gospels, the historic biblical Christ, has
relevance for faith through preaching. Kähler
essentially identified the historical Jesus and the
historic Christ. He insisted that this picture itself
was the ground and content of faith, not some content
supplied by subjectivity per se.

    In 1941 Bultmann, Kähler's twentieth-century
proponent, published a famous essay in which he
advocated his program of demythologization. Bultmann
claimed that it was no longer possible for moderns to
accept a three-story universe, or the picture of the
reign of an eschatological figure, or even that of a
resuscitated corpse. Such beliefs, Bultmann argued,

involved too much of a _sacrificium_ _intellectus_. He
went on to suggest that some effort was necessary to
reappropriate the content of mythological speech in
terms that moderns could appreciate. "The real purpose
of myth is not to present an objective picture of the
world as it is, but to express man's understanding of
himself in the world in which he lives."[26] The point
now is to interpret myth, not to do away with it as was
the case with the old liberals.[27] And the means by
which New Testament myth can be appropriated for today
is given in existential philosophy. Bultmann went on
to suggest how New Testament mythology speaks of human
beings being grounded in alien powers from which there
is need for redemption. Furthermore, Bultmann
distinguished act of God/resurrection language from
other kinds of myth. He believed that the former kind
of myth expresses something of more enduring significance than the "traditional" mythology. So Bultmann
acknowledged that there is a point beyond which
demythologization cannot go. His views, nonetheless,
were radical.[28]

          Bultmann's radicalism is evident in other post-
war works of his. In his Theology of the New
Testament, he states that Jesus is simply the presupposition for the post-Easter theological developments.[29] Jesus understood as God's decisive action is
the Dass; the Easter kerygma is the Was.[30] In many
ways Bultmann retains a quasi-liberal separation
between the Jesus of history and the Christ of faith.
The emphasis is different, however. As exegete and
historian, Bultmann is said to be sceptical about the
extent to which the actual Jesus can be known.[31] Van
Harvey and Schubert Ogden have shown how much Bultmann
can and does say about the historical Jesus.[32] And

Bultmann's book on Jesus could say much about Jesus'
(or the oldest Jesus tradition's) message. For
Bultmann the Christian, however, the stress falls upon
the kerygma about the Christ, because for him the Jesus
of history is hardly relevant to faith.

Much debate has focused around the historical
and theological ramifications of Bultmann's work.[33]
Norman Perrin has characterized the positions in this
post-Bultmannian debate in terms of center, right, and
left wing. In the center is Ernst Käsemann, a former
student of Bultmann. Käsemann delivered a famous
lecture in 1953 in which he expressed fundamental
historical and theological reservations about
Bultmann's scepticism regarding the connection between
Jesus and the kerygma. Käsemann points out that
Bultmann's later position heavily depends upon Paul and
John. Yet the presence of the Synoptic gospel material
in the canon must prove to be somewhat of an embar-
rassment for Bultmann, because it shows the early
Christians more concerned with the historical Jesus
than Bultmann will allow.[34] Käsemann sees in the
Synoptic tradition a movement against the docetic
stance of Christian "enthusiasts."[35] He senses also
that Bultmann's position likewise tends toward
docetism.[36] A Christ without some connection to the
historical Jesus is simply a ghost!

On the right stands Joachim Jeremias. Jeremias
has spent much time and effort studying the Jewish
milieu of Jesus. He concerns himself with the
ipsissima verba of Jesus or the question whether the
Last Supper was really a Passover meal. Perrin writes
of his former teacher: " . . . he has done more than
any other single scholar to add to our knowledge of the
historical Jesus."[37] Understandably, Jeremias's

Jerusalem in the Time of Jesus (German 1923, 1962[3]; ET
1969) has acquainted many New Testament scholars with
first-century Palestinian society. Jeremias also has
produced one of the fundamental modern works on the
parables of Jesus. He believes that Bultmann fundamentally erred by slighting the historical nature of
Christianity. For Jeremias there must be an essential
historical connection between Jesus and his ministry
and the post-Easter developments. So Jeremias can
claim that Jesus is indeed the presupposition for the
kerygma, but (pace Bultmann) only in the sense that
Jesus' words and his actions are carried on in the
early church:

> The gospel of Jesus and the kerygma of the early
> church must not be placed on the same footing, but
> they are related to one another as call and
> response.[38]

The left-wing criticism of Bultmann comes from
people like Schubert Ogden and Karl Jaspers. This
position queries that if Jesus only provides us with an
existential self-understanding, how can he be absolutely necessary to the process? Could such an understanding be gained through some other means? These
critics, then, stand even closer than Bultmann to the
older liberal view of "Jesus as example."[39] Jesus
conveys a timeless truth, but is himself dispensable.
Ogden suggests that the reverse of this argument is the
dispensability of Bultmann's "act of God" language.
This is radical demythologization.

The New Quest of the historical Jesus,
represented particularly by Ernst Fuchs, Gerhard
Ebeling, and James M. Robinson, pursues what was
thought to be a whole new approach to the problem of
the Jesus of history and the Christ of faith.[40] It

attempts to move beyond Bultmann's historical scepticism, as well as his theological conclusions. The New
Quest devotes itself to documenting how an essential
connection lies in the understanding of existence con-
veyed by Jesus to the church. This existential understanding is seen by the New Quest to be fundamentally
the same in each case. Even more than Bultmann and
Jeremias, the New Quest understands the link between
the church and Jesus to be the Word--Jesus' word brings
faith to expression, which evokes faith and the
church's testimony.[41] So the New Quest speaks of
Sprachereignisse or Wortgeschehen ("language-" or
"word-events").

        Van Harvey in his book The Historian and the
Believer (1969) raises the same question of the New
Quest as the left-wing critics raised against Bultmann:
If the fundamental concern of the kerygma is with
Jesus' existential self-understanding or faith, then is
it not possible to detach that self-understanding from
the bearer of it? Is this not in essence to speak of a
timeless truth?[42] Herbert Braun has perceived this
problem as a result of his theological study of the New
Testament: He states that the anthropology of the New
Testament is the constant, the christology is the
variable.[43] If this declaration is true, and Käsemann
at least vociferously denies its validity,[44] then New
Testament scholarship must reevaluate the particularism
of its claims about Jesus.[45] As Harvey has seen, the
New Quest really represents a retrogression to a
position similar to Wilhelm Herrmann's. Herrmann, it
will be recalled, resolved the tension between the
historical Jesus and the Christ of faith by saying that
Jesus constituted the ground of Christian faith, which
participated in Jesus' inner faith-consciousness. This

is, _mutatis_ _mutandis_, precisely the existentialist
position of the New Quest. Bultmann too noticed
this.[46]

Norman Perrin, commenting upon the essay by
Käsemann mentioned above and the by-path taken from it
in the New Quest, writes:

> So the discussion [sc. after Käsemann] ought to
> have turned to an intensive consideration of the
> synoptic tradition, especially since we now had
> form criticism to guide us as to the true nature of
> that tradition, but unfortunately it did this only
> in part. The issues which were taken up most
> immediately and most vigorously in the subsequent
> discussion were, rather, those of the question of
> continuity between the Christ of the kerygma and
> the historical Jesus, and of the significance of an
> existentialist view of history in connection with
> the 'problem of the historical Jesus.'[47]

As both Käsemann and Perrin stress, the reason there is
a problem at all regarding the historical Jesus is
because of the presence of the Synoptic gospels in the
New Testament canon. The rest of the New Testament
(with a few exceptions) would seem to support a
Bultmann-type position. The Synoptic material by
contrast has some paraenesis and mythological overlay,
but also historical material and historicizing
tendencies.[48] What does this fact mean?

Perrin makes a fundamental set of distinctions
in his book on the teaching of Jesus. Perrin believes
it is imperative for the clarification of the whole
debate about the historical Jesus to distinguish three
kinds of knowledge: First, there is knowledge about
Jesus that must meet criteria applied to all historical
knowledge. Secondly, there is the knowledge of Jesus

that would see him as a significant historical figure
like any other of the past. Thirdly, there is
knowledge of Jesus that is significant only in the
context of specifically Christian faith. Thus, Perrin
points out, Bultmann's position fairly well distinguishes and keeps separate the three categories of
Jesus-knowledge, although Bultmann admits only a small
amount to the first category. The right-wing critics
of Bultmann collapse the first and third categories of
knowledge: Jesus-as-he-was is very closely tied to
faith in him. The left-wing critics collapse the
second and third categories: Jesus is only a significant figure of the past. Perrin himself declares that
he too, like Bultmann, wants to keep the three kinds of
knowledge separate. Each of these kinds of knowledge
is subject to different kinds of tests.[49] All categories are, nonetheless, interrelated.

As corroboration for the fundamental accuracy of
Perrin's epistemological procedure here, the work of
Van Harvey can be mentioned. Harvey makes a similar
set of distinctions. He speaks of "levels of meaning"
in regard to Jesus of Nazareth.[50] It is possible to
speak of Jesus as he really existed (1), although no
one except his contemporaries can ever know him in this
way. The actual Jesus supports inferences about the
historical Jesus (2) via all available sources about
his life. Next Harvey refers to a memory-impression of
Jesus (3), related to the historical Jesus but
distinct, which Harvey compares to a kind of bas-
relief: All irrelevant details are chiseled away; only
the essential elements of a memory-picture remain.
This memory-impression conveys a sympathetic perspective of Jesus. Finally, it is possible to speak of the
biblical Christ (4) or "the transformation and altera-

tion of the memory-impression (or perspectival image)
under the influence of the theological interpretation
of the actual Jesus by the Christian community."[51]

That twentieth-century New Testament scholarship
has been preoccupied with the interrelationship of
history and theology, as well as the tension between
the historical Jesus and the Christ of faith, is amply
documented in its concern with eschatology and
christology.

Since the work of Weiss and Schweitzer, the role
of eschatology and apocalypticism in the message and
ministry of Jesus has been of central concern in New
Testament scholarship. It is a commonplace of contemporary New Testament studies that the message of Jesus
centers upon the imminent arrival of the kingdom of
God.[52] Over the past decades, the theological significance of this message has been explored again and
again.[53] Along with this discussion of the meaning
behind Jesus' proclamation of the kingdom, there has
been debate regarding the interrelationship in Jesus'
message between the future references to the kingdom
and the present references.[54] Furthermore, it has been
a continuous point of contention among biblical
scholars as to just how the eschatological reference in
the proclamation is to be correlated with human ethical
behavior. A. Schweitzer thus came to speak of an
interim ethic in this regard, believing that Jesus'
apocalyptic stance rendered all human activity super-
fluous.[55] Others have demurred, arguing that the
strenuous statements attributed to Jesus in the Sermon
on the Mount express the essence of life in the coming
kingdom.

Many of the words and parables of Jesus, far
from carrying an apocalyptic flavor, are preoccupied

with the mundane sphere. That is to say, many of Jesus'
recognizably authentic words themselves point to the
here and now and dissolve the problem of eschatology
and ethics by grounding response to the message in
"what is perfectly natural." Bornkamm has noted this:

> We have repeatedly drawn attention to the signifi-
> cance of the 'wisdom sayings' in Jesus' preaching.
> Their characteristic is this, that they appeal
> immediately to the knowledge, experience and under-
> standing of man, and reject all necessity for out-
> side proof . . .[56]

A similar observation is made by Conzelmann.[57] The
point is underscored by Jesus' use of a typical wisdom
form, the parable.

Too-great an attribution of apocalyptic thinking
or eschatological orientation to Jesus might utterly
mislead, so far as understanding the significance of
his ministry is concerned. Apocalyptic thinking, as it
has been preserved for us in the ancient Jewish
pseudepigrapha, was manifestly an esoteric intellectual's game. Jesus' message and ministry was, as far
as now can be determined, exoteric in intention.
Treatments of his message like those found in Mark 4
and 13--painting Jesus' parabolic teaching as intentionally opaque and attributing apocalyptic discourses
to him--are now seen to be later constructs of the
primitive Christian community. Jesus' parabolic
teaching was not intentionally esoteric, unless
political factors forced Jesus to veil his speech.[58]
Furthermore, it seems hard to square the Synoptic
Apocalypse with statements of Jesus like that in Lk.
17:20-21.[59]

The historical judgment that Jesus did not
promulgate esoteric teaching and did not formulate his

message directly upon apocalyptic speculations would
seem to be corroborated by the work of G. Vermes, who
places Jesus generally within the category of the
Galilean Hasidim.[60] He argues that the Hasidim in
Galilee advocated a Judaism quite different from that
in Jerusalem. These were not the Torah-zealous of
Jerusalem, i.e. the Pharisees, nor were they ultra-
conservative like the wealthy Sadducees. Rather, like
Hanina ben Dosa, these Galilean Hasidim would seem to
have been charismatic leaders recognized by the
peasantry. Jesus' miracle-working and his storehouse
of agrarian wisdom confirm this general impression.

Along with the rigorous discussion of the
significance of eschatology in the words and activity
of Jesus, has gone a concern for the christological
titles attributed to him in the tradition. Much
research has been devoted to ascertaining whether any
of these titles reflect a "messianic consciousness" on
the part of Jesus. The general consensus seems now to
be that the christological titles have all been
attributed to Jesus by the early Christian tradition.[61]

As can be seen, the tension between history and
theology remains. What becomes clear for the student
of the historical Jesus is that there is still the need
for an Old Quest "flavor" in our thinking about the
tradition. The Old Quest in its innermost essence was
both a quest for the Jesus who provided the impetus for
the early Christian movement and an anti-ideological
exercise--first against the dogmatic conceptions of
Jesus in the church and later (when that battle was
fairly much won) against any tendentious reading of the
Christian past. Thus, Bultmann was bound to come under
attack for his position on the essential irrelevance of
Jesus for Christian proclamation. Bultmann's position

represents the mature fruit of a consistently applied
existential ideology. A similar critique needs to be
written, however, for virtually every effort to get
back to Jesus. Jeremias, whose work in every respect
has been admirable, might be accused, by a more
extensive application of the same methods he uses, of
an overstatement of the uniqueness and authority of
Jesus. The historical deficiencies of Jeremias's
theological position can be seen quite easily by
comparing it with Bultmann's: Whereas Bultmann emphasizes the continuity of Jesus with his environment and
the discontinuity between Jesus and Christianity,
Jeremias takes the reverse tack and emphasizes the
discontinuity of Jesus and his environment (authority
and uniqueness) and the continuity of Jesus' authority,
word, and work with the post-Easter church.[62] Yet both
positions paradoxically imply (as a function of their
German provenance?) that the church or Jesus
respectively is the end of Judaism!

In this way the theological _Tendenzen_ of
Jeremias and Bultmann are evident. Every student of
history and the gospels must be aware of those
ideological factors that play into historical and
theological work. While some of these, as indicated in
the two cases above, may well be philosophical or
theological in nature, others are definitely psycho-
logically, sociologically, nationally, geographically,
and historically determined. This consideration leads
us on to our third problem.

The third problem that confronts the student of
Jesus has been perceived at least since the end of the
nineteenth century and the Social Gospel movement.[63]
It is, namely, the problem of formulating the difficult
relationship between the religious ministry and message

of Jesus and the social conditions which shaped and
were addressed by that ministry and message. As
indicated just above, it is also a problem of
determining what are the predominantly "external"
factors working upon the exegete, influencing the kinds
of questions he asks and the kinds of information he
solicits from the past.

There seems to be in the biblical scholarly
establishment a certain amount of ambivalence toward,
if not outright rejection of, explicitly sociological
approaches in the discipline.[64] This might at first
sight seem surprising, since a sociological approach to
the New Testament was already advocated by the German
A. Deissmann in the early part of this century.[65]
Furthermore, the work of S. J. Case in America shows
that Deissmann did not constitute a lone voice in the
matter.[66] Even the work of the form critics in the
1920s might have urged a more comprehensive sociological study of the New Testament in the concern for
the setting of the early Christian traditions.

As the survey above has shown, these overtures
did not carry the day in New Testament studies. In
mid-century the scholarly establishment as a whole was
far more concerned with biblical texts, biblical
theology, and hermeneutical issues. The pendulum had
swung not only away from the historical concerns
evident in biblical studies at the turn of the century,
but also away from the incipient treatment of the past
from the standpoint of sociological thinking (the work
of Max Weber is the greatest monument to the possibilities of this approach to history). To be sure,
redaction critics, like the form critics, may have
sensed the "gravitational pull" of their subject matter
toward explicating the early history of Christianity

sociologically and showing the interrelationship of
Christian groups and the larger environment. If the
redactional work of an Evangelist, or a body of tradition, was to be understood in a communal context, why
not broaden horizons even further? Willi Marxsen,
pursuing some of the insights of E. Lohmeyer, can be
said to have pointed toward an incipient sociology of
early Palestinian Christianity. The only person who
seems to have worked consistently toward understanding
the environment was Jeremias.

The ambivalence or hostility of the scholarly
biblical establishment seems conditioned by its
reaction to the historical "firstfruits" of the
Enlightenment in the nineteenth century. Those
firstfruits came to clear articulation in the work of
Troeltsch, the Religionsgeschichtliche Schule, and in
the incipient sociological treatment of early
Christianity. Granted that American scholarship has
always remained somewhat more "liberal" than
Continental scholarship, even in America today there is
discomfort over the return to the use of such methods
in the heretofore (under the influence of the Germans)
exclusively theological domain. Is there any substance
to this aversion?

If sociological study shares in some of the evil
taint of Troeltsch's "purely historical" method, and
certainly shares similar philosophical presuppositions
(critical judgment, analogy as the basis for comparison, the interrelationship of social causes and
effects) there can be no doubt that the use of sociology in a theological discipline will introduce
problems. When all is said and done, however, what
really is at the root of these problems?

The chief points of contention for the establishment regarding the use of sociological models and
explanations would seem in substance to be two: 1) The
objection of historical particularism and 2) the objection of theological particularism.[67]

1) The objection of historical particularism is
the objection of the historical specialist. The use of
sociological models and theory for the study of the
past, it is claimed, is inappropriate to a unique
subject matter. The specialist argues that the bark on
the individual trees of the forest is of such uniqueness that it is inappropriate to class the trees together as forest. The specialist refuses to see the
forest! Data get played off against similarities
perceived through comparison. The specialist says,
"Dilettantes compare." If this argument is not sufficient, it is urged that there are insufficient data in
the Bible (if not all historical study) for a truly
sociological analysis.[68] Such a lack of data intro-
duces the danger of circularity into the historical
argument: The data are used to justify the comparative
theory, which in turn is used to explain the data.[69]

2) The use of sociological models and theory for
the study of ancient religion, particularly the history
of early Christianity, is also inappropriate to a
unique subject matter. The theological claims of Jesus
and the early church, in other words, cannot simply be
explained (implicit is "explained away") by sociology
in terms of other factors or variables.[70] Furthermore,
the interpretation of the Bible today is a special
province requiring special methods; the church's book
cannot be approached without certain faith presuppositions, or if it is, it cannot be expected to yield
purely historical information.

To 1) it may be countered that true, data cannot
simply be manipulated to fit into a theory, but will
"data" ever be intelligible without some advance notion
of "what they are" and without some a priori framework
with which to evaluate the data? To borrow Bultmann's
version of this question: "Is exegesis without presuppositions possible?" Furthermore, there are levels of
generalization recognized even among sociologists;
generalizations can be built up from or related to data
without doing violence to the data. It is not as if
the sole task of sociologists were to impose an alien
theory upon some sacrosanct body of data. Perhaps the
most damning critique of the particularist position,
however, is the one already leveled by Troeltsch (see
above): How can the past ever be understood by us
unless it is not totally unique? Analogy is as much a
tool of the historian as it is of the sociologist.

To 2) it may be countered that the relationship
between religio-theological expression and other
factors in society is more complex than either a strict
independence (as for theological particularists) or a
strict dependence (as for a materialist interpretation). The task of the social historian of early
Christianity must then be to explore the interrelationship, rather than to make a priori pronouncements
about the outcome of investigation. The particularist
historian of ancient Israel or Christianity is also
forced to acknowledge some relationship here anyway.

The foregoing objections are interrelated. They
can be helpfully elucidated by a methodological debate
that has existed for some time in the social sciences
regarding whether ethnography is best done by insiders
or outsiders, that is, whether the external interpretation or the internal interpretation is most valid.

Out of this debate have come the two terms emic and etic (on analogy with phon<u>emic</u> and phon<u>etic</u>) to describe the two approaches. The emic approach, then, requires learning the language and accepting more or less the values, principles, and viewpoint of the people to be understood, interpreted, or described. The etic approach requires the development of models and theories to elucidate one group or society on the basis of a comparative body of information on, or a comprehensive knowledge of, societies in general. The etic approach demands the comparative method. The emic approach assumes the absolute, incomparable uniqueness of the group studied. The biblical guild has traditionally, then, adopted an emic stance. It senses somehow a threat in any move to an etic stance.[71]

Why should the comparative method be so much of a threat? In truth, the question requires us to ask why <u>both</u> history and sociology should pose so great a threat to the theological guild. The Enlightenment is still with us, though its contours have taken on familiar shape by now. The resurgence of sociological interest among biblical scholars, perhaps because of the "re-enlightenment" of the 1960s, is in fact a return to the great questions of the nineteenth century.[72] The theological detours of the intervening years; the social experience of total war, colonialism, and imperialism, along with the realization in our times of human liberation in a multitude of forms; and finally the entry of the Third World into the discussion of the human condition--these must modify any naïve return to liberalism on our part. Nevertheless, there are certain interests of liberalism that need to be appreciated and reappropriated. Among them is a return to the consideration of the importance of Jesus for the human struggle.

Notes to Appendix 1

[1]Perrin, (1967) 24f.

[2]Harrisville, (1964) 172-196.

[3]Bornkamm, (1960) 13ff. Jeremias, (1969b) 8:
"Testimonies of faith."

[4]The characterization of Morgan, (1973) 10f.

[5]Cf. Conzelmann, (1973) 12-16, especially the
references there to Klausner and Goguel.

[6]James Robinson has outlined a similar set of
phases in his introduction to a recent edition of
Schweitzer, (1968) xi-xxxiii.

[7]Schweitzer, (1968) 78-95; Dahl, (1962) 140.

[8]Perrin, (1969) 5.

[9]Schweitzer, (1968) 4.

[10]Ibid.: 370.

[11]Ibid.: 330.

[12]Perrin, (1969) 7-13.

[13]Ibid.: 14.

[14]Dahl, (1962) 143.

[15]Perrin, (1969) 15.

[16]Bultmann, (1958) 14.

[17]Dibelius (1949); Schmidt, (1969) 1·93-168.

[18]Perrin, (1969) 21.

[19]Idem, (1967) 25.

[20]Ibid.: 219ff.

[21]Quoted in Harvey, (1969) 5.

[22]On these see Harvey, (1969) 14ff.

[23]Kähler (1964).

[24]Braaten's introduction to Kähler, (1964) 11.

[25]Ibid.: 14-15.

[26]Bultmann, (1957) 10.

[27]Cf. Fuller, (1962) 3.

[28]Cf. Harvey, (1969) 139ff.

[29]Bultmann, (1951) 1:3.

[30]Harvey, (1969) 144.

[31]Perrin, (1967) 222.

[32]Harvey and Ogden, (1964) 205 and n. 21.

[33]Käsemann, (1964) 16.

[34]Ibid.: 30.

[35]Ibid.: 25.

[36]Cf. Käsemann, (1969) 57. See also Jeremias's statement, in (1969b) 22: "To isolate the message of Jesus leads to Ebionitism; to isolate the kerygma of the early church leads to Docetism."

[37]Perrin, (1967) 224.

[38]Jeremias, (1969b) 23.

[39]Perrin, (1967) 224.

[40]Harvey, (1969) 164ff.

[41]Ebeling, (1963) 296f.

[42]Harvey, (1969) 196.

[43]Ibid.: 178, 200; cf. Bultmann, (1964b) 36.

[44]Käsemann, (1969) 37.

[45]Cf. Bultmann, (1964b) 39.

[46]Ibid.: 30ff.

[47]Perrin, (1967) 226f.

[48]Perrin, (1967) 234; Käsemann, (1964) 24.

[49]Perrin, (1967) 240f.

[50]Harvey, (1969) 266.

[51]Ibid.: 267.

[52]Dodd (1961); Perrin (1967). Bornkamm, (1960) ch. 4.

[53]See, for example, Klein, (1972) 387-418.

[54]See the passages listed in Bornkamm, (1960) 90.

[55]Cf. Sanders, (1979) 474ff.

[56]Bornkamm, (1960) 106.

[57]Conzelmann (1976) especially under "3. Wisdom material in the NT. a. Jesus and the Synoptic gospels."

[58]See discussion in Chapter 3, Section B.

[59]Cf. Bornkamm, (1960) 69. Bultmann, (1963) 39f.

[60]Vermes (1973).

[61]Bornkamm, (1960) 226-231 [Appendix III]; Conzelmann, (1973) 36-50, 87-96 (+ lit.).

[62]The latter viewpoint also seems to be that of the New Questers, cf. Bornkamm, (1960) 83.

[63]E.g. Mathews (1971 = 1928); the work of Rauschenbusch; Case (1914); also Troeltsch (1980 = 1911). See Hopkins (1940); Scroggs, (1980) 165.

[64]See for instance these articles: Rodd, (1981) 95-106; Harrington, (1980) 181-190; Holstein, (1975) 159-179.

[65]See Deissmann, (1965) 190 and (1957).

[66]See the fascinating account of the work of Case and the "Chicago School" in Hynes (1981).

[67]On what follows see particularly the articles of Cyril Rodd and Jay Holstein previously cited (Note 64).

[68]Scroggs, (1980) 166. Cf. Rodd, (1979) 468.

[69]Rodd, (1981) 99.

[70]Scroggs labels this "reductionism," (1980) 167.

[71]Cf. Rodd, (1979) 466f. On the concepts of emic and etic, see Kaplan and Manners, (1972) 22.

[72]Scroggs, (1980) 171.

APPENDIX 2

A BASIC LANGUAGE COMPUTER PROGRAM TO ASSIST IN
THE STUDY OF ANCIENT WEIGHTS, MEASURES,
COINS, AND SUBSISTENCE

The following computer program has been utilized
in Part One of this book as the basis for many of the
calculations. The program is published here, not as a
finished product, but with the hope that others will
find it useful or improve upon it. The commentary in
this appendix is not designed to explain how the
program works. A certain amount of computer literacy
is assumed on the part of the reader. The commentary
is intended rather as an explication of typical
conversions and calculations that can be done by the
program.

The value of a computer program like this is not
that it does something that could not be done with a
piece of paper and a pencil. Obviously not. The value
is that the computer program does everything so much
faster. Thus, the program facilitates quick comparisons, say, between Jewish and Roman systems of measurement. This program also centralizes information. This
makes quantitative studies and comparisons relating to
the ancient economies much easier.

The danger of a computer program like this lies
in the false sense of security it gives in terms of
results. Ancient measures, as was emphasized in the
text, were not often uniform. This program can only
give better or worse approximations. The following
commentary tries to indicate where the best results can
be expected, as well as where uncertainties must be
lived with.

A. The Computer Program

```
10 DEF FNEQ(X)=X
20 PRINT "A CONVERSION PROGRAM FOR ANCIENT WEIGHTS,
       MEASURES, COINS, AND CALORIC REQUIREMENTS"
30 PRINT:PRINT "SELECT FUNCTION:"
40 PRINT "A: CAPACITY & AREA CONVERSION"
50 PRINT "B: YIELD (GIVEN QUANTITY SOWN)"
60 PRINT "C: SEED REQUIREMENT (GIVEN HARVEST)"
70 PRINT "D: MONEY AND MONEY EQUIVALENTS IN KIND"
80 PRINT "E: CALORIC CONTENT OR EQUIVALENT"
90 PRINT "F: CALORIE SYNTHESIZER"
100 PRINT "T: TERMINATE"
110 INPUT "",A$
120 IF A$="A" THEN GOTO 220
130 IF A$="B" THEN GOTO 500
140 IF A$="C" THEN GOTO 570
150 IF A$="D" THEN GOTO 1480
160 IF A$="E" THEN GOTO 640
170 IF A$="F" THEN GOTO 1970
180 IF A$="T" THEN END
190 REM CHANGE PERMISSIBLE UNITS AT 1400
200 REM CHANGE CONSTANTS AT 950
210 REM IF CHANGES MADE AT 1400, CHANGE UNITS AT 310,
       390, 460
220 GOSUB 1400
230 PRINT
240 PRINT "TYPE IN UNIT AND AMOUNT TO BE CONVERTED"
250 PRINT "FORMAT #1: X,'CAPACITY UNIT',0,0 OR 0,0,X,
       'AREA UNIT'"
260 INPUT "FORMAT #2: X,'UNIT',Y,'UNIT'";A,A$,B,B$
270 GOSUB 950
280 IF A=0 THEN GOTO 560
290 IF B=0 THEN GOTO 380
300 PRINT:PRINT A;"/";B;A$;"/";B$;" ="
```

```
310 PRINT DD/JJ"HL/HA";KGW/JJ"KG-WHEAT/HA";KGB/JJ"KG-
    BARLEY/HA"
320 PRINT AA/JJ"QUINTALS-WHEAT/HA";BB/JJ"QUINTALS-
    BARLEY/HA"
330 PRINT LBW/JJ"LBS-WHEAT/HA";LBB/JJ"LBS-BARLEY/HA"
340 PRINT EE/KK"BU/ACRE";FF/LL"ARTABA(S)/AROURA"GG/LL
    "MODII/IUGERUM"
350 PRINT HH/NN"COR(S)/CORS-SPACE"
360 PRINT:INPUT "PRESS <CR> TO END DISPLAY",A
370 GOTO 30
380 PRINT:PRINT A;A$;" ="
390 PRINT LBW"LBS-WHEAT";KGW"KGS-WHEAT";LBB"LBS-BARLEY"
    ;KGB"KGS-BARLEY"
400 PRINT AA"QUINTAL(S)-WHEAT";BB"QUINTAL(S)-BARLEY";CC
    "LITER(S)"
410 PRINT DD"HECTOLITER(S)";EE"BUSHEL(S)";FF"ARTABA(S)"
    ;MM"MEDIMNI"
420 PRINT GG"MODII"HH"COR(S)";II"SEAH(S)";OO"QAB(S)";PP
    "LOG(S)"
430 PRINT:INPUT "PRESS <CR> TO END DISPLAY",A
440 GOTO 30
450 PRINT:PRINT:PRINT B;B$;" ="
460 PRINT JJ"HA";KK"ACRES";LL"AROURAS";LL"IUGERA";NN
    "CORS-SPACE(S)"
470 PRINT:INPUT "PRESS <CR> TO END DISPLAY",A
480 GOTO 30
490 REM YIELD; CONSTANTS IN 950, 1400; PRINTOUT AT 280
500 GOSUB 1400
510 PRINT
520 PRINT "SPECIFY AVERAGE RELATIVE YIELD EXPECTED
    (XFOLD), QUANTITY SOWN"
530 INPUT "'UNIT OF CAPACITY','UNIT OF AREA'";A,B,A$,B$
540 C=A*B:B=1:A=FNEQ(C):GOSUB 950
550 GOTO 280
```

```
560 REM SEED REQUIREMENTS; CONSTANTS IN 950, 1400;
    PRINTOUT AT 280
570 GOSUB 1400
580 PRINT
590 PRINT "SPECIFY AVERAGE RELATIVE YIELD (XFOLD),
    ABSOLUTE YIELD"
600 INPUT "'UNIT OF CAPACITY','UNIT OF AREA'";A,B,A$,B$
610 C=B/A:B=1:A=FNEQ(C):GOSUB 950
620 GOTO 280
630 REM CALORIC CONVERSION; CONSTANTS IN 680-690, 900-
    910
640 PRINT:PRINT:INPUT "A: CALORIC CONTENT OF BULK
    GRAIN, B: GRAIN EQUIVALENT (GIVEN CALORIES)";A$
650 IF A$="B" THEN GOTO 890
660 PRINT:PRINT "A: WHEAT, B: BARLEY"
670 PRINT:INPUT "WHICH GRAIN COMMODITY";C$
680 IF C$="A" THEN CALKG=3150:CALLB=1429
690 IF C$="B" THEN CALKG=3307:CALLB=1500
700 PRINT:INPUT "QUANTITY BY VOLUME OR WEIGHT (V OR W)"
    ;V$
710 IF V$="V" THEN GOTO 800
720 PRINT:PRINT "USE POUNDS (LB) OR KILOGRAMS (KG)"
730 INPUT "WEIGHT (FORMAT: X,'UNIT')";A,A$
740 IF A$="LB" THEN RES=CALLB*A
750 IF A$="KG" THEN RES=CALKG*A
760 PRINT:PRINT:PRINT A;A$;" =":PRINT
770 PRINT RES"CALS";365*RES"CALS/YR";RES/365"CALS/DAY"
780 PRINT:INPUT "PRESS <CR> TO END DISPLAY",A
790 GOTO 30
800 GOSUB 1400
810 PRINT:INPUT "DRY VOLUME (FORMAT: X,'UNIT',0,0)";
    A,A$,B,B$
820 GOSUB 950
830 IF C$="A" THEN RES=LBW*CALLB:GOTO 850
```

```
840  RES=LBB*CALLB
850  PRINT A;A$;" =":PRINT
860  PRINT RES"CALS";365*RES"CALS/YR";RES/365"CALS/DAY"
870  PRINT:INPUT "PRESS <CR> TO END DISPLAY",A
880  GOTO 30
890  PRINT:INPUT "NO. OF CALORIES";A
900  WH=A/85680!:PRINT WH"BU WH";" ="WH*27.2"KG";" ="
     365*WH"BU/YR"
910  BAR=A/59856.7:PRINT BAR"BU BAR";" ="BAR*18.1"KG"
     ;" ="365*BAR"BU/YR"
920  PRINT:INPUT "PRESS <CR> TO END DISPLAY",A
930  GOTO 30
940  REM X=BUSHEL AS COMMON UNIT
950  IF A=0 THEN GOTO 1110
960  IF A$="KG-W" THEN X=A/27.2
970  IF A$="LB-W" THEN X=A/60
980  IF A$="Q-W" THEN X=A/.272
990  IF A$="KG-B" THEN X=A/18.1
1000 IF A$="LB-B" THEN X=A/40
1010 IF A$="Q-B" THEN X=A/.181
1020 IF A$="L" THEN X=A/35.238
1030 IF A$="MED" THEN X=A/.6725
1040 IF A$="BU" THEN X=A
1050 IF A$="ART" THEN X=A*1.114
1060 IF A$="MOD" THEN X=A/4.035
1070 IF A$="COR" THEN X=A*11.15
1080 IF A$="SEAH" THEN X=A*(11.15/30)
1090 IF A$="QAB" THEN X=A*(11.15/180)
1100 IF A$="LOG" THEN X=A*(11.15/720)
1110 IF B=0 THEN GOTO 1170
1120 IF B$="HA" THEN Y=2.47*B
1130 IF B$="ACRE" THEN Y=FNEQ(B)
1140 IF B$="AR" THEN Y=B*.625
1150 IF B$="IUG" THEN Y=B*.625
```

```
1160 IF B$="CORS-SP" THEN Y=B*5.27
1170 IF A=0 THEN GOTO 1340
1180 AA=.272*X
1190 KGW=27.2*X
1200 LBW=60*X
1210 BB=.181*X
1220 KGB=18.1*X
1230 LBB=40*X
1240 CC=35.238*X
1250 DD=.01*CC
1260 EE=X
1270 MM=X*.6725
1280 FF=X/1.114
1290 GG=4.035*X
1300 HH=X/11.15
1310 II=30*HH
1320 OO=180*HH
1330 PP=720*HH
1340 IF B=0 THEN GOTO 1390
1350 JJ=Y/2.47
1360 KK=Y
1370 LL=Y/.625
1380 NN=Y/5.27
1390 RETURN
1400 PRINT "USE THESE SYMBOLS FOR VARIOUS UNITS:"
1410 PRINT "'KG-, LB-, Q(UINTAL)-W(HEAT) OR -B(ARLEY)',
     'L(ITER)', 'BU(SHEL)'"
1420 PRINT "'ART(ABA)', 'MED(IMNUS)', 'MOD(IUS)', 'COR'
     , 'SEAH'"
1430 PRINT "'QAB', 'LOG'"
1440 PRINT:PRINT "'HA', 'ACRE', 'AR(OURA)', 'IUG(ERUM)'
     , 'CORS-SP(ACE)'"
1450 RETURN
1460 REM MONEY; MAKE CHANGES AT 1540, 1620, AND 1910
```

```
1470 REM CONSTANTS AT 1580-1590
1480 GOSUB 1900
1490 PRINT
1500 PRINT "TYPE IN UNIT AND AMOUNT TO BE CONVERTED"
1510 INPUT "FORMAT: X,'UNIT'";A,A$
1520 GOSUB 1620
1530 PRINT:PRINT A;A$;" ="
1540 PRINT "JEWISH: "BB"LEPTONS";DUP"DUPONDIONS";AA
     "SHEKELS"
1550 PRINT "GREEK: "CC"DRACHMAS";DD"STATERS=TETRA
     DRACHMAS";EE"TALENTS"
1560 PRINT "ROMAN: "FF"QUADRANSES";GG"ASSES";II
     "SESTERCES";HH"DENARII";JJ"AUREI"
1570 PRINT:PRINT "EQUIVALENT TO PALESTINIAN STAPLES:"
1580 PRINT "WHEAT "HH*(11.15/30)"BU, ";"WINE "HH*2"L"
1590 PRINT "OIL "HH"-"HH*20"L, ";"FIGS "HH*96"-"HH*320
1600 PRINT:INPUT "PRESS <CR> TO END DISPLAY",A
1610 GOTO 30
1620 REM X=DENARIUS AS COMMON UNIT
1630 IF A$="DUP" THEN X=A/12
1640 IF A$="LEP" THEN X=A/128
1650 IF A$="SH" THEN X=A*4
1660 IF A$="DR" THEN X=A
1670 IF A$="ST" THEN X=A*4
1680 IF A$="TAL" THEN X=A*6000
1690 IF A$="QUAD" THEN X=A/64
1700 IF A$="AS" THEN X=A/16
1710 IF A$="DEN" THEN X=A
1720 IF A$="SES" THEN X=A/4
1730 IF A$="AU" THEN X=A*25
1740 AA=X/4
1750 BB=X*128
1760 DUP=X*12
1770 CC=X
```

```
1780 DD=X/4
1790 EE=X/6000
1800 FF=X*64
1810 GG=X*16
1820 HH=X
1830 II=X*4
1840 JJ=X/25
1850 KK=0
1860 LL=0
1870 MM=0
1880 NN=0
1890 RETURN
1900 PRINT "USE THESE SYMBOLS FOR VARIOUS UNITS:"
1910 PRINT "'DUP(ONDION)', 'LEP(TON)', 'SH(EKEL)',
     'DR(ACHMA)', 'ST(ATER)'"
1920 PRINT "'TAL(ENT)', 'QUAD(RANS)', 'AS',
     'DEN(ARIUS)'"
1930 PRINT "'SES(TERTIUS)', 'AU(REUS)'"
1940 RETURN
1950 REM CALORIE SYNTHESIZER; CONSTANTS IN 2110, 2130,
     2170
1960 REM 2210, 2250, 2410-2420
1970 ZZ=0:YY=0:XX=0:WW=0:W=0:VV=0:UU=0:B=0:B$="0"
1980 GOSUB 1400:PRINT
1990 PRINT:INPUT "WHEAT (X, CAPACITY UNIT)";A,A$
2000 IF A=0 THEN GOTO 2040
2010 GOSUB 950
2020 C$="A":GOSUB 2410
2030 ZZ=FNEQ(RES)
2040 INPUT "BARLEY (X, CAPACITY UNIT)";A,A$
2050 IF A=0 THEN GOTO 2090
2060 GOSUB 950
2070 C$="B":GOSUB 2410
2080 YY=FNEQ(RES)
```

```
2090 INPUT "FIGS (NO., 0 OR X, CAPACITY UNIT)";A,A$
2100 IF A=0 THEN GOTO 2140
2110 IF A$="0" THEN XX=A*30:GOTO 2140
2120 GOSUB 950
2130 XX=EE*62500!
2140 INPUT "LEGUMES (X, CAPACITY UNIT)";A,A$
2150 IF A=0 THEN GOTO 2180
2160 GOSUB 950
2170 W=(EE*27.2)*2681
2180 INPUT "WINE (X, LIQ. UNIT)";A,A$
2190 IF A=0 THEN GOTO 2220
2200 GOSUB 950
2210 WW=(EE*35.238)*966.23
2220 INPUT "OIL (X, LIQ. UNIT)";A,A$
2230 IF A=0 THEN GOTO 2260
2240 GOSUB 950
2250 VV=(EE*35.238)*8108.88
2260 UU=VV+WW+W+XX+YY+ZZ
2270 INPUT "ARE THESE FOR A SPECIFIED NO. OF DAYS
     (=/DAY), /WK, OR /YR";T$
2280 IF T$="/DAY" THEN INPUT "HOW MANY DAYS";T
2290 PRINT:PRINT "WHEAT"ZZ"CALS"
2300 PRINT "BARLEY"YY
2310 PRINT "FIGS"XX
2320 PRINT "LEGUMES"W
2330 PRINT "WINE"WW
2340 PRINT "OIL"VV
2350 PRINT "TOTAL"UU"CALS";UU/1800"1800-CAL SUBSISTENCE
     UNITS"
2360 IF T$="/DAY" THEN PRINT UU/T"CALS/DAY"
2370 IF T$="/WK" THEN PRINT UU/7"CALS/DAY"
2380 IF T$="/YR" THEN PRINT UU/365"CALS/DAY"
2390 PRINT:INPUT "PRESS <CR> TO END DISPLAY",A
2400 GOTO 30
```

```
2410 IF C$="A" THEN CALKG=3150:CALLB=1429
2420 IF C$="B" THEN CALKG=3307:CALLB=1500
2430 IF C$="A" THEN RES=LBW*CALLB:GOTO 2450
2440 RES=LBB*CALLB
2450 RETURN
2460 END
```

B. Commentary on the Program

The above program is written in the standard
Basic of Microsoft. With modifications, it undoubtedly
can be rewritten to run in any Basic. The program
itself is "modularized" and relatively straightforward.
None of the advanced features of Microsoft's Basic are
utilized.

Lines 120-170 locate the branches to the various
parts of the program or "modules." Lines 40-90 give
summary indications of what the modules do. Briefly,
Function A permits the user to rapidly compare ancient
units of area and capacity (dry, some liquid).
Function B permits calculations of crop yields, given
the knowledge of how much was sown. Function C
reverses the process of Function B to calculate seed
requirements. Function D calculates money values in
terms of other coins and indicates the approximate
buying power of money (in kind) in first-century
Palestine. Functions E and F permit the user to assess
caloric content of a given quantity of grain or in a
given subsistence diet respectively.

In general, the most accurate calculations can
be assumed to be those within a given system of
weights, capacities, or money (e.g. Roman), since these
are calibrated through historical or archaeological
research. The most precarious calculations will be
those between systems. The relationship between the

various systems was often complex and subject to
historical vicissitude. As Dr. Gildas Hamel has
pointed out:

> What characterizes most descriptions [sc. of
> weights and measures] is the attempt to give a
> coherent picture, a system, and the assumption that
> it had a wide application.[1]

Understandably, to make a computer program like
this work, some compromises need to be effected to
provide a coherence the computer can understand. Certain assumptions about average weights and measures
need to be made. Some of these compromises and assumptions are indicated below.

The "guts" of Function A are stored in the
lookup table of conversion factors after line 940. The
computer "reads" what is input in lines 950-1170. The
common units are the bushel (though for liquid
conversions from logs or liters, this is simply a
cipher) and the acre. Lines 1180 1300 reconvert what
was input into all other units provided for in the
program. Some of the numbers printed out will be
nonsense numbers. The user has to keep in mind that
calculations of weight specified in wheat will not
convert properly to barley. Modifications to the
program could eliminate this, but the work involved
would not necessarily be commensurate with the
meagerness of the problem. This lookup table, it
should be noted, can be expanded to any units the user
wishes (as long as the computer memory is large
enough). The "permissible units" table (lines 1400-
1450) as well as the readout sections, then need to be
modified accordingly.

Some of the values in lines 960-1020 are taken
from the USDA's Agricultural Statistics.[2] Others are

drawn from Clark and Haswell (1970) and Moritz
(1958). The wheat or barley are assumed to be in an
unprocessed form, not ground into flour.

     The value of the Roman artaba, which was used
for taxation, is ascertainable from archaeological
study.[3] It essentially equalled four and a half modii,
a little larger than an English bushel. The medimnus
has been set equal to 6 modii (Cicero, Verrine Orations
2.3.44.106).

     The modius measure can be determined fairly
accurately on the basis of surviving artifacts, as well
as on the basis of literary information about this
measure. The older work of Hultsch gave a result of
8.75 liters, but Duncan-Jones has disputed this. He
prefers a value of 8.62 liters.[4] Since the difference
between these two valuations of the modius would give
less than one-half percent error to the bushel anyway,
this slight difference is not significant.

     The value for the modius chosen in this computer
program is 8.73 liters. The readouts in the computer
program have been adjusted to give correct correspondence between several of the various units. The most
important consideration is the equation of the Roman
sextarius and the Jewish log.[5] The Jewish seah then
corresponds to the modius castrensis (= 1.5 Italic
modii).[6]

     The Jewish cor is calibrated in the same way as
the Italian modius--through modern study of archaeological artifacts and literary sources. However, since
the Jewish system was being brought into alignment with
the Roman during the early first century, this measure,
familiar from the Old Testament, was nearly twice the
size of its Old Testament counterpart. All of the
Jewish capacity measures retained their proportional

relationship to each other. The calibration of the log
with the Roman sextarius, however, increased the size
of the other capacity units.[7] Thus, the cor is around
11 bushels.

Turning to the land area section, it must first
be recognized that two different systems of land
measurement prevailed in antiquity.[8] In the ancient
Near East, lands were measured by the quantities of
grain that could be sown on them. This is the type of
measuring system attested in the Talmud. The Romans,
by contrast, measured land in terms of area that could
be plowed in a given time. This area was much more
predictable than area determined by the oriental
method.

The aroura, though originally perhaps calibrated in the eastern manner with the artaba, had also
a definite measurement under the Romans. It was set
nearly equal to the Roman iugerum.[9] The iugerum,
comprised of two actus (= 120 x 120 Roman feet), equals
about 5/8 of an English acre.

The readout for cor's-spaces, that is, the area
covered by a cor of seed, is perhaps the most inaccu-
rate of the area readouts. The space covered varied
according to the quality of the ground, less so
according to the density of seed sown per each unit of
area.[10] The Talmud allows an estimation of the cor's-
space in terms of the cubit--75,000 square cubits.[11]
This unit, however, had a number of definitions.
Assuming with Jeremias that the talmudic cubit is the
Philetarian cubit, and taking its value as 1.75 English
feet, we get the following: 75,000 cubits^2 = (274
cubits)^2 = (480 ft)^2 = 229,920 ft^2 = 5.3 acres.[12]
Hamel gives 700-1000 m^2 as an estimate for the seah's-
space. The cor's-space would then be 30 x 700 = 21,000

to 30 x 1000 = 30,000 m^2. This works out to a range of
5.2 - 7.4 acres. The lower range of his scale agrees
with our calculation. Thus, the conversion value in
the computer program is 5.3; this represents a minimum
value.

The lookup table for money conversions is given
in lines 1630-1840. Here again the problem of a number
of historically developed systems and their interrelationship comes to light. The Romans permitted the
older Hellenistic coinage to remain circulating, and
some municipalities like Antioch and Tyre continued to
mint silver and copper denominations. Augustus
reorganized imperial issues into a three-metal
system.[13] The imperial money is assumed as the basis
for the lookup table values, but there is uncertainty
as to how to relate Jewish and Greek coinage. Talmudic
references are frequently oriented to the Greek denominations, but it is difficult to align these simply with
the imperial issues.

All of the Roman denominations are related step-
wise in lines 1690-1730. This is straightforward.

The lepton in all sources is equal to 1/2 the
Roman quadrans. The drachma and the stater are kept to
the Tyrian standard; hence, the drachma equals the
silver denarius. The Syrian (Antioch) drachma
apparently was worth 3/4 the Roman denarius.[14] The
Syrian as likewise was only worth 1/24 of the denarius,
though the imperial and Tyrian asses were worth 1/16.
The value of the eastern dupondion suffered from
similar confusion. Sperber and Hamel equate the shekel
to 2 denarii, but Mt. 17:27 seems to indicate 4
denarii.[15]

Turning to the buying power of the denarius for
the early first century, lines 1580-1590 represent an

attempt to give first-century values. The basis for
the wheat calibration is rabbinic evidence.[16] The
basic equivalence was 1 seah per 1 denarius. Heichelheim has collected evidence for wine prices.[17]
Josephus (Life 75) gives an indication of oil prices
around mid-century. The readout, therefore, reflects
the price range from areas where oil was plentiful
(Upper Galilee) to areas where oil was dear. The price
of figs comes from talmudic evidence. Again, a range
is given.[18]

     A few more assumptions need to be made to get an
indication of the nutritional value of quantities of
food-stuffs. These assumptions are facilitated by
modern studies of the nutritional values of foods. The
general structure of all such calculations is as
follows: First, some idea is gained of the absolute
caloric value of a given quantity of food. Modern
scientific lists of such values are readily available.[19] Next, some way is found to convert ancient
food quantities into modern equivalences. The body, of
course, will not always utilize the absolute caloric
value.

     The figures given in lines 680-690, 2130, 2170,
2210, 2250, and 2410-3420 represent the standard
caloric values present in a given weight of a given
item.[20] Volume conversions from ancient evidence, of
course, will not give the same accuracy as weight
conversions. Wheat densities are assumed to be 27.2
kg/bu. The volume-ratio of wheat to balance an equal
weight of barley has been set at 1::1.8.[21] The
readouts for Functions E and F display total calories,
calories per unit of time, and in the latter function,
1800-cal subsistence units.

Notes to Appendix 2

[1]Hamel, (1983) 500; cf. Rostovtzeff, (1941) 2:1296-1301.

[2]"WEIGHTS, MEASURES, AND CONVERSION FACTORS," in USDA, (1983) IV-IX.

[3]Duncan-Jones, (1982) 372.

[4]Ibid.: 371.

[5]This correspondence apparently was established in the Herodian period. It undoubtedly obtained subsequently. See Sperber, (1971) 388 and Hamel, (1983) 499.

[6]Duncan-Jones, (1982) 372.

[7]Compare Sellers, (1962) and Sperber, (1971).

[8]Sperber, (1971) 390.

[9]Duncan-Jones, (1982) 372.

[10]Hamel, (1983) 501 makes the former point in his discussion of the beth-se'ah: ". . .the unit of volume of cereals sown or harvested was more stable than the unit of area."

[11]Danby, (1933) 798.

[12]See Chapter 2, Note 87.

[13]Koester, (1982) 1:88-91; Sutherland, (1970).

[14]Heichelheim, (1959) 212.

[15]Sperber, (1971) 388; Hamel, (1983) 499.

[16]Jeremias, (1969a) 122; Heichelheim, (1959) 184.

[17]Heichelheim, (1959) 184.

[18]In Heichelheim, (1959) 185.

[19]See the references in Chapter 2, Notes 63-67.

[20]Assuming the standard 4 calories/gm of carbohydrate, 9 cal/gm of fat, 4 cal/gm of protein: See Passmore, Nicol, et al., (1974) 7.

[21]Chapter 2, Note 66.

SELECTED BIBLIOGRAPHY

A. Primary Texts, Editions, and Ancillary Tools

Aland, K., ed. 1973. Synopsis Quattuor Evangeliorum. 8. Aufl. Stuttgart: Württembergische Bibelanstalt.

The Apostolic Fathers. 1912–13. 2 vols. Tr. K. Lake. LCL. Cambridge: Harvard University.

Bagnall, R., and Derow, P. 1981. Greek Historical Documents: The Hellenistic Period. Sources for Biblical Study, 16. Chico: Scholars.

Bauer, W.; Arndt, W. F.; Gingrich, F. W.; and Danker, F., eds. 1979. A Greek English Lexicon of the New Testament and Other Early Christian Literature. University of Chicago.

Billerbeck, P. 1922–61. Kommentar zum Neuen Testament aus Talmud und Midrasch. 7 vols. Munich: Beck'sche.

Blackman, P. 1965. Mishnayoth. 7 vols. 3rd ed. New York: Judaica.

Blass, F. and Debrunner, A. 1961. A Greek Grammar of the New Testament and Other Early Christian Literature. Tr. and rev. by R. W. Funk. University of Chicago.

Cato, (M. Porcius), and Varro, (M. Terrentius). 1954. De re rustica. Tr. W. D. Hooper, rev. by H. B. Ash. LCL. Cambridge: Harvard University.

Charles, R. H., ed. 1913. The Apocrypha and Pseudepigrapha of the Old Testament. Vol. 2: Pseudepigrapha. Oxford: Clarendon.

271

Charlesworth, J. H., ed. 1983-85. The Old Testament
    Pseudepigrapha. 2 vols. Garden City, NY:
    Doubleday.

Cicero, (M. Tullius). 1953. The Verrine Orations. 2
    vols. Tr. L. H. G. Greenwood. LCL. Cambridge:
    Harvard.

Columella, (L. Junius Moderatus). 1941-55. Res
    rustica and De arboribus. 3 vols. Tr. H. B.
    Ash, et al. LCL. Cambridge: Harvard
    University.

Danby, H. 1933. The Mishnah. London: Oxford
    University.

Epstein, I. 1961 [1935-52]. The Babylonian Talmud.
    18 vols. London: Soncino.

Eusebius. 1926-32. The Ecclesiastical History. 2
    vols. Tr. K. Lake and J. E. L. Oulton. LCL.
    Cambridge: Harvard University.

Funk, R. W. 1985. New Gospel Parallels. 2 vols.
    Philadelphia: Fortress.

Hennecke, E., and Schneemelcher, W. 1963. The New
    Testament Apocrypha. Vol. 1: Gospels and
    Related Writings. Tr. R. McL. Wilson.
    Philadelphia: Westminster.

Holladay, C. R. 1983. Fragments from Hellenistic
    Jewish Authors. Vol. 1: Historians. Texts and
    Translations, 20. Chico: Scholars.

Josephus, Flavius. 1926-65. Josephus. 9 vols. Tr.
    H. St. J. Thackeray, R. Marcus, A. Wikgren, and
    L. H. Feldman. LCL. Cambridge: Harvard
    University.

Liddell, H. G.; Scott, R.; and Jones, H. S., et al.
    1968. A Greek English Lexicon with A
    Supplement. Oxford: Clarendon.

May, H., and Metzger, B., eds. 1973. The New Oxford
    Annotated Bible With the Apocrypha. Revised
    Standard Version. New York: Oxford.

Moulton, W. F., and Geden, A. S. 1963. A Concordance
    to the Greek Testament. Edinburgh: T. & T.
    Clark.

Moulton, J. H., and Milligan, G. 1980 [1930]. The
    Vocabulary of the Greek Testament. Reprint ed.
    Grand Rapids: Eerdmans.

Nestle, E., and Aland, K. 1979. Novum Testamentum
    Graece. 26. Aufl. Stuttgart: Deutsche
    Bibelstiftung.

Petronius and Seneca. 1969. Satyricon and Apocolo-
    cyntosis. Tr. M. Heseltine and W. H. D. Rouse.
    LCL. Cambridge: Harvard University.

Pliny (Plinius Secundus Gaius). 1949-62. Natural
    History. 10 vols. Tr. H. Rackham, et al. LCL.
    Cambridge: Harvard University.

Richardson, C. 1970. Early Christian Fathers. New
    York: Macmillan.

Rosenthal, F. 1961. A Grammar of Biblical Aramaic.
    Wiesbaden: Otto Harrassowitz.

Tacitus, (P. Cornelius). 1925-37. The Histories and
    The Annals. 4 vols. Tr. C. H. Moore and J.
    Jackson. LCL. Cambridge: Harvard University.

Varro. See under Cato.

Virgil. 1978. Eclogues, Georgics, and Aeneid (Bks.
    1-6). Tr. H. R. Fairclough. LCL. Cambridge:
    Harvard University.

B. Secondary Literature

Alt, A. 1953-64. Kleine Schriften zur Geschichte des
    Volkes Israel. 3 vols. München: Beck.

Applebaum, S. 1975:125-128. "The Struggle for the
    Soil and the Revolt of 66-73 C.E." Eretz Israel
    12 (in Hebrew, with English summary).

_____. 1976:631-700. "Economic Life in Palestine."
    In Safrai and Stern, (1976) vol. 2.

Aulén, G. 1976. Jesus in Contemporary Historical
    Research. Tr. I. Hjelm. Philadelphia:
    Fortress.

Austin, M. M., and Vidal-Naquet, P.   1977.   Economic
     and Social History of Ancient Greece: An
     Introduction.   Tr. and rev. by M. M. Austin.
     Berkeley: University of California.

Avi-Yonah, M., ed.   1975.   The World History of the
     Jewish People.   First Series, Vol. 7: The
     Herodian Period.   Jerusalem: Massada.

_____ .   1977.   The Holy Land from the Persian to
     the Arab Conquests. An Historical Geography.
     Grand Rapids: Baker.

Bailey, K. E.   1976.   Poet and Peasant: A Literary
     Cultural Approach to the Parables in Luke.
     Grand Rapids: Eerdmans.

_____ .   1980.   Through Peasant Eyes: More Lucan
     Parables, Their Culture and Style.   Grand
     Rapids: Eerdmans.

Balsdon, J. P. V. D.   1970.   Rome: The Story of an
     Empire.   New York: McGraw-Hill.

Baly, D.   1974.   The Geography of the Bible.   New and
     rev. ed.   New York: Harper & Row.

Balz, H.   1972:127-39.   "TESSARES, KTL."   In TDNT 8.

Bammel, E., and Moule, C. F. D.   1984.   Jesus and the
     Politics of His Day.   Cambridge University.

Baron, S. W.   1952.   A Social and Religious History of
     the Jews.   Vol. 1: Ancient Times.   2d ed.   New
     York: Columbia University.

Baron, S.; Kahan, A.; et al.; edited by N. Gross.
     1975.   Economic History of the Jews.   Jerusalem:
     Keter.

Barrois, A.-G.   1939-53.   Manuel d'archéologie
     biblique.   2 vols.   Paris: Picard.

_____ .   1962a:809-10.   "Debt, Debtor."   In IDB 1.

_____ .   1962b:677-78.   "Trade and Commerce."   In
     IDB 4.

Bellah, R. N.   1970.   Beyond Belief: Essays on
     Religion in a Post-Traditional World.   New York:
     Harper & Row.

Belo, F. 1981. A Materialist Reading of the Gospel of
    Mark. Tr. M. J. O'Connell. Maryknoll: Orbis.

Bengtson, H. 1970. Introduction to Ancient History.
    Tr. R. I. Frank and F. D. Gilliard. University
    of California.

Benoit, P.; Milik, J. T.; and de Vaux, R. 1961. Les
    Grottes de Murabba'at. Discoveries in the
    Judaean Desert, 2. Oxford: Clarendon.

Berger, A. 1953. Encyclopedic Dictionary of Roman
    Law. Philadelphia: American Philosophical
    Society.

Béteille, A. 1969. Social Inequality. Penguin Modern
    Sociology Readings. Baltimore: Penguin.

Black, M. 1963. An Aramaic Approach to the Gospels
    and Acts. 3d ed. Oxford: Clarendon.

Blair, E. P. 1962:631-32. "Thomas." In IDB 4.

Blau, L. 1927:96-151. "Der Prosbol im Lichte der
    griechischen Papyri und der Rechtsgeschichte."
    In L. Blau, ed., Festschrift zum 50 jährigen
    Bestehen der Franz Josef Landesrabbinerschule
    in Budapest. Budapest.

Blok, A. 1969:365-78. "Variations in Patronage."
    Sociologische Gids 16.

Blümner, H. 1912. Technologie und Terminologie der
    Gewerbe und Künste bei Griechen und Römern. 4
    vols. Leipzig und Berlin: Teubner.

Boissevain, J. 1969:379-86. "Patrons as Brokers."
    Sociologische Gids 16.

Borg, M. J. 1984. Conflict, Holiness, and Politics in
    the Teachings of Jesus. Studies in the Bible
    and Early Christianity, 5. New York and
    Toronto: Edwin Mellen.

Bornkamm, G. 1960. Jesus of Nazareth. Tr. I. and F.
    McLuskey, with J. Robinson. New York: Harper &
    Row.

Braaten, C. E., and Harrisville, R. A., eds. 1964.
    The Historical Jesus and the Kerygmatic Christ:
    Essays on the New Quest of the Historical Jesus.
    New York and Nashville: Abingdon.

Brandon, S. G. F. 1967. Jesus and the Zealots. A
    Study of the Political Factor in Primitive
    Christianity. Manchester University.

Braun, H. 1979. Jesus of Nazareth. The Man and His
    Time. Tr. E. Kalin. Philadelphia: Fortress.

Breech, J. 1983. The Silence of Jesus: The Authentic
    Voice of the Historical Man. Philadelphia:
    Fortress.

Brengle, K. G. 1982. Principles and Practices of
    Dryland Farming. Boulder: Colorado Associated
    University.

Brown, R. E. 1965:254-64. "Parable and Allegory
    Reconsidered." In New Testament Essays.
    Milwaukee: Bruce Publishing Co.

_____. 1966-70. The Gospel According to John. 2
    vols. The Anchor Bible. Garden City, NY:
    Doubleday.

Brueggemann, W. 1979:161-85. "Trajectories in Old
    Testament Literature and the Sociology of
    Ancient Israel." JBL 99.

Brunt, P. A. 1971. Social Conflicts in the Roman
    Republic. New York: W. W. Norton.

_____. 1977:149-53. "Josephus on Social Conflicts
    in Roman Judaea." Klio 59.

Büchler, A. 1973. "The Economic Conditions of Judaea
    after the Destruction of the Second Temple." In
    J. Agus, et al., eds., Foundations of Jewish
    Life: Three Studies. The Jewish People:
    History, Religion, Culture. New York: Arno.

Bultmann, R. 1951-55. Theology of the New Testament.
    2 vols. Tr. Kendrick Grobel. New York:
    Scribner's.

_____. 1957:1-44. "New Testament and Mythology."
    In H. W. Bartsch, ed., Kerygma and Myth. Tr.
    Reginald Fuller. London: SPCK.

_____. 1958. Jesus and the Word. Tr. L. P. Smith
    and E. H. Lantero. New York: Scribner's.

Bultmann, R. 1963. The History of the Synoptic
     Tradition. Tr. J. Marsh. New York: Harper &
     Row.

_____. 1964a:509-12. "APHIĒMI, KTL." In TDNT 1.

_____. 1964b:15-42. "The Primitive Christian
     Kerygma and the Historical Jesus." In Braaten
     and Harrisville, (1964).

Burridge, K. 1969. New Heaven, New Earth: A Study of
     Millenarian Activities. New York: Schocken.

Caird, G. B. 1962:601-602. "Chronology of the New
     Testament." In IDB 1.

Carney, T. F. 1975. The Shape of the Past: Models and
     Antiquity. Lawrence, KS: Coronado.

Case, S. J. 1914. The Evolution of Christianity.
     University of Chicago.

_____. 1925:561-75. "The Life of Jesus during the
     Last Quarter Century." Journal of Religion 5.

_____. 1927. Jesus, A New Biography. University
     of Chicago.

_____. 1932. Jesus Through the Centuries.
     University of Chicago.

_____, ed. 1928. Studies in Early Christianity.
     New York and London: The Century Co.

Chaney, M. L. 1983:39-90. "Ancient Palestinian
     Peasant Movements and the Formation of
     Premonarchic Israel." In Freedman and Graf
     (1983).

Childe, V. Gordon. 1964. What Happened in History.
     New York: Penguin.

Clark, C., and Haswell, M. 1970. The Economics of
     Subsistence Agriculture. 4th ed. New York: St.
     Martin's.

Clévenot, M. 1985. Materialist Approaches to the
     Bible. Tr. W. J. Nottingham. Maryknoll: Orbis.

Coffin, T. P. 1983:317-329. "Folklore." In L. Bram,
    R. Phillips, N. Dickey, gen. eds., Funk and
    Wagnalls New Encyclopedia 10. R. R. Donnelley &
    Sons.

Conzelmann, H. 1973. Jesus. (The classic article
    from RGG[3] expanded and updated.) Tr. J. R.
    Lord. Edited, with an introduction, by J.
    Reumann. Philadelphia: Fortress.

_____. 1976:956-960. "Wisdom in the New
    Testament." In IDBSup.

Countryman, L. W. 1980. The Rich Christian in the
    Church of the Early Empire. Texts and Studies
    in Religion, 7. New York: Edwin Mellen.

Cowell, F. R. 1967. Cicero and the Roman Republic.
    4th ed. Baltimore: Penguin.

Crossan, J. D. 1973. In Parables: The Challenge of
    the Historical Jesus. New York: Harper & Row.

_____. 1983. In Fragments: The Aphorisms of Jesus.
    San Francisco: Harper & Row.

Cullmann, O. 1970. Jesus and the Revolutionaries.
    Tr. G. Putnam. New York: Harper & Row.

Dahl, N. A. 1951:132-65. "The Parables of Growth."
    Studia Theologica 5.

_____. 1962:138-71. "The Problem of the Historical
    Jesus." In C. E. Braaten and R. A. Harrisville,
    eds., Kerygma and History. New York: Abingdon.

Dalman, G. 1930. Die Worte Jesu. 2 Bände. 2. Aufl.
    Leipzig: Hinrichs.

_____. 1964 [1928-42]. Arbeit und Sitte in
    Palästina. 7 vols. Reprint ed. Hildesheim:
    G. Olms.

David, M., and van Groningen, B. A. 1965.
    Papyrological Primer. 4th ed. Leiden: E. J.
    Brill.

Davisson, W. I., and Harper, J. E. 1972. European
    Economic History. Vol. 1: The Ancient World.
    Appleton Century Crofts.

Day, J. 1932:166-208. "Agriculture in the Life of
    Pompeii." Yale Classical Studies 3.

Deissmann, A. 1957 [German 1925^2, ET 1927]. Paul: A
    Study in Social and Religious History. Tr. W.
    Wilson. New York: Harper Torchbooks.

_____. 1965 [German 1922^4, ET 1927]. Light From
    the Ancient East. Tr. L. Strachan. Reprint ed.
    Grand Rapids: Eerdmans.

Delling, G. 1972:216-25. "TREIS, KTL." In TDNT 8.

Dibelius, M. 1935. From Tradition to Gospel. Tr. B.
    L. Woolf. New York: Scribner's.

_____. 1949. Jesus. Tr. Charles B. Hedrick and F.
    C. Grant. Philadelphia: Westminster.

Dickey, S. 1923. The Constructive Revolution of
    Jesus New York: Doran.

_____. 1928:393-416. "Some Economic and Social
    Conditions of Asia Minor Affecting the Expansion
    of Christianity." In Case (1928).

Dodd, C. H. 1961. The Parables of the Kingdom. New
    York: Scribner's.

Donahue, J. 1971:39-61. "Tax Collectors and Sinners."
    CBQ 33.

Duncan-Jones, R. 1982. The Economy of the Roman
    Empire: Quantitative Studies. 2d ed. Cambridge
    University.

Ebeling, G. 1963:288-304. "The Question of the
    Historical Jesus." In Word and Faith. Tr. J.
    Leitch. London: SCM.

Eisenstadt, S. N., and Roniger, L. 1980:42-77.
    "Patron Client Relations as a Model of
    Structuring Social Exchange." Comparative
    Studies in Society and History 22.

Elliott, J. H. 1981. A Home for the Homeless: A
    Sociological Exegesis of 1 Peter, Its Situation
    and Strategy. Philadelphia: Fortress.

_____, ed. 1986. Semeia. Vol. 35: Social-
    Scientific Criticism of the New Testament
    and its Social World. Scholars Press.

Elliott-Binns, L. E. 1956. Galilean Christianity.
     Studies in Biblical Theology, 16. London: SCM.

Encyclopaedia Judaica (EJ) 5. 1971:1042-45. S. v.
     "Crafts: Post-Biblical and Talmudic Period."

FAO. See United Nations, Food and Agriculture
     Organization.

Finegan, J. 1969. The Archeology of the New Testa-
     ment: The Life of Jesus and the Beginning of
     the Early Church. Princeton, NJ: Princeton
     University.

Finley, M. I. 1973. The Ancient Economy. Sather
     Classical Lectures, 43. Berkeley: University of
     California.

Fitzmyer, J. A. 1970:501-31. "The Languages of
     Palestine in the First Century A.D." CBQ 32.

_____. 1974. Essays on the Semitic Background of
     the New Testament. Society of Biblical
     Literature Sources for Biblical Study, 5.
     Missoula, MT: Scholars.

_____. 1981-85. The Gospel According to Luke. 2
     vols. Anchor Bible, 28-28A. New York:
     Doubleday.

Frank, T. 1927. An Economic History of Rome. 2d ed.
     Baltimore: Johns Hopkins.

_____. 1959. "Rome and Italy of the Empire." In
     Frank, (1959) vol. 5.

Frank, T., ed. 1959 [1933-40]. An Economic Survey of
     Ancient Rome. 6 vols. Reprint. Paterson, NJ:
     Pageant Books.

Frayn, J. M. 1979. Subsistence Farming in Roman
     Italy. London: Centaur.

Freedman, D. N., and Graf, D. F. 1983. Palestine in
     Transition: The Emergence of Ancient Israel.
     Sheffield: The Almond Press.

Frend, W. H. C. 1984. The Rise of Christianity.
     Philadelphia: Fortress.

Freyne, S. 1980a. Galilee From Alexander the Great to
     Hadrian: 323 B.C.E. to 135 C.E. University of
     Notre Dame Center for the Study of Judaism and
     Christianity in Antiquity, 5. University of
     Notre Dame.

_____. 1980b. The World of the New Testament.
     New Testament Message, 2. Wilmington, Delaware:
     Michael Glazier.

Fuller, R. 1962. The New Testament in Current Study.
     New York: Scribner's.

Gager, J. 1975. Kingdom and Community. Englewood
     Cliffs: Prentice Hall.

Galling, K. 1977. Biblisches Reallexikon. 2. Aufl.
     Tübingen: Mohr.

Gil, M. 1970:11-53. "Land Ownership in Palestine
     under Roman Rule." Revue Internationale des
     Droits de L'Antiquité 17.

Goguel, M. 1960 [French 1932, ET 1933]. Jesus and the
     Origins of Christianity. Vol. 2: The Life of
     Jesus. Tr. O. Wyon. New York: Harper
     Torchbooks.

Golomb, B., and Kedar, Y. 1971:136-40. "Ancient
     Agriculture in the Galilee Mountains." IEJ 21.

Goodman, M. 1982:417-27. "The First Jewish Revolt:
     Social Conflict and the Problem of Debt." JJS
     33.

_____. 1903. State and Society in Roman Galilee,
     A.D. 132-212. Totowa, NJ: Rowman & Allanheld.

Göppelt, L. 1980. Apostolic and Post-Apostolic Times.
     Tr. R. Guelich. Grand Rapids: Baker.

_____. 1981-82. Theology of the New Testament.
     2 vols. Tr. John Alsup, ed. Jürgen Roloff.
     Grand Rapids: Eerdmans.

Gottwald, N. 1983a:25-37. "Early Israel and the
     Canaanite Socio-economic System." In Freedman
     and Graf (1983).

_____. 1983b. The Bible and Liberation: Political
     and Social Hermeneutics. Maryknoll: Orbis.

Grant, F. C. 1923-24:196-213, 1924-25:281-89. "The
     Economic Significance of Messianism." Anglican
     Theological Review 6 and 7.   .

_____ . 1926. The Economic Background of the
     Gospels. New York: Oxford University.

_____ . 1962:869-96. "Jesus Christ." In IDB 2.

Gregory, J. R. 1975:73-92. "Image of Limited Good,
     or Expectation of Reciprocity?" Current
     Anthropology 16.

Hamburger, H. 1962:423-35. "Money, Coins." In IDB 3.

Hamel, G. 1983. "Poverty and Charity in Roman
     Palestine." Ph.D. dissertation. Santa Cruz:
     University of California.

Harrington, D. J. 1980:181-90. "Sociological Concepts
     and the Early Church: A Decade of Research."
     Theological Studies 41.

Harrisville, R. A. 1964:172-96. "Representative
     American Lives of Jesus." In Braaten and
     Harrisville (1964).

Harvey, A. E. 1982. Jesus and the Constraints of
     History. Philadelphia: Westminster.

Harvey, V. A. 1969. The Historian and the Believer.
     New York: Macmillan.

Harvey, V., and Ogden, S. 1964:197-242. "How New Is
     the 'New Quest of the Historical Jesus'?" In
     Braaten and Harrisville (1964).

Hauck, F. 1967a:559-66. "OPHEILŌ, KTL." In TDNT 5.

_____ . 1967b:744-61. "PARABOLĒ, KTL." In TDNT 5.

Haywood, R. M. 1959. "Roman Africa." In Frank (1959)
     vol. 4.

Heichelheim, F. M. 1959. "Roman Syria." In Frank
     (1959) vol. 4.

Heitland, W. E. 1970 [1921]. Agricola: A Study of
     Agriculture and Rustic Life in the Graeco Roman
     World from the Point of View of Labour.
     Westport, Conn.: Greenwood.

Hengel, M. 1968:1-39. "Das Gleichnis von den
      Weingaertnern Mc 12:1-12 im Lichte der
      Zenonpapyri und der rabbinischen Gleichnisse."
      ZNW 59.

_____. 1971. Was Jesus a Revolutionist? Tr. W.
      Klassen. Philadelphia: Fortress Press Facet
      Books.

_____. 1973. Victory Over Violence. Jesus and the
      Revolutionists. Tr. D. E. Green. Philadelphia:
      Fortress.

_____. 1974a. Property and Riches in the Early
      Church. Tr. by J. Bowden. Philadelphia:
      Fortress.

_____. 1974b. Judaism and Hellenism. 2 vols. Tr.
      J. Bowden. Philadelphia: Fortress.

_____. 1976. Die Zeloten. 2. Aufl. Leiden:
      Brill.

Herskovits, M. J. 1952. Economic Anthropology: The
      Economic Life of Primitive Peoples. New York:
      Knopf.

Herz, D. J. 1928:98-113. "Grossgrundbesitz in
      Palästina im Zeitalter Jesu." PJB 24.

Hock, R. 1980. The Social Context of Paul's Ministry:
      Tentmaking and Apostleship. Philadelphia:
      Fortress.

Hoehner, H. 1972. Herod Antipas. SNTS Monographs,
      17. Cambridge University.

Hollenbach, P. 1983:61-78. "Recent Historical Jesus
      Studies and the Social Sciences." In SBLSP 22.

_____. 1985:151-157. "Liberating Jesus for Social
      Involvement." BTB 15.

Holstein, J. 1975:159-79. "Max Weber and Biblical
      Scholarship." HUCA 46.

Holzner, W., and Numata, M. 1982. Biology and
      Ecology of Weeds. London: Dr W. Junk.

Hopkins, C. 1940. The Rise of the Social Gospel in
      American Protestantism: 1865-1915. New Haven:
      Yale University.

Hunzinger, C.-H. 1971:287-91. "SINAPI." In TDNT 7.

Hynes, W. J. 1981. Shirley Jackson Case and the
    Chicago School. Society of Biblical Literature:
    Biblical Scholarship in America, 5. Chico:
    Scholars.

Isaac, B. 1984:44-50. "Judaea after AD 70." JJS 35.

Isenberg, S. R. 1974:26-46. "Millenarianism in
    Greco-Roman Palestine." Religion 4.

Jeremias, J. 1963. The Parables of Jesus. Rev. ed.
    New York: Scribner's.

_____. 1964. Unknown Sayings of Jesus. Tr. R.
    Fuller. 2d ed. London: SPCK.

_____. 1967:82-107. "The Lord's Prayer in the
    Light of Recent Research." In The Prayers of
    Jesus. Tr. J. Reumann. Studies in Biblical
    Theology, Second Series, 6. London: SCM.

_____. 1969a. Jerusalem in the Time of Jesus. Tr.
    F. H. and C. H. Cave. Philadelphia: Fortress.

_____. 1969b. The Problem of the Historical Jesus.
    Tr. N. Perrin. Rev. ed. Facet Books: Biblical
    Series, 13. Philadelphia: Fortress.

Jolowicz, H. F, and Nicholas, B. 1972. Historical
    Introduction to the Study of Roman Law. 3d ed.
    Cambridge University.

Johnson, A. C. 1959. "Roman Egypt to the Reign of
    Diocletian." In Frank, (1959) vol. 2.

Johnson, S. E. 1957. Jesus in His Homeland. New
    York: Scribner's.

Jones, A. H. M. 1931:78-85. "The Urbanization of
    Palestine." JRS 21.

_____. 1967. The Herods of Judaea. 2d ed.
    Oxford: Clarendon.

_____. 1971. The Cities of the Eastern Roman
    Provinces. 2d ed., rev. by M. Avi-Yonah, et al.
    Oxford: Clarendon.

Jones, A. H. M. 1974:151-85. "Taxation in Antiquity."
In P. Brunt, ed., The Roman Economy: Studies in
Ancient Economic and Administrative History.
New York: Rowman and Littlefield.

Kähler, M. 1964. The So Called Historical Jesus and
the Historic, Biblical Christ. Tr. C. Braaten,
Foreword by P. Tillich. Philadelphia: Fortress.

Käsemann, E. 1964:15-42. "The Problem of the
Historical Jesus." In Essays on New Testament
Themes. Tr. W. J. Montague. Philadelphia:
Fortress.

_____. 1969:23-65. "Blind Alleys in the 'Jesus of
History' Controversy." In New Testament
Questions of Today. Tr. W. J. Montague.
Philadelphia: Fortress.

Kaplan, D. 1968:228-51. "The Formal-Substantive
Controversy in Economic Anthropology: Some
Reflections on its Wider Implications."
Southwestern Journal of Anthropology 24.

Kaplan, D., and Manners, R. A. 1972. Culture Theory.
Foundations of Modern Anthropology Series.
Englewood Cliffs: Prentice-Hall.

Kee, H. C. 1980. Christian Origins in Sociological
Perspective. Philadelphia: Westminster.

Kingsbury, J. D. 1969. The Parables of Jesus in
Matthew 13. Richmond, VA: John Knox.

_____. 1977. Matthew. Proclamation Commentaries.
Philadelphia: Fortress.

Kippenberg, H. G. 1978. Religion und Klassenbildung
im antiken Judäa. SUNT 14. Göttingen:
Vandenhoeck and Ruprecht.

Kissinger, W. S. 1979. The Parables of Jesus: A
History of Interpretation and Bibliography.
ATLA Bibliography Series, 4. Metuchen, N.J.:
American Theological Association.

Klausner, J. 1925 [Hebrew 1922]. Jesus of Nazareth:
His Life, Times, and Teaching. Tr. H. Danby.
New York: Macmillan.

Klausner, J. 1975:179-205. "The Economy of Judea in
     the Period of the Second Temple." In Avi-Yonah
     (1975).

Klein, G. 1972:387-418. "The Biblical Understanding
     of 'Kingdom of God'." Interpretation 26.

Koester, H. 1982. Introduction to the New Testament.
     2 vols. Philadelphia: Fortress.

Koester, H., and Robinson, J. M. 1971. Trajectories
     Through Early Christianity. Philadelphia:
     Fortress.

Koffmahn, E. 1968. Die Doppelurkunden aus der Wüste
     Juda. Leiden: Brill.

Kornemann, E. 1924a: cols. 83-108. "Bauernstand." In
     PWSup 4.

_____. 1924b: cols. 227-68. "Domänen." In PWSup
     4.

Krauss, S. 1966 [1911]. Talmudische Archäologie. 3
     vols. Reprint ed. Georg Olms, Hildesheim.

Kreissig, H. 1969:223-54. "Die Landwirtschaftliche
     Situation in Palästina vor dem judäischen
     Krieg." Acta Antiqua 17.

Lang, B. 1982:47-63. "The Social Organization of
     Peasant Poverty in Biblical Israel." JSOT 24.

Lee, C. 1971:121-38. "Social Unrest and Primitive
     Christianity." In S. Benko and J. J. O'Rourke,
     The Catacombs and the Colosseum. Valley Forge:
     Judson.

Lenski, G. 1966. Power and Privilege. New York:
     McGraw Hill.

Lenski, G., and Lenski, J. 1974. Human Societies: An
     Introduction to Macrosociology. 2d ed. New
     York: McGraw Hill.

Linnemann, E. 1966. Jesus of the Parables:
     Introduction and Exposition. Tr. J. Sturdy.
     New York: Harper & Row.

Liphschitz, N., and Waisel, Y. 1973:30-36.
     "Dendroarchaeological Investigations in
     Israel." IEJ 23.

Löw, I. 1926-34. Die Flora der Juden. 4 vols. Wien
      und Leipzig: R. Löwit Verlag.

MacMullen, R. 1966. Enemies of the Roman Order:
      Treason, Unrest, and Alienation in the Empire.
      Harvard University.

_____. 1974. Roman Social Relations: 50 B.C.
      to A.D. 284. New Haven: Yale University.

Madden, F. W. 1881. Coins of the Jews. London:
      Trübner & Co.

Malherbe, A. 1983. Social Aspects of Early
      Christianity. 2d ed. Philadelphia: Fortress.

Malina, B. 1981. The New Testament World: Insights
      from Cultural Anthropology. Atlanta: John
      Knox.

Manson, T. W. 1935. The Teaching of Jesus. 2d ed.
      Cambridge University.

_____. 1949. The Sayings of Jesus. London: SCM.

Mathews, S. 1971 [1928 = 1897 The Social Teaching of
      Jesus]. Jesus on Social Institutions. Ed. K.
      Cauthen. (Lives of Jesus Series, L. E. Keck
      ed.) Philadelphia: Fortress.

Mayer, A. 1983. Der zensierte Jesus: Soziologie des
      Neuen Testaments. Olten: Walter Verlag.

McArthur, H. K. 1971:198-201. "The Parable of the
      Mustard Seed." CBQ 33.

McCown, C. C. 1928:173-89. "HO TEKTŌN." In Case
      (1928).

_____. 1929. The Genesis of the Social Gospel.
      New York: Knopf.

_____. 1940. The Search for the Real Jesus. New
      York: Scribner's.

_____. 1962:626-39. "Palestine, Geography of." In
      IDB 3.

Mealand, D. L. 1980. Poverty and Expectation in the
      Gospels. London: SPCK.

Meeks, W. 1983. The First Urban Christians: The
    Social World of the Apostle Paul. New Haven:
    Yale University.

Mendelsohn, I. 1962:383-91. "Slavery in the OT." In
    IDB 4.

Meyers, E. M. 1976:93-101. "Galilean Regionalism as a
    Factor in Historical Reconstruction." BASOR 21.

Meyers, E., and Strange, J. 1981. Archaeology, the
    Rabbis, and Early Christianity. Nashville:
    Abingdon.

Michaelis, W. 1971:736-42. "SYNGENĒS, SYNGENEIA." In
    TDNT 7.

Michel, O. 1967:149-53. "OIKONOMOS, OIKONOMIA." In
    TDNT 5.

_____. 1972:88-105. "TELŌNĒS." In TDNT 8.

Millar, F. 1970:1093. "Tributum." In OCD.

Miranda, J. 1974 [Spanish 1971]. Marx and the Bible:
    A Critique of the Philosophy of Oppression. Tr.
    J. Eagleson. Maryknoll: Orbis.

Mittwoch, A. 1955:352-61. "Tribute and Land tax in
    Seleucid Judea." Biblica 36.

Moldenke, H., and Moldenke, A. 1952. Plants of the
    Bible. New York: Ronald.

Monson, J., et al. 1979. Student Map Manual:
    Historical Geography of the Bible Lands. Grand
    Rapids: Eerdmans.

Morgan, R. 1973. The Nature of New Testament
    Theology. Studies in Biblical Theology, Second
    Series, 25. Naperville: Alec R. Allenson, Inc.

Moritz, L. A. 1958. Grain Mills and Flour in
    Classical Antiquity. Oxford: Clarendon.

Mowry, L. 1962:649-54. "Parable." In IDB 3.

Nash, M. 1968:359-65. "Economic Anthropology." In
    International Encyclopedia of the Social
    Sciences (IESS) 4.

Neusner, J. 1971. The Rabbinic Traditions About the
     Pharisees Before 70. 3 vols. Leiden: Brill.

_____. 1973. From Politics to Piety: The
     Emergence of Pharisaic Judaism. Englewood
     Cliffs: Prentice-Hall.

Nicholas, B. 1962. Introduction to Roman Law.
     Oxford: Clarendon.

Nineham, D. E. 1963. The Gospel of St. Mark. The
     Pelican New Testament Commentaries. Baltimore:
     Penguin.

North, R. 1954. Sociology of the Biblical Jubilee.
     Analecta Biblica, 4. Rome: Pontifical Biblical
     Institute.

Oakman, D. 1985:57-73. "Jesus and Agrarian Palestine:
     The Factor of Debt." SBLSP 24.

Oertel, F. 1928:382-424. "The Economic Unification of
     the Mediterranean Region." In CAH 10.

Passmore, R.; Nicol, B. M.; et al. 1974. Handbook on
     Human Nutritional Requirements. FAO Nutritional
     Studies, 28. Rome: Food and Agriculture
     Organization of the United Nations.

Pearson, L. C. 1967. Principles of Agronomy. New
     York: Reinhold.

Pellett, P. L., and Shadarevian, S. 1970. Food
     Composition Tables for Use in the Middle East.
     2d ed. American University of Beirut.

Perrin, N. 1963. The Kingdom of God in the Teaching
     of Jesus. Philadelphia: Westminster.

_____. 1967. Rediscovering the Teaching of Jesus.
     New York: Harper & Row.

_____. 1969. What is Redaction Criticism?
     Philadelphia: Fortress.

Pixley, G. V. 1981. God's Kingdom. A Guide for
     Biblical Study. Maryknoll: Orbis.

Polanyi, K. 1957:243-70. "The Economy as Instituted
     Process." In Polanyi, Arensberg, and Pearson
     (1957).

Polanyi, K. 1968. *Primitive, Archaic and Modern Economies. Essays of Karl Polanyi*. Ed. by George Dalton. Garden City, NY: Anchor.

Polanyi, K.; Arensberg, C. M.; and Pearson, H. W., eds. 1957. *Trade and Market in the Early Empires*. Glenco: Free Press.

Post, G. E. 1932-33. *Flora of Syria, Palestine and Sinai*. 2 vols. 2d ed., rev. by J. E. Dinsmore. Beirut: American Press.

Postan, M. M., ed. 1966. *The Cambridge Economic History of Europe*. Vol. 1: *The Agrarian Life of the Middle Ages*. 2d ed. Cambridge University.

Preisigke, Fr. 1915. *Fachwörter des öffentlichen Verwaltungsdienstes Ägyptens*. Göttingen.

_____. 1927. *Wörterbuch der griechischen Papyrus-kunden*. Berlin.

Premnath, Devadasan N. 1984. "The Process of Latifundialization Mirrored in the Oracles Pertaining to the 8th Century B.C.E. in the Books of Amos, Hosea, Isaiah and Micah." Ph.D. dissertation. Berkeley: Graduate Theological Union.

Redfield, R. 1960. *The Little Community* and *Peasant Society and Culture*. Chicago: Phoenix.

Reicke, B. 1968. *The New Testament Era*. Tr. D. Green. Philadelphia: Fortress.

Reifenberg, A. 1965. *Ancient Jewish Coins*. 4th ed. Jerusalem: R. Mass.

Rengstorf, K. 1964:49. "OIKODESPOTĒS." In *TDNT* 2.

Reumann, J. 1968. *Jesus in the Church's Gospels: Modern Scholarship and the Earliest Sources*. Philadelphia: Fortress.

Ringe, S. H. 1985. *Jesus, Liberation, and the Biblical Jubilee*. Overtures to Biblical Theology Series. Philadelphia: Fortress.

Robinson, E. S. G. 1970:258-61. "Coinage, Greek." In *OCD*.

Robinson, J.   1983.   A New Quest of the Historical
    Jesus. Rev. ed. Philadelphia: Fortress.

Rodd, C.   1979:457-69.   "Max Weber and Ancient
    Judaism." SJTh 32.

_____.   1981:95-106.   "On Applying a Sociological
    Theory to Biblical Studies." JSOT 19.

Rohrbaugh, R. L.   1978.   The Biblical Interpreter: An
    Agrarian Bible in an Industrial Age.
    Philadelphia: Fortress.

Ron, Z.   1966:33-49, 111-22.   "Agricultural Terraces in
    the Judean Mountains." IEJ 16.

Rostovtzeff, M.   1904.   Geschichte der Staatspacht in
    der römischen Kaiserzeit. Philologus,
    Supplementband IX. Leipzig.

_____.   1910.   Studien zur Geschichte des römischen
    Kolonates. Archiv für Papyrusforschung, Beiheft
    I. Leipzig und Berlin: Teubner.

_____.   1941.   The Social and Economic History of
    the Hellenistic World. 3 vols. Oxford:
    Clarendon.

_____.   1957.   The Social and Economic History of
    the Roman Empire. 2 vols. 2d ed., rev. by P.
    M. Fraser. Oxford: Clarendon.

Safrai, S.   1975:282-337.   "The Temple and the Divine
    Service." In Avi-Yonah (1975).

Safrai, S.; Stern, M.; et al., eds.   1974-76.   The
    Jewish People in the First Century. 2 vols.
    Compendia Rerum Iudaicarum ad Novum Testamentum.
    Amsterdam: Van Gorcum.

Sahlins, M.   1968.   Tribesmen. Foundations of Modern
    Anthropology Series. Englewood Cliffs:
    Prentice-Hall.

Ste. Croix, G. E. M. de.   1981.   The Class Struggle in
    the Ancient Greek World From the Archaic Age to
    the Arab Conquests. Ithaca: Cornell University.

Salisbury, E. J.   1961.   Weeds and Aliens. London:
    Collins.

Sanders, E. P.   1979.   Paul and Palestinian Judaism.
     Philadelphia: Fortress.

Sanders, J. A.   1962:520-22.   "Tax, Taxes."   In IDB 4.

Schalit, A.   1969.   König Herodes.   Tr. Jehoschua Amir.
     Berlin: de Gruyter.

Schmidt, K. L.   1964:579-93.   "BASILEIA."   In TDNT 1.

_____.   1969:93-168.   "Jesus Christ."   In J.
     Pelikan, ed., Twentieth Century Theology in the
     Making 1. 3 vols.   Tr. from the RGG² article by
     R. Wilson.   New York: Harper & Row.

Schmidt, S. W., et al.   1977.   Friends, Followers, and
     Factions: A Reader in Political Clientelism.
     University of California.

Schottroff, L., and Stegemann, W.   1981.   Jesus von
     Nazareth--Hoffnung der Armen.   2. Aufl.
     Stuttgart: Kohlhammer.

Schrage, W.   1964.   Das Verhältnis des Thomas Evangel-
     iums zur Synoptischen Tradition.   BZNW 29.
     Töpelmann.

Schürer, E.   1973-79.   The History of the Jewish
     People in the Age of Jesus Christ (175 B.C.--
     A.D. 135).   2 vols.   Rev. ed., G. Vermes, F.
     Millar, and M. Black, eds.   Edinburgh: T & T
     Clark.

Schweitzer, A.   1968 [German 1906, ET 1910].   The
     Quest of the Historical Jesus.   Tr. W.
     Montgomery, with a new Introduction by J.
     Robinson.   New York: Macmillan.

Scramuzza, V. M.   1959.   "Roman Sicily."   In Frank,
     (1959) vol. 3.

Scroggs, R.   1980:164-79.   "The Sociological Interpre-
     tation of the New Testament: The Present State
     of Research."   NTS 26.

Sellers, O. R.   1962:828-39.   "Weights and Measures."
     In IDB 4.

Semple, E. C.   1922:3-38.   "The Influence of Geographic
     Conditions Upon Ancient Mediterranean Stock
     Raising."   Annals of the Association of
     American Geographers 12.

Shanin, T. 1971. Peasants and Peasant Society.
     Baltimore: Penguin.

_____. 1973:186-204. "The Nature and Logic of
     Peasant Economics." JPS 1.

Sherwin-White, A. N. 1981 [1963]. Roman Society and
     Roman Law in the New Testament. Twin Brooks
     Series. Grand Rapids: Baker.

Sloan, H. S., and Zurcher, A. J. 1970. Dictionary of
     Economics. 5th ed. Barnes & Noble.

Smith, B. T. D. 1937. The Parables of the Synoptic
     Gospels. Cambridge University.

Sorokin, P.; Zimmermann, C.; and Galpin C. 1930-32.
     A Systematic Source Book in Rural Sociology. 3
     vols. Minneapolis: University of Minnesota.

Sperber, D. 1971: cols. 388-90. "Weights and
     Measures: In the Talmud." In EJ 16.

Sprenger, (Pastor Dr.). 1913:79-97. "Jesu Säe und
     Erntegleichnisse." PJB 9.

Stager, L. 1976:11-13. "Agriculture." In IDBSup.

Stegemann, W. 1984. The Gospel and the Poor. Tr. D.
     Elliott. Philadelphia: Fortress.

Stein, S. 1971: cols. 244-53. "Moneylending." In EJ 12.

Stern, M. 1974:308-76. "The Province of Judaea." In
     Safrai and Stern, (1974) vol. 1.

_____. 1975:71-123. "The Reign of Herod." In
     Avi-Yonah (1975).

Stevenson, G. H. 1939. Roman Provincial Administra-
     tion: Till the Age of the Antonines. New York:
     G. E. Stechert and Co.

Strauss, David F. 1972 [German 1835, ET 1846]. The
     Life of Jesus Critically Examined. Tr. G.
     Eliot, ed. P. C. Hodgson. (Lives of Jesus
     Series, L. E. Keck ed.) Philadelphia: Fortress.

Sugranyes de Franch, R. ,1946. ,Études sur le droit
     palestinien a l' époque évangelique. Fribourg.

Sutherland, C. H. V. 1970:261-63. "Coinage, Roman."
     In OCD.

Talbert, C. H., ed. 1970 [German 1780²]. Reimarus:
     Fragments. Tr. R. S. Fraser. (Lives of Jesus
     Series, L. E. Keck ed.) Philadelphia: Fortress.

Tarn, W. W., and Griffith, G. 1952. Hellenistic
     Civilisation. 3d ed. London: Arnold.

Taylor, V. 1953. The Gospel According to St. Mark.
     London: Macmillan.

Tcherikover, V. 1937:9-90. "Palestine Under the
     Ptolemies." Mizraim 4-5.

_____. 1979 [1959]. Hellenistic Civilization and
     the Jews. New York: Atheneum.

Theissen, G. 1976:144-58. "Die Tempelweissagung
     Jesu: Prophetie im Spannungsfeld von Stadt und
     Land." TZ 32.

_____. 1977:161-96. "'Wir haben Alles verlassen'
     (Mk 10, 28): Nachfolge und soziale Entwurzelung
     in der jüdisch palästinischen Gesellschaft des
     1. Jahrhunderts n. Chr." NovTest 19.

_____. 1978. Sociology of Early Palestinian
     Christianity. Tr. John Bowden. Philadelphia:
     Fortress.

_____. 1982. The Social Setting of Pauline Christ-
     ianity: Essays on Corinth. Ed., tr., introduc-
     tion by J. Schütz. Philadelphia: Fortress.

_____. 1983. The Miracle Stories of the Early
     Christian Tradition. Tr. F. McDonagh.
     Philadelphia: Fortress.

Thomson, W. M. 1880-85. The Land and the Book. 3
     vols. New York: Harper & Bros.

Thorner, D. 1968:503-11. "Peasantry." In IESS 11.

Toutain, J. 1951. The Economic Life of the Ancient
     World. Tr. M. R. Dobie. New York: Barnes &
     Noble.

Trever, J. C. 1962a:355. "Barley." In IDB 1.

Trever, J. C.   1962b:267.   "Fig Tree, Fig."   In IDB 2.

_____.   1962c:596.   "Olive Tree."   In IDB 3.

_____.   1962d:839-40.   "Wheat."   In IDB 4.

Tristram, H. B.   1880.   The Natural History of the
     Bible.   6th ed.   London: Society for Promoting
     Christian Knowledge.

Trocme, A.   1973.   Jesus and the Nonviolent Revolution.
     Tr. M. H. Shank and M. E. Miller.   Scottdale,
     PA: Herald.

Troeltsch, E.   1981 [German 1911, ET 1931].   The Social
     Teachings of the Christian Churches.   2 vols.
     Tr. O. Wyon.   Reprint ed.   University of
     Chicago.

Turkowski, L.   1968:21-33, 1969:101-12.   "Peasant Agri-
     culture in the Judaean Hills."   PEQ 100 and 101.

United Nations, Food and Agriculture Organization
     (FAO).   1984. FAO Production Yearbook, 1983.
     Vol. 37. Rome.

U.S., Department of Agriculture.   1971.   Nutritive
     Value of Foods.   Home and Garden Bulletin, 72.
     Washington, D.C.: Government Printing Office.

U.S., Department of Agriculture.   1983.   Agricultural
     Statistics.   Washington, D.C.: Government
     Printing Office.

Vaux, R. de.   1965.   Ancient Israel.   2 vols.   New
     York: McGraw Hill.

Vermes, G.   1973.   Jesus the Jew.   New York: Macmillan.

Waetjen, H. C.   1976.   The Origin and Destiny of
     Humanness: An Interpretation of the Gospel
     According to Matthew.   San Rafael, CA: Omega.

Wallace, A.   1956:264-81.   "Revitalization Movements."
     American Anthropologist 58.

Warriner, D.   1965.   The Economics of Peasant Farming.
     2d ed.   New York: Barnes & Noble.

Watson, G. R.   1970:1014.   "Stipendium."   In OCD.

Weber, M. 1924. Wirtschaftsgeschichte. Ed. S.
     Hellmann and M. Palyi. München: Duncker &
     Humblot.

_____. 1976. The Agrarian Sociology of Ancient
     Civilizations. Tr. R. I. Frank. Atlantic
     Highlands: Humanities Press.

_____. 1978. Economy and Society. 2 vols. Tr. E.
     Fischoff, H. Gerth, et al.; edited by G. Roth
     and C. Wittich. Berkeley: University of
     California.

Weiss, J. 1971 [German 1892]. Jesus' Proclamation of
     the Kingdom of God. Tr., ed., and introduction
     by R. H. Hiers and D. L. Holland. (Lives of
     Jesus Series, L. E. Keck ed.) Philadelphia:
     Fortress.

Weiss, K. 1974:56-87. "PHERŌ, KTL." In TDNT 9.

White, K. D. 1964:300-307. "The Parable of the
     Sower." JTS 15.

_____. 1967:62-79. "Latifundia." Bulletin of the
     Institute of Classical Studies 14.

_____. 1970a. A Bibliography of Roman Agriculture.
     Institute of Agricultural History. University
     of Reading.

_____. 1970b. Roman Farming. Ithaca, N.Y.:
     Cornell University.

_____. 1973:439-97. "Roman Agricultural Writers,
     I. Varro and His Predecessors." In ANRW I, 4.

Widtsoe, J. A. 1911. Dry Farming: A System of
     Agriculture for Countries Under a Low Rainfall.
     New York: Macmillan.

Wilder, A. N. 1939. Eschatology and Ethics in the
     Teaching of Jesus. New York: Harper & Brothers.

Woess, F. von. 1922:485-529. "Personalexekution und
     Cessio Bonorum im römischen Reichsrecht."
     Zeitschrift der Savigny Stiftung für Rechts-
     geschichte 43.

Wolf, C. U. 1962a:539. "Carpenter." In IDB 1.

Wolf, C. U. 1962b:843-44. "Poor." In IDB 3.

Wolf, E. 1966. Peasants. Foundations of Modern Anthro-
    pology Series. Englewood Cliffs: Prentice-
    Hall.

_____. 1969:172-90. "The Hacienda System and Agri-
    cultural Classes in San José, Puerto Rico." In
    Béteille (1969).

_____. 1974. Anthropology. New York: W. W.
    Norton.

Wrede, W. 1971 [German 1901]. The Messianic Secret.
    Tr. J. Greig. Greenwood, SC: Attic.

Wright, G. E. 1962. Biblical Archaeology. Rev. and
    expanded ed. Philadelphia: Westminster.

Wuellner, W. 1976:339. "Fisherman." In IDBSup.

Yoder, J. H. 1972. The Politics of Jesus. Grand
    Rapids: Eerdmans.

Zohary, M. 1962:284-302. "Flora." In IDB 2.

_____. 1982. Plants of the Bible. Cambridge
    University.

INDEX OF PASSAGES

A. Biblical Passages

1. Old Testament

2. New Testament

B. **Extra-Biblical Passages**

1. New Testament Apocrypha and
Early Christian Writings

2. Old Testament Apocrypha
and Pseudepigrapha

3. Rabbinic Literature

4. Other Ancient Writings

INDEX OF MODERN NAMES

INDEX OF SUBJECTS

Cicero, 60, 63, 64, 67,
    69, 88 n, 264
Circumcellions, 75
Cities, 39, 44, 41, 48,
    210
    See Rural-urban
    distinction
Claudius, 74, 157
Cleopas, see Clopas
Client, 193
Client kingship, 45
Clopas, 184, 187, 201 n
Consumption (of food),
    12 n
Creditors, 75, 149-52,
    171 n
Criteria of authenticity,
    8
Crops, subsistence, 25
    yields, absolute, 26,
    64
    yields, relative, 63
    See also cash
    cropping
Cultivation, 21
    and Darnel parable,
    116-18
    in parable of the
    Sower, 106
    lack of in Seed
    Growing Secretly,
    110

Darnel, 13 n, 95, 96,
    109, 114, 115, 116-
    118, 119, 121, 122,
    127, 129, 136 n
Dead Sea Scrolls, 204 n
Debt, 72ff, 141, 148,
    149, 207
    and commerce, 73
    and money economy, 76
    and politics, 162
    and population, 74
    and taxation, 74-75
    natural causes, 74
    remission, 148, 153-
    55
    remission as a
    revolutionary
    demand in

antiquity, 73
Distribution, 6, 12 n,
    141-169, 205
Domitian, 38, 184
Dosa, Hanina b., 242

Ebionite, ebionism, 183,
    250 n
Economic, 141, 159
Economic anthropology,
    17, 30 n, 219 n
Economy, agrarian, 31 n
Edenic dreams, 131, 135 n
Egypt, 38, 39, 40, 41,
    56, 60, 63, 81 n,
    85 n, 153, 199 n
Elisha traditions, 133 n
Elizabeth, 184
Emmaus, 47, 184
Enclosure walls, 21
    See also Terrace
Endzeit, 113
Enlightenment, 2, 223,
    245, 248
Eschatology, 98
    and Seed Growing
    Secretly, 110
    and the Sower, 104
    material eschatology,
    111, 112-13, 135 n
    millenarian move-
    ments, 143, 171 n
    See Kingdom of God
Esdraelon Plain, 19, 39,
    71, 178, 198
Essenes, 43, 204 n, 207
Estates, large, 47, 77
Eupolemus, 70, 88 n
Execution against the
    person, 149, 170 n
Exploitation, 56, 79, 208
Expropriation of land,
    73-75, 79, 80, 211

Factors of production,
    18-19, 30 n
Famine, 74, 130-31
Fig, fig tree, 27, 145
Flowers as ambivalent
    symbols, 161
Fodder, 65